GUIDE TO AUSTRALIAN
HERITAGE TRAINS
AND RAILWAY MUSEUMS

CW00735393

Compiled by
ROBERT F McKILLOP

7th EDITION

AUSTRALIAN RAILWAY HISTORICAL SOCIETY

NEW SOUTH WALES DIVISION

ROBERT PARNELL

Top: The Cowra Roundhouse is where the Lachlan Valley Railway stables its locomotives. Seen here on an early winter's morning are steam locomotives 3013 (under restoration), 5367 and 3026T; diesel-electrics 4464, 4703, 4702 and 4716. Some of the diesel locos depicted here were transferred to Sydney for commercial freight operations.

Bottom: The Zig Zag Railway Coop Ltd operates tourist services on the former route using ex-QGR locomotives and rolling stock. The DD17-class 4-6-4T No 1047 is operating a service past one of the historic stone viaducts on the top road.

HIGH JINX PHOTO LIBRARY / ZIG ZAG RAILWAY

LINDSAY LUCAS

Top: Locomotives 3801/3830, the first and last of the NSWGR 38-class, double-head a 3801 Limited mainline tourist train down Spaniards Hill on the Main Southern Line to Sydney on 6 December 1998. Streamlined loco 3801 was, following overhaul, released to traffic in August 1999 in black rather than green livery. It was expected to be repainted green a few months later.

Bottom: Locomotive 3830 powers a southbound tourist service at Yanderra on the Main South on 23 May 1999.

STEVE MUNRO

MARK CARTER

Top: The ex-Western Australian W-class 4-8-2 locomotive W 934 is seen in the heart of the Pichi Richi Pass in South Australia with a return working from Woolshed Flat to Quorn.

Bottom: A Don River Railway special train in Tasmania is progressing up one of the waterway's banks near Launceston being double-headed by steam locomotives M4 and MA2.

LINSAY LUCAS

INTRODUCTION

AT THE DAWN OF A NEW MILLENNIUM the time is opportune for an all-new edition of the *Guide to Australian Heritage Railways and Museums*. It is a time of rapid change in the structure and operation of Australia's railways and these changes are also affecting heritage and tourist train operations. This 7th edition of the Guide presents the heritage/ tourist train operations, heritage sites and museums that will be open to the public in the year 2000.

Entries for tourist railways, museums and heritage sites are presented by state and region. There has been some adjustment of regional boundaries from the 6th edition to incorporate changes made by various state tourist bodies. The entries cover the many tourist attractions created by the efforts of railway preservation groups working tirelessly to re-create the nostalgia of steam and to conserve significant items of railway heritage. These museums and heritage railways trace the contribution of railways to social and economic development. There are also entries describing heritage sites and walking tracks, which provide the opportunity to further explore the history and infrastructure of Australian railway systems.

Australia's rich and diverse historic heritage is listed on the National Estate (RNE). The RNE category 'historic' refers to places associated with people since European settlement of Australia. Railway heritage listings include civil engineering items such as bridges, tunnels and cuttings, safe working systems, track work and a wide range of architectural structures from grand stations that dominate country towns to the humble nineteenth century gatekeeper's cottage. These historic places all have a particular story to tell about Australia and the people who have lived here. The Great Zig Zag near Lithgow and the Cairns-Kuranda railway have inter-national significance as outstanding feats of Victorian era engineering.

The need to effectively manage this railway heritage is receiving increased attention. Individual states have heritage legislation requiring government authorities to identify and manage heritage items under their ownership. Rail operators are therefore under pressure to manage heritage items that are still required for their regular services and to dispose of surplus items to those best able to manage them. These include the many preservation groups listed in this Guide.

Various groupings of railway preservation groups have been established to build linkages with heritage bodies, share information and help promote preserved railways. In South Australia, the Council of Historical Railways and Tramways of South Australia (CHRTSA) offers a consultative and advisory service on behalf of its members. In New South Wales a Railway Heritage Committee provides advice on heritage matters, as does the Association of Tourist Railways in Victoria and the Tasmanian Association of Tourist Railways.

Acknowledgements: Thanks are due to Peter Neve and David Jackson (NSW), Graham Wilson and John Browning (Queensland), Steve York (South Australia), Michael Dix (Tasmania), Stuart Turnbull (Victoria) and David Whiteford (Western Australia) for their assistance.

PASSENGER TRAIN OPERATORS

Rail passenger operators serving several states of regions are listed below. Local operators are described in the relevant regions.

Countrylink

Operates an extensive network of passenger services in eastern Australia serving 334 destinations in New South Wales, the Australian Capital Territory, Victoria and Queensland. *Countrylink* operates a modern fleet of high-speed XPT and *Explorer* trains.

Bookings: Countrylink Travel & Tours Centres
11 York Street, Sydney, and throughout NSW.
Phone: 13 22 32 for bookings and service information during the hours 0630-2000 daily.

Great South Pacific Express

This world-class, luxury heritage train operates between Sydney, Brisbane, Cairns and Kuranda. The train has been designed to accommodate standard gauge bogies, thereby permitting operation in all Australian mainland states. It is operated by the *Heritage Train Company*, a joint-venture between QR and Venice Simplon-Orient Express. The luxurious state room car *Abraham Fitzgibbon*, has two suites are fitted out with double beds and fully equipped hotel style en-suites finished in opulent Victorian-era decor.

Bookings: Traveltrain Holidays 1800 627 655

Great Southern Railway

Operator of some of Australia's best known trains, the *Indian Pacific*, *The Ghan* and *The Overland*. The twice-weekly *Indian Pacific* links the Pacific Ocean at Sydney with the Indian Ocean at Perth on a 4352km journey through the Blue Mountains, the Outback of Broken Hill to Adelaide and then across the desolate Nullaboar Plain. *The Ghan* operates from Melbourne or Sydney via Adelaide to the mysterious Red Centre.
Bookings: Phone 132 147 or (08) 8213 4696
Home Page: www.gsr.com.au

QR Traveltrain

QR long distance passenger trains include some of the world's most luxurious long-distance trains and high-speed electric tilt trains.

Bookings: Central Reservations Bureau, Phone (07) 132 232 or Brisbane Transit Centre, Roma Street Station.

QR Web Page http://powerup.com.au/~qroti/

V/Line Passenger, operated by *National Express*, services operates air-conditioned trains and luxury coaches to destinations throughout Victoria. Most arrive and depart from the Melbourne Spencer Street Terminal and from here connections are made to Met trains and trams. *V/Line* offers a number of special fares, including *Victoria Pass*, which offers 14 day unlimited travel on the network.

A 7-day Victoria Pass is available for international visitors.

V/Line Travel Centres are located at Transport House, 589 Collins Street, Melbourne (Phone: 03 9619 1549) a▮ 377 Centre Road, Bentleigh (Phone: 03 9563 9055). Train Information and Reservations 132 232.

Westrail Country Passenger

Westrail operates daily rail passenger services to Bunbury (▮ *Australind*), Northam (*AvonLink*) and Kalgoorlie (the *Prospecto*▮ New high-speed trains for the Kalgoorlie and *Avon Link* servic▮ will enter service in 2001.

Country Road passenger service operates to country cent▮ throughout the south-west of the State.

Bookings: Westrail Travel Centre, Perth Rail Station, Wellington Street, Perth WA 6000

Phone: (08) 9326 2159/9326 2195; Fax: (08) 9326 2063

NATIONAL VOLUNTEER RAILWAY SOCIETIES

Association of Railway Enthusiasts

The ARE was formed in 1961 to cater for all those who are interested in railways and tramways. The Association's aim is to foster an awareness of the part played by our rail transport in everyday life as well as to facilitate the interchange of information between people interested in the operation and development of our railways and tramways. Special trains are run several times a year to places of interest. Generally they operate in Victoria, but also occasionally travel over interstate lines. The Association operates a retail shop called *The Railfan Shop*, which is located at

> 40 Market Street (Cnr Flinders Lane)
> Melbourne VIC 3000
Phone/fax   (03) 9621 2238

Australian Railway Historical Society

The ARHS dates from 1933. It helps people interested in Australian railways meet others with similar interests and actively encourages the compilation and preservation of authentic historical records. Branches in each state maintain ARHS Archives which provide a valuable research base; hold regular members' meetings; publish monthly magazines, notably the *ARHS Bulletin* (historically focussed) and *Railway Digest* (current events); publish books on appropriate subjects; and arrange tours and visits to places of railway significance. ARHS NSW offers Australia's best selection of railway books, magazines and videos by mail order, Online through the Internet and through the ARHS Bookshop at

> 67 Renwick Street, Redfern NSW 2016
Phone/fax: (02) 9699 1714

Australian Rails to Trails Society

The Society aims to promote and support local Rails to Trails groups to establish an Australia-wide network of paths and linear nature reserves along closed railway lines. It provides and documents co▮ tacts, shares information and acts as a national resource centre ▮ Rails to Trails activities.

The Society can be contacted at

> PO Box 223, East Melbourne VIC 3002
> Phone 0500 587 254

Light Railway Research Society of Australia

The Light Railway Research Society of Australia Inc is a non-pro▮ organisation which was founded in 1961. Its purpose is to enco▮ age interest into specialised railways, both past and present, a▮ the industries they have served.

The LRRSA covers the fields of: industrial archaeology; ▮ dustrial locomotive history; the social history of industrial are▮ locating and recording sites of abandoned operations; research in▮ industries or communities associated with light railways; mappi▮ or photography of railway and industrial sites and relics; and ra▮ ways, towns, and industries in remote and rugged locations. T▮ Society publishes a quality bi-monthly magazine, *Light Railwa*▮ featuring the results of members' research and news items relati▮ to light railways.

Contact: The Secretary, PO Box 21, Surrey Hills VIC 3127

Rail 2000 Incorporated

Rail 2000 is Australia's leading community based rail transpo▮ lobby and education organisation, with over 150 members acro▮ the country. With a national focus, Rail 2000 seeks to promote ra▮ as a viable alternative to road transport through the maximum u▮ lisation of new and existing rail links.

> Rail 2000, 135 Waymouth Street, ADELAIDE SA 500▮
> Postal Address: PO Box 29, HINDMARSH SA 5007
> Phone: (08) 8410 0024; Fax: (08) 8212 4441

NEW SOUTH WALES

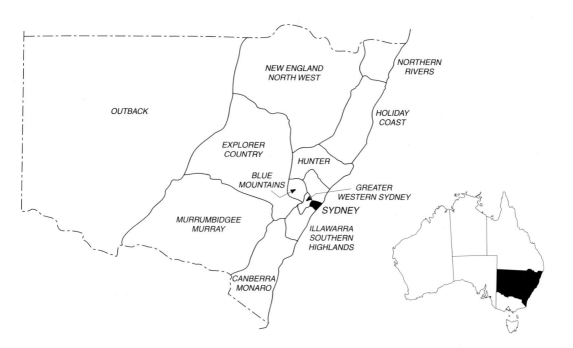

NEW SOUTH WALES offers a wealth of railway heritage and travel experiences for the visitor. Scenic coastal journeys on the *CityRail* network from Sydney to Newcastle in the north and Wollongong in the south take the traveller to regions rich in railway heritage. The Blue Mountains to the west of Sydney required innovative engineering feats to build the railway that connects the vast hinterland with the port of Sydney.

Mainline tours by 3801 Limited, the NSW Rail Transport Museum, Federal City Express, the Rail Motor Society and two electric train societies offer a variety of heritage trains, including steam-hauled operations. 3801 Limited also operates a regular tourist train over the spectacular line from Port Kembla to Robertson and return.

The Great Zig Zag near Lithgow is both an engineering marvel of the 19th century and the location of one of the state's major heritage train operation. The Zig Zag Railway operates on a daily basis (steam on weekends and public holidays), offering visitors spectacular views and an appreciation of the engineering feats of yesteryear. Complementary experiences of industrial railways at Lithgow and the mountains locomotive depot at Valley Heights are offered by the State Mine Railway Heritage Park & Railway and the Valley Heights Locomotive Depot Heritage Museum.

Sydney's Powerhouse Museum includes important railway items and is open daily, while Central Railway Station and the Australian Technology Park at Eveleigh offer public access to some of the State's most significant railway heritage items. The Sydney Tramway Museum (open Sundays) has Australia's largest collection of electric trams, with regular trips into the Royal National Park. The NSW Rail Transport Museum at Thirlmere, south-west of Sydney, with its extensive collection of locomotives and rolling stock under cover, is open daily. Steam trains operate over a branch line on Sundays, public holidays and Wednesday during school holidays. Other railway museums operate at Canberra, Yass, Junee (housed in Australia's finest roundhouse), Broken Hill, Richmond Main (coalfields industrial), Dorrigo, Armidale and Tenterfield.

In addition to Zig Zag and the RTM's Loop Line Railway, heritage railways operate over branch lines at Cowra (the Lachlan Valley Railway), Canberra to Michelago (Michelago Tourist Railway), Cooma and Murwillumbah. Narrow gauge enthusiasts can enjoy steam operations at the Illawarra Train Park, Albion Park (second Sunday of the month), Timbertown at Wauchope and Melaleuca Station in northern NSW.

State Rail is responsible for conserving heritage items under its control. A *Heritage and Conservation Register* lists items of heritage significance. The Association of Railway Preservation Groups (ARPG) is a peak grouping of railway preservation societies in NSW and the ACT. It provides advice to State Rail and other organisations on heritage matters and technical support to member organisations on accreditation under the *Rail Safety Act*.

MAINLINE RAIL TOURS

3801 Limited Heritage Steam Train

R HODGES

Locomotive 3801 approaching the Picton Tunnel with a tour train on 6 September 1997.

3801 Limited was formed for the purpose of restoring and operating Australia's most famous steam locomotive No 3801 a▮ a fleet of historical carriages. Operations are carried out on main lines under the control of the Rail Access Corporation NSW. The Large Erecting Shop at Eveleigh Workshops in Sydney serves as the base for 3801 Limited.

Locomotives: 3801 is the class leader of 30 *Pacific* steam locomotives designed and built in New South Wales between 1943 and 1949. 3801 undertook Australia's first steam locomotive transcontinental railway journey to Perth in 1972. It was rebuilt to operating condition in 1985-86, and will return to service following heavy overhaul. 3801 Limited also manages 3830, the last of the 38-class locomotives, owned by Powerhouse Museum, which was restored to operating condition between 1994 and 1997.

Heritage diesels include main-line Co-Co DE 4401 and diesel-hydraulic B-B DH 7344, with Alco mainliner 4401 on hire for special trains.

Rolling Stock: 16 accredited vintage carriages, including 5 MFS cars, 3 FN-type and 2 HFS.

Operations: 3801 Limited provides a range of steam tours to interesting destinations along the scenic routes of the New South

Wales railway system. Group charters from one carriage to the ent▮ train can be arranged as well as special event or promotional tou▮ Contact 3801 Limited for itineraries and times.

Regular services include the *Long Lunch Train* from Sydn▮ Terminal to Moss Vale, over the scenic line down the Illawar▮ Escarpment to Wollongong and back to Sydney on Wednesday▮ 3801 Limited is the operator of the Illawarra Scenic Mounta▮ Railway.

Location: Trains depart from Sydney Terminal Station in Sydne▮
Contact: 3801 Limited
103 Regent Street (PO Box 3801)
Redfern NSW 2016
Phone: 1300 65 3801
Web Page http://www.wollongong.asn.au/3801/

Federal City Express

Mainline Tours (Steam/Diese▮

Federal City Express is the "tour train" of the ACT Division of the ARHS. It operates both long distance and local dine▮ sleeping and tourist outings to varied locations on Australia's standard gauge network.

Tours: Federal City Express operates diesel-hauled tours from Canberra Railway Station using hired locomotives and the Society's extensive collection of passenger carriages and sleeping cars. Long distance excursions are periodically operated to various destinations.

Bookings and Timetable Information:
ARHS ACT Tours Operation Centre
Room G10, Griffin Centre, Bunda Street
Canberra City (PO Box 112, Civic Square) ACT 260▮
Phone: (02) 6239 6707 or 6295 7909
Fax: (02) 6284 2791

Heritage Train
NSW Rail Transport Museum

Heritage Tours (Steam/Diesel)
1435 mm gauge

DON TREVENA

Vintage diesel-electric locomotives 4520/4490 with the Silver City Aurora tourist train at Broken Hill railway station on 4 April 1999.

Heritage Train tours using classic carriages hauled by steam locomotives or vintage diesels are organised by the **NSW Rail Transport Museum** from time to time. Trains recreate the romance of a great rail journey in genuine 1920s style, travelling aboard comfortable and authentic 'end platform' timber panelled carriages. Our scenic steam adventures are a great, convenient way to go - there's a friendly atmosphere, no traffic hassles and they're ideal for families and groups. The RTM also operates modern air-conditioned carriages with dining cars formerly used on the *Southern Aurora Express* between Sydney and Melbourne to provide luxury tours.

Train: *The Heritage Train* comprises four classic end-loading Pullman-style carriages. The carriages, with six-wheel bogies and clerestory monitor-type roofs, were among 24 built by NSWGR workshops between 1892 and 1902. They are finished in a purple-brown livery which was the colour scheme used by the NSWGR from 1874 until the 1920s. Former *Southern Aurora* carriages and dining cars are a popular attraction. Steam locomotives or vintage diesels from the RTMs operating fleet are used (see RTM Thirlmere).

Other: The RTM operates a Sydney office and shop at 27/15A Belmore Street, Burwood.

Operations: The RTM operates tours to a wide variety of destinations including Sydney suburban locations, the Southern Highlands, Blue Mountains, the South Coast, and Newcastle and the Hunter Valley. Contact the Burwood office for current operating schedules. Prior reservations are essential on these tours. The train is available for charter.

Location: Tours operate from Sydney Terminal station.
Contact: General Manager, Rail Transport Museum
27/15A Belmore Street, (PO Box 31)
Burwood NSW 1805
Phone: Office (02) 9744 9999; fax (02) 9745 2530

Rail Motor Museum, Paterson
The Rail Motor Museum Society Inc

Mainline Tours (Rail Motor)

The Society restores and operate members of a fleet of the rail motors which once served the New South Wales railways. Rail motor tours are run on a regular basis and are available for charter.

Tours information: phone (02) 4938 8000 (see Hunter Region for further details).

Historic Electric Traction

1435 mm gauge

This company was established in 1997 to preserve Sydney's historical electric past in order that future generations can enjo former rail transport experience. HET is involved in the preservation of single-deck electric rolling stock dating from 191 through to the first double-deck carriages of 1964, in conjuction with *CityRail*.

Trains: The focus is on the "red trains" that travelled the Sydney system from electrification in 1927 till the early 1990s, plus the "silver" inter-city trains introduced with electrification of the Blue Mountains line in the late 1950s. HET members are actively involved in the preservation of representative examples of the electric fleet.

Operations: HET utilises rolling stock from the State Rail heritage fleet for tours within the CityRail electrified system. Tours are advertised through *Railway Digest* and on local radio stations.

Notes: The HEC has its registered office at 56 Magnolia Street, St Marys and holds its meetings at the Canterbury Bowling Club, Clo Street, near Canterbury railway station. Three public meetings p year.

Location: Trains operate from Sydney Central Station and oth suburban locations as advertised.

Contact: Historic Electric Traction
PO Box 246, Lidcombe NSW 2141
Infoline: (02) 9623 4111
Home Page: members.optusnet.com.au/~paulmat/trains.html

Sydney Electric Train Society

Mainline Tours (Electric)
1435 mm gauge

The Society was formed in 1991 to encourage the preservation of historic electric suburban trains and to foster interest i Sydney's rail transport heritage, namely its electric trains and the technology and environment in which they operate Historically significant examples of this pioneer electric rolling stock have been retained for the benefit of present and futu generations to see and experience. Tours are operated to destinations within the electrified network.

Trains: SETS utilises trains from the State Rail heritage fleet. The cars retained span the entire single-deck car construction era, from the original wooden Bradfield Motor Cars through to the steel cars of the post-war period, including the 1955 interurban carriages (known as U-boats). These single-deck carriages serve as living examples of the evolution in electric carriage technology that eventually brought us the new *Tangara* double-deck train, and shows exactly why the cars were renowned for decades as being the "World Leaders in Electric Traction".

Operations: The Society operates tours using preserved electr trains, holds monthly meetings and publishes a bi-monthly jou nal, *Under the Wires*.

Location: Trains operate from Sydney Central Station.

Contact: Sydney Electric Train Society Inc
PO Box 275, Broadway NSW 2007
Info Line: (02) 9526 1864
Home Page: www.ozemail.com.au/~utwww

SYDNEY REGION

Sydney is Australia's oldest, largest and most spectacular city (population 3.8 million). It presents the heritage of Australia foundations and the vision of the future as a modern global financial centre and the *Olympic 2000* city. Sydney's magnifice harbour, Opera House and Harbour Bridge are well-known international symbols of Australia. As Host City for the Ye 2000 Olympic Games, Sydney will feature a wide range of attractions over the coming years. The first railway opened from Sydney to Parramatta in 1855 and an extensive network of suburban railways developed over the following decades. Th system was electrified in 1926. Horse-operated street tramways date from 1861 and steam trams commenced operations 1869. Electric trams were introduced in 1890. The Sydney tramway system was Australia's largest with a route length of 290k and 1400 trams in 1933. The system closed in 1961, but modern light rail vehicles have recently returned to Sydney streets.

Public Transport: Sydney is the hub of the State's railway system. *CityRail* services connect underground CBD stations with an extensive suburban network using modern double-deck electric trains over 10 lines. Automatic ticketing machines are in service at all stations, but a range of special tickets are also available from sales outlets.

A train journey across the Harbour Bridge, especially in the evening sunlight, offers spectacular views of the harbour and city. The Airport Line opens in the year 2000. Regular shuttle services operate from Lidcombe to Olympic Park station with high frequency and service during major events.

State Transit operates public bus and ferry services and there are also numerous private bus operators. Sydney's ferry services are part of the city's fabric and the fleet has been modernised in recent years. Sydney buses run special Explorer bus services to popular attractions and there are scenic ferry cruises of Sydney Harbour. Details of services are presented in the Sydney Public Transport Directory and telephone directory.

A *Sydney Pass* provides unlimited travel on trains, buses and ferries for 3, 5 or 7 days, including the *Sydney Explorer* bus a special harbour cruises ($70 for 3-day pass). Passes are availab from CityRail ticket offices and Sydney Bus Information Office

Metro Light Rail & Monorail: The light rail currently operat from Central Terminal Station to Pyrmont (3.6km). The line, whi uses state-of-the-art low-floor light rail vehicles, operates 24 hou a day with 10-15 minute schedules. It is to be extended to Lilyfie (6.5km from Central).

The **monorail** links the tourist features of the Darling Harbo complex with the CBD. A monorail day pass is available for $6.
Public Transport Infoline: 131 500 between the hours 0600-220

ARHS Sales. The ARHS (NSW Division) operates Australia's lar est railway bookstore, together with extensive archives on NS railways at
67 Renwick Street, Redfern
(250m east of Redfern railway station.)
Phone: (02) 9699 1714
Open: Weekdays 1200-1730; Saturdays 0900-1600

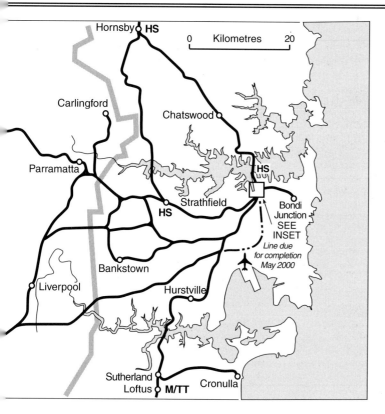

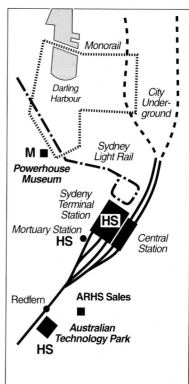

HERITAGE SITES

Hornsby Station and Yard: Located at the junction of the Short North and North Shore lines, the original station building was constructed in 1886, while the island platform building is a standard design dating from 1894. Up to 1999, the railway yard was the oldest remaining in its original state.

The 1920s 'J-type' signal box was one of the most elaborate used in NSW and Hornsby remains the last example in original condition. The 120-lever Type H power interlocking machine was manufactured in NSW railway workshops. It and the adjacent electric sub-station are under development as the NSW Railway Signalling Museum.

Lewisham viaduct/bridge: The original Long Cove Creek viaduct was a stone and brick arch bridge with eight 9.1 metre spans completed in 1855 as part of the original Redfern to Parramatta railway. It was replaced in 1886 by a two-track metal truss bridge, while adjacent bridges were built on the northern side in 1891 and 1927. An unusual whipple truss bridge was in use until recent years and a section of this is on display at the lower (road) level.

Sydney Harbour Bridge: Opened in 1932, this is one of the most remarkable feats of bridge construction. The 1,163.12 metre length bridge originally carried four rail tracks (2 used for trams). At the time of its construction and until recently it was the longest single span bridge in the world. It has been an important factor in the growth of Metropolitan Sydney, particularly since World War II.

The bridge, its pylons and approaches are all important elements in the townscape of areas both near and distant from it. The curved northern approach gives a grand sweeping entrance to the bridge with continually changing views of the Bridge and Harbour.

Sydney Terminal Station: Opened in 1906, Sydney Terminal Station is the grandest in the Southern Hemisphere and a high point in nationalist (Federation) architectural design. The clock tower is one of Australia's finest examples, while the main building provides the major civic focus for the southern part of Sydney. Planning of the present station site was marked by outstanding integration and segregation of goods and passengers: rail, tramways, motor vehicles and pedestrians were separated by a two level access system and a series of service tunnels and lifts.

The electric platforms, opened in 1924, mark the transition from British to American influence. Popularly known as "Central", the station was Sydney's major transport interchange during the period 1855-1955. It continues to serve this function for suburban, commuter and country train and coach passengers, with some 2000 trains daily serving its 25 platforms. The station building and clock tower have been restored to their former glory.

Sydney Railway Square: Sydney's central Railway Square is being redeveloped into a public plaza. In addition to the Terminal Station, heritage items include Mortuary Station and the Parcels Post Office building. Sydney yard dates back to the first railway terminus and shows the evolution of such facilities in Australia.

Tempe Tram Depot: Tempe tram depot is the last surviving Sydney depot which is reasonably intact. The large tramshed (which could hold up to 104 cars) with its *castellated* facade and superb offices have been retained and, since 1986, as Sydney's Bus and Truck Museum.
Location: Gannon Street, Tempe NSW 2044. The depot is a short walk from Tempe railway station. Vintage buses operate Route 444 from Newtown Bridge to the Museum and St Peters Station on Sundays.

Eveleigh Railway Precinct
Australian Technology Park, Sydney Ltd.
Eveleigh Locomotive Workshops Heritage Working Group
3801 Limited

Heritage Site

Eveleigh Railway Workshops is the most significant railway heritage site in the state and one of the most important histor railway workshops remaining in the world. Eveleigh was where Australia's railway technologies were developed and used, and was an important occupational community that revolved around extended family networks and continuous employment. handsome industrial buildings, mainly constructed in the 1880s, housed the men and machines who built over 170 locomotive and maintained the locomotive and rolling stock fleet of New South Wales. The machinery and technology housed in them is chronology of industrial development from the 1880s to the present day.

Much of this important precinct has been redeveloped as the Australian Technology Park (ATP) following strict conservatic principles to preserve the heritage items. The Large Erecting Shop has been retained in its original condition and serves as th operating base for 380 Limited, and the Eveleig Carriage Workshops to th north are to be redevelope as a Transport Heritag Park.

The 0-4-0 crane locomoti 1072 stands to salute th former New Engine Shop Eveleigh.

BOB McKILLOP

Heritage Significance: The Eveleigh precinct has seven heritage protected sites, including the locomotive workshops, works managers office, an administrative building and the booking office at Redfern railway station. The Large Erecting Shop has been retained in its original condition and serves as a depot for 3801 Limited [Not accessible to public]. Locomotives 3801, 3830 and 3265 are housed here together with 3801 Limited carriages and State Rail's special state carriages.

Features: The ATP has restored the 1906 New Engine Shop to house the National Innovation Centre, while the 1887 Locomotive Workshop has been restored for tenancies, exhibition/convention space and a range of educational facilities. The original fabric of the buildings has been retained, including the cast iron columns and significant items of equipment. The National Innovation Centre retains a 35-ton overhead crane (Craven Bros, 1907), while a 7-ton 0-4-0T locomotive crane 1082 (RSH 7542/1950) is on display in Innovation Plaza between the National Innovation Centre and Locomotive Workshops.

Bays 1 and 2 of the Locomotive Workshops contain operational and static displays of heritage-protected machinery, including an operating iron foundry, a Davey 1500 ton steam press, four 36-class locomotive boilers, a steam hammer, lathes and forges. An exten-

sive range of workshop tools is also on display. Future display will provide the visual medium for explaining the way peop worked at Eveleigh. They are to be backed by Information Tec nologies (IT) currently being developed to help visitors naviga around the site during different periods of history. Photograph archival and recent film, and oral history extracts will help demo strate the broad range of functions and machines that were use and built at Eveleigh.

Opening Times: ATP is open from 0900-1700, Monday to Frida

Location: Adjacent to Redfern railway station on the edge the CBD.

Contact: Angus M Robinson, General Manager
Suite 145, National Innovation Centre
Australian Technology Park, Eveleigh NSW 143C

Phone: (02) 9209 4141; Fax (02) 9319 3874
E-mail: a.robinson@atp.com.au

♿ ☕ 🪑 RNE

Powerhouse Museum
NSW Museum of Science & Technology

Technology Museum

Sydney's Powerhouse is one of the world's great museums dedicated to promoting awareness and understanding of the past, present and future of Australian society. The technology of transport and industry, everyday life in Australia and decorative arts are all featured in the exhibitions.

POWERHOUSE MUSEUM

NSWGR Locomotive No 1 of 1855 and replica carriages displayed on Barlow track in the Wran Building of the Powerhouse Museum.

Displays: Locomotive No 1, an 0-4-2 mixed traffic engine built in England (RS 954/1854), together with replica 1st, 2nd and 3rd class carriages and artefacts of the 1860s, has place of honour on original Barlow track in the Wran Building. The display simulates a journey from Sydney to Penrith in 1865. The former Sydney Station destination board, locomotives, rolling stock and models are displayed in the transport section. A Boulton-Watt steam engine of 1785 operates on steam power during open hours. As the world's oldest surviving rotating steam engine, it is regarded as the most important existing icon of the Industrial Revolution in Australia.

The *Steam Revolution* exhibition features live-steam engines and illustrates how steam revolutionised the world. Powerhouse Museum has its own railway siding for interchange of locomotives and carriages.

Locomotives and rolling stock: The museum has an extensive collection of locomotives and trams. In addition to locomotive No 1, Sydney steam tram motor No 28 (Henry Vale 52 of 1891) displayed as No 1A; ex-NSWGR express passenger 4-4-0 1243 (Atlas Eng., built 1882); the Governor's Carriage (built 1891); and a tram hearse are on display. Museum 4-6-2 express locomotive 3830, has been restored to its original operating condition for tour trains (see 3801 Limited) and restoration work is currently in progress on 4-6-0 locomotive 3265.

Facilities: Restaurants, bookshop, function rooms, wheelchair access, services for visually and hearing impaired, Kings cinema (railway films are regularly shown). Special parking rates at Entertainment Centre Secure Parking.

Opening Times: Daily from 1000-1700. Visiting steam locomotives are displayed in the courtyard on special occasions (eg, during school holidays).

Admission: Adults $8, children $2, concession $3, family$18.
Location: 500 Harris Street, Ultimo; a 10 minute walk from Central Station.
Public Transport: STA buses 456 and 501, Metro Light Rail line from Central or *HarbourLink* monorail (Haymarket station).

Contact: PO Box K346
                Haymarket NSW 2000
Phone: (02) 9217 0111   **Information line:** 9217 0444

RNE

Sydney Tramway Museum, Loftus
South Pacific Electric Railway Co-operative Society Ltd

Tram Museum (Electric)
1435 mm gauge

BOB McKILLOP

O-class trams in Tramway Avenue at the Sydney Tram Museum on an open day.

The Sydney Tramway Museum preserves Sydney's tramway heritage. The museum, established in 1957, was a pioneer in transport preservation. Electric operations commenced at the museum on 13 March 1965. The *Parklink* public passenger service operates over the former branch railway line from Loftus to National Park station (2km), from where a range of bushwalks are available.

Features: Visitors can relive the tramway era, riding the trams over a 1.1km section of tramway to the outskirts of Sutherland. The Museum's main street, Tramway Avenue, is being reconstructed as a street scene in the 1930s, featuring old tramway buildings and ornamental steel span poles. The tramway waiting shed, built in Railway Square near Central Railway station in 1907, has been restored and re-erected on site.

The Display Hall houses historic trams and an extensive range of photographs of Sydney's street transport during the tramway era, together with associated relics. The displays show the importance of trams in the development of Sydney and other cities during the early decades of this century. There are picnic facilities, a food kiosk and bookshop.

Electric Trams: The largest tram museum in the southern hemisphere with 47 vehicles representing Sydney, Brisbane, Melbourne, Ballarat, San Francisco, Berlin, Munich and Nagasaki tramways. The collection includes Australia's oldest electric tram (C 290 of 1896 and sister tram C 29 of 1898), three of the famous O-class toastrack trams (1910-13), modern R-class corridor trams, the only prison tram in the southern hemisphere and the unique counterweight dummy from the Balmain line, together with many other restored trams. Twelve trams are kept in operating condition.

Operations: The Museum is open every Sunday and Public Holiday from 1000 to 1700 and every Wednesday from 0930 to 1530. Trams run on Sundays and public holidays from the museum at 0 and 30 minutes past the hour and from Sutherland terminus at 8 and 38 minutes past the hour. On Wednesdays trams run as required. *Parklink* services every Sunday and public holiday, with hourly services departing Pitt Street at 15 past the hour from 0915 to 1615 returning from Royal National Park at 35 past the hour.

Admission: All inclusive fee; adults $8, child/concession $4 which covers entry to the Display Hall, unlimited tram rides on the Museum line and use of facilities. Group concessions available (contact Bookings Officer). *Parklink:* Adult $4, concession $2.

Location: Adjacent to Loftus railway station. By road, 1.5km south of Sutherland shopping centre on the old Princes Highway (renamed Rawson Avenue). Travelling time is approximately 40 minutes from Sydney.

Public Transport: *CityRail* Waterfall trains to Loftus.

Contact: Sydney Tramway Museum
        Box 103, Sutherland NSW 2232

Phone: (02) 9542 3646; Fax (02) 9545 3390

GREATER WESTERN SYDNEY
Australia Starts Here

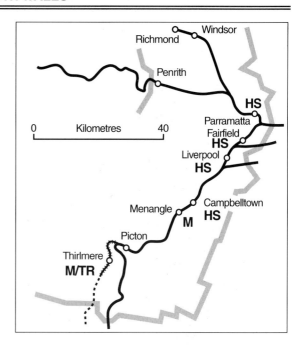

This dynamic region of 1.4 million people has emerged as a grouping of 12 local government areas seeking improved prospects for employment, business investment and public infrastructure. With Australia's second oldest European settlement, Parramatta established in 1788, the region has an important cultural and heritage-based tourist industry. Parramatta was the terminus for the first railway in 1855.

The area is served by CityRail electric trains to Penrith, Richmond and Macarthur (first station after Campbelltown) and diesel trains to Picton and Mittagong. *RiverCat* ferries link Parramatta with Circular Quay.

Parramatta: Australia's second oldest permanent settlement is the commercial and industrial centre of the region. The city has over 20 historic buildings and sites including Elizabeth Farm (Australia's oldest building), Hambledon Cottage, Old Government House (Australia's oldest public building) and St Johns Cathedral. A number of walks link the city's scenic and heritage sites.

Menangle Narrow Gauge Railway
Campbelltown Steam and Machinery Museum

Steam Museum
610mm gauge

The NSW Steam Preservation Cooperative Society has established a museum devoted to the preservation of steam and internal combustion tractors, road rollers, portable and stationary engines and old farm machinery. The narrow-gauge railway operates on the site.

Locomotives: The English-built Hudson/Hudswell Clarke 0-4-0WT locomotive (1423/1922) is unique, being the only one of its type in the Southern Hemisphere; pioneer Fowler 0-6-0DM (16830/1926) ex-Condong Sugar Mill, NSW; 5 small canefield/industrial diesel locomotives; 4 battery-electric locomotives.

Rolling Stock: 4-wheel inspection car, 2 bogie carriages, 8 4-wheel carriages, 15 flat-top, 4-wheel munitions wagons and various other wagons.

Operation: Two Expo weekend Steam & Machinery rallies are held each year, usually on the weekend before Easter and the second weekend of November.

Admission: Adult $5, concession/child $2 entry on Expo weekends.

Location: On Menangle Road, 57km south-west of Sydney; 5 km from Campbelltown.

Public transport: *CityRail* train to Macarthur shopping centre, thence taxi.

Address: Secretary, PO Box 905
Campbelltown NSW 2560
Phone: Site Manager (02) 4628 6655

HERITAGE SITES (Register of the National Estate)

Fairfield Railway Station: The station building and adjacent residence were opened when the railway was extended to Liverpool in 1856. The original buildings are still standing and are among Australia's oldest surviving railway buildings.

Menangle Railway Bridge: The bridge over the Nepean River at Menangle is the oldest railway bridge in NSW still existing. Four sandstone piers support three iron spans of 60.3m. Opened in 1863, it was the first iron structure built in NSW.

Parramatta Railway Station. This station precinct is one of Australia's most significant rail heritage sites. The original Georgian-style station building (1860) is the oldest in use in NSW and presents an impressive facade to the street. The island platform buildings were constructed in 1886 to match the original structure.

The platform also incorporates a rare elevated 1886 signal box with one of the oldest frames on the NSW system. The modern construction (1996) was located at the eastern end to maintain the heritage buildings in their original setting.

Rail Transport Museum, Thirlmere
NSW Rail Transport Museum

Museum/Tourist Line (Steam)
1435mm gauge

LINDSAY LUCAS

Volunteers servicing the various heritage locomotives at the Rail Transport Museum at Thirlmere.

This railway museum has a fascinating and historically important collection of some 55 locomotives and 100 carriages, most of which are housed under cover. The RTM tourist railway operates over 14 km of the branch line from Picton to Colo Vale which was built as the Great Southern Railway in 1867 and bypassed by the existing main line in 1919. A large workshop area is used by volunteers to keep the fleet of operating locomotives and carriages maintained for trips during the steam operating season.

Locomotives: Steam locomotives on display from the NSW Government Railways and industrial operators range from No18, an 0-6-0 built by Robert Stephenson (B/No 1542) in 1864, to the giant 260 ton Beyer Garratt No 6040 built in 1956. Of historical significance are No 1905, an 0-6-0 goods locomotive of 1877; 1219 a 4-4-0 express loco of 18??; 3203 and 3214 of the famous P-class 4-6-0s of 1891; three 36-class express 4-6-0 of 1928, 5711, the only survivor of the 226-ton 4-8-2s of 1930; and 3820 from Australia's most famous class of *Pacific* express locomotives. Vintage diesel and electric locomotives are also on display.

Operating Locomotives: Steam locomotives ex-NSWGR express passenger 4-4-0 1709 (VF 1172/1887); mixed traffic 2-6-0, 2705 (Hunslet 1115/1913); mixed traffic 4-6-0, 3001T (BP 4444/1903); express 4-6-0, 3642 (Clyde 376/1926); and 2-8-2, 5910 (BLW 75579/1952). The Museum has a number of Vintage diesels, including AIA-AIA 4306 (Goninan 1956), Co-Co 4201 (Clyde 1955), branch line unit 4916 and Alco-engined locos 4490, 44211, 4520 and 4803.

Rolling Stock: Assorted passenger carriages, sleeping cars, cranes, prison van, horse transporter, goods wagons and rolling stock from our railway past.

Opening Times: The museum is open every day of the year (except Good Friday and Christmas Day): weekdays from 1000-1500, week-ends and public holidays from 0900-1700. Guided tours of the locomotive restoration and maintenance workshops are conducted most Sundays. The *Thirlmere Festival of Steam* is held on the first Sunday in March.

Loop Line Railway: Steam trains operate on the loop line between Thirlmere and Buxton every Sunday, public holiday and Wednesday during school holidays.

Admission: Museum adult $6, senior citizens $4, school students $2.

Location: Barbour Road, Thirlmere which is 83km SW of Sydney. By road, take the F5 Freeway from Liverpool to the Picton exit, then 1km south of Picton, turn right at sign and travel 5km to the Museum.

Public Transport: To be updated.

Contact: General Manager, Rail Transport Museum
27/15A Belmore Street, (PO Box 31)
Burwood NSW 2134

Phone: Office (02) 9744 9999; fax (02) 9745 2530
Museum (7 days) (02) 4681 8001

ILLAWARRA - SOUTHERN HIGHLANDS

The Illawarra and Southern Highlands region, with a population of 450,000 is a major coal mining and heavy industry centre, which is also emerging as a centre of excellence in information technology, research and development. The region is noted for its beautiful landscapes from the fine beaches and coastal scenery of the coast to the national parks and nature forests of the Southern Highlands.

Railway construction to link Sydney with its agricultural hinterland, and eventually Victoria, was a priority for the colonial government. The main southern railway reached Mittagong in March 1867, opening up the Southern Highlands region for grazing and resort development at Bowral and Moss Vale. The Illawarra railway with its difficult descent down the escarpment through six tunnels, was opened to Kiama in 1887.

Wollongong (population 240,000) located 85km south of Sydney, is Australia's eighth largest city, incorporating coal mining settlements and the industrial centre of Port Kembla. European settlement dates from 1826. The town initially developed as an agricultural and dairy centre, but coal mining expanded from 1849. The railway from Sydney opened in 1887. The city grew rapidly from the 1950s as a service centre for steel works and heavy industry at Port Kembla, but suffered severe economic recession in the mid-1980s.

The BHP steelworks railway, Port Kembla, operates a 190km industrial railway with 30 locomotives. 0-6-0ST *Bronzewing* (Clyde 57/1937) and vintage diesel-electric D6 (ComEng 1951) have been restored to operating condition and are used to haul passenger trains during open days, including the *Illawarra Florawarra Festival* in September.

Wollongong Visitors Centre: 93 Crown Street, Wollongong.
  Phone: (02) 4228 0300

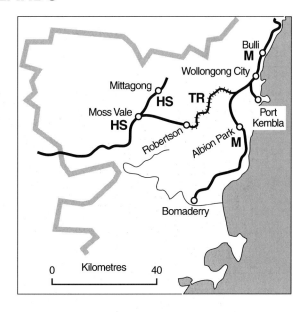

Access: *CityRail* electric trains connect Wollongong, Port Kembla and Dapto with Sydney at regular intervals, offering spectacular vistas of the Illawarra Escarpment and coast from the carriage windows. Modern diesel trains operate from Dapto to Kiama and Bomaderry (Nowra).

CityRail offers regular commuter services to Southern Highland centres between Campbelltown and Goulburn using modern *Endeavour* railcars. Off-peak fares are available on weekends and public holidays.

HERITAGE SITES (Register of the National Estate)

Mittagong Railway Station: The station was opened in March 1867 with the existing small, single-story building on platform 1. The refreshment room, opened in 1873, was the first such facility in NSW. A well-proportioned two story brick building with parcels office and a Station Master's residence were built over the next decade.

Moss Vale Station: Also dating from 1867, the Moss Vale station was upgraded in 1890 to provide a Vice Regal waiting room, complete with chandeliers, for the Governor travelling to his Southern Highlands retreat located nearby. A hotel and refreshment room was added in 1891. The whole precinct is heritage-listed (RNE).

Stanwell Creek Viaduct: This brick and arch viaduct, constructed for the Illawarra line deviation in 1920, is the highest in Australia and offers train passengers magnificent views over the Illawarra Escarpment.

Stonequarry Creek Railway Viaduct, Picton: The sandstone viaduct, opened in 1867, has 5 arches the highest measuring 30 metres. The structure is 84 metres long and a small fence has been added on one side. The structure presents a picturesque sight spanning the commencement of The Gorge and is an excellent example of John Whitton's engineering work.

Black Diamond District Heritage Centre, Bulli   *Local History Museum*

The historic down Bulli Railway Station building (built 1887) has been restored as a heritage museum featuring the early coal mining era of Bulli district.

Exhibits: The museum features the signal box room, which houses local railway memorabilia, and a local history display, including many old photographs, housed in the former waiting room. Former colliery 0-6-0T locomotive, *South Bulli* (H/Clarke 297/1888) is on static display outside the museum, together with a period coal wagon and brakevan.

Opening Times: Sundays 1000-1600.
Admission: Adults $2, children $1.

Location: Bulli Railway Station, Franklin Street. By road, turn into Park Road from Princes Highway at traffic lights at Bulli Shopping Centre.
Public Transport: Served by *CityRail* trains from Sydney and Wollongong.
Contact: Mick Roberts, Publicity Officer
          1A O'Brien Street, Bulli NSW 2516
Phone: (02) 4267 3675

Illawarra Scenic Mountain Railway
3801 Limited

Tourist Line (Steam/Diesel)
1435mm gauge

STEPHEN PRESTON, COURTESY OF 3801 LT

Vintage locomotive 4833 ascending the Illawarra Scenic Mountain Railway amid the rainforest setting on the long 1 in 30 grade to Summit Tank.

This tourist train is operated by *3801 Limited* over the scenic line between Port Kembla, Unanderra (2km west of Wollongong) and Robertson. The line is one of the most scenic in Australia and the train offers a unique "railway experience."

Features: The Unanderra-Moss Vale line has a 600 metre ascent from the Pacific Ocean to the Southern Highlands offering spectacular views over the Illawarra escarpment. At Robertson, the railway station provides a classic example of 1930s railway architecture and is the site of the Robertson Rural Railway development.

Train: The vintage passenger cars offer the traditional style of the 1930s and 1940s. The buffet car offers morning and afternoon teas, light refreshments and souvenirs. Trains are hauled by former South Maitland Railways 2-8-2T steam locomotive No 18 or heritage diesel locomotives.

Operations: Thursday-Sunday between March and November, departing Port Kembla at 1050 (1115 from Unanderra, connecting with the 0938 train from Sydney) and arriving Robertson at 1310.

The return service departs Robertson at 1500 and arrives Unanderra at 1625, connecting with 1636 train to Sydney. Some evening dinner trains are also operated. Contact 3801 Limited for details.

Return Fares: Adult $26, seniors $23, children$17, family $70 Group bookings and discounts are available.

Bookings: Free call: 1300 65 3801
Wollongong Tourism Office: (02) 4228 0300
Countrylink Wollongong Travel Centre: (02) 4223 5627
or any *Countrylink* Travel Centre. Bookings are essential.

Illawarra Train Park, Albion Park
Illawarra Light Railway Museum Society Limited

Industrial Railway Museum (Steam)
610mm gauge

BOB McKILLOP

The Illawarra Light Rail Society's 0-6-0 locomotive and train at the Illawarra Train Park, Albion Park.

The Illawarra Light Railway Museum Society was established in 1972 to preserve the industrial railway heritage of the Illawarra and Australia generally. The 610mm gauge Corrimal Colliery railway provided the initial impetus for the museum, which now features items from industrial and canefield lines. The Society has an active restoration program, with four steam locomotives, industrial diesels and an interesting range of carriages in operation.

Features: Operating steam locomotives, internal combustion units, battery-electric locomotive, small railcars, passenger cars and mine personnel carriers. Visitors can ride 610mm gauge tracks in vintage carriages behind steam locomotives, while a miners' tram operates a shuttle service from the Tongarra Road entrance to the former Yallah station. The station formerly served Yallah south of Wollongong on the Illawarra line until 1974 and was transported to the ILRNS site in 1976. The Otford signal box and 18-lever mechanical frame which date from 1890. It was restored in 1986-87. A variety of restored steam stationary engines and pumps powered by a large vertical boiler are demonstrated in motion. There is a souvenir shop, a kiosk and the ticket office is in the original Yallah station building. Children's play areas, picnic and barbecue facilities and free parking are available.

Locomotives: Operating steam locos are *Burra* 0-4-0ST (H/Leslie 1574/1923), ex-Corrimal Colliery; 0-6-2T Perry Engineering 7967/9/1 of 1949, ex-Tully Sugar Mill No 3; *Cairns* 0-6-0 (H/Clarke 706/1939), ex-Victoria Sugar Mill; and *Kiama* 0-4-0ST (Davenport 1596/1917), ex-Quarries Ltd, Kiama;; with Fowler 0-4-0T (JF 16089/1923) ex-Kiama Quarries under restoration. Diesel locomotives include *Seymour* 0-6-0DM (Baguley 2392/1952) ex-Victoria Sugar mill 1994, two Hudson-Hunslet 4wDM locomotives ex-ER&S Port Kembla copper refinery and two Ruston 4wDM; while there are two underground mining locomotives, a Mancha 4wBE and a GEMCO 4wBE converted to trolley wire operation. A Shay geared locomotive is under construction, using parts of several vintage locomotives.

Rolling Stock: Passenger carriages include two ex-Melbourne cable tram trailers (Nos 110 and 430) and ex-Sydney Tramways end-loading saloon car of 1899. There is a large collection of mining and industrial rolling stock which form demonstration trains of typical operations.

Operations: 1100-1700 (1630 in winter) second Sunday of each month, 2nd and 4th Sunday during January. Also open Sunday of public holiday weekends and selected school holidays. Parties and visits can be arranged by prior notification. Museum work days 0930-1600 Tue, Thu and Sat.

Train fares: Adults $2.50, all-day ticket $5.

Location: Tongarra Road, 700 metres from the Albion Park railway station (105km south of Sydney) in the Wollongong suburban system. Electric trains operate from Sydney to Dapto, then change to Albion Park.

Contact: Illawarra Light Railway Museum Society Ltd
                PO Box 244, Albion Park NSW 2527
Phone: (02) 4256 4627 (Tue, Thur, Sats)
                (02) 4232 2488 Operations Manager.

CANBERRA - MONARO REGION

Australia's National Capital, Canberra, is the dominant force driving the economy of the south-eastern region, which also includes the Australian Alps and the beaches of the South Coast. Mt Kosciusko (2228 metres) is Australia's highest peak. The Mt Kosciusko National Park has become a major tourist destination with extensive ski fields in winter, mountain walks in summer and water sports on the many lakes of the Snowy Mountains Scheme constructed in the 1950s.

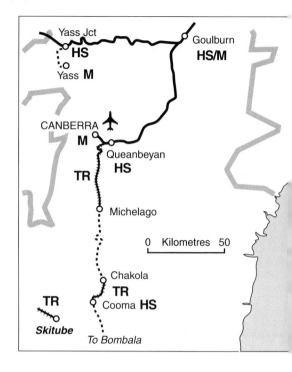

Canberra (population 320,000) was planned by the Chicago architect Walter Burley Griffin and construction commenced in 1913. It was connected to the NSW railway system in 1914. Today, the city is a popular tourist destination with many fine public buildings, including the Parliament House, National Gallery of Australia, National Library of Australia and the Australian War Memorial.
Transport: *Countrylink* operates between Canberra and Sydney, with three daily *Xplorer* train services in either direction. Daily (except Sunday) coordinated rail-coach services ex-Melbourne and Adelaide. ACTION Bus Services provide public transport within Canberra and suburbs seven days a week. ACTION operates one of Australia's most modern bus fleets and has outstanding mass transit infrastructure.
For timetable information, phone (02) 6207 7611.
Tourist Information: Visitors Information Centre
　　　　　　　Northbourne Avenue, Dickson ACT 2602
Phone:　　(02) 6205 0044 or toll free 1-800 026166
Facsimile:　(02) 6205 0776

Queanbeyan (population 27,000), 8km east of Canberra, dates from 1838, but owes its growth to its proximity to Canberra's post-war expansion. The city is a thriving multi-cultural centre catering for a tourist support industry for visitors from all corners of the world. There are regular bus services from Canberra to Queanbeyan.
　　The 1886 heritage-listed railway station is leased by ARHS (ACT Division) and serves as the Michelago Tourist Railway operations centre, a *Countrylink* ticketing office and base for the Society's library and archives.
Phone (02) 6297 1242.

Goulburn (population 24,000) was established in 1833 and became Australia's first inland city in 1863. With the opening of the main southern railway in 1869, Goulburn developed as a major railway centre. The city actively promotes its railway heritage.
Information and booking: Goulburn Visitors Centre
　　　　　　　6 Montague Street, Goulburn NSW 2580
Phone:　　(02) 4821 5343
Countrylink Phone (02) 4823 2485

Goulburn Rail Heritage Centre
Goulburn Roundhouse Preservation Society Inc

Heritage Depot
1435mm gauge

This Society was formed to manage the historic Goulburn roundhouse and steam locomotive depot to provide a restoration base for persons owning locomotives and/or rolling stock. The 25-road 1918 roundhouse and the machine shop, located in the historic former Wellington locomotive shed, have been restored together with workshop machinery.

Locomotives: Branch-line diesel locomotive 4821 was allocated to Goulburn and 2-6-0 B-class steam locomotive No 390 (Dubs 2641/1891) was restored as a static exhibit. Privately-owned locomotives currently at Goulburn include 73-class diesel-hydraulic and mainline de 42101.

Rolling Stock: A large number of carriages and freight wagons are under restoration at the Centre.

Opening Times: 1300-1700 Saturday or by appointment. Open days are held about four times a year.

Admission: Individual $2, family $5.
Location: Braidwood Road, Goulburn, 211km south-west of Sydney on Hume Highway.

Public Transport: Regular *CityRail* and *CountryLink* trains.

Contact:　PO Box 711, Goulburn NSW 2580
Phone:　　(02) 4822 1210

RNE

Canberra Railway Museum
Australian Railway Historical Society (ACT Division)

Railway Museum
1435mm gauge

The Canberra Railway Museum presents the Golden Age of Railways and serves as an operating base for heritage steam rail tours. The museum complex provides storage facilities for carriages and locomotives, and provides a static display of vintage railway rolling stock, together with railway memorabilia.

Locomotives: 4-4-0 No 1210 and 4-6-0 No 3016 restored to working condition for tour operations. No 1210 was built in 1878 and hauled the first train into Canberra in 1914. Other locomotives on display include Beyer Garratt No 6029 built in 1954, the largest and most powerful steam locomotive class in Australia, and No 2413, a 2-6-0 of 1891. Operating diesel locomotives include 73-class B-B DH locos.

Rolling Stock: A wide range of vintage carriages on display provide the visitor with the experience of past train travel, from the rudimentary comfort of a 2nd class *dogbox* to the luxury of classic sleeping and dining cars. The ornate polished timber and metal ceilings created by the craftsmanship of carriage builders is featured. Four CPH-class rail motors (Nos 2, 13, 27 and 37), which provided branch line passenger services throughout the state, and rail bus FP11 are among the self-propelled vehicles. Memorabilia and photographs of the railways of the Canberra and Monaro districts are on display.

Opening Times: 1300-1600 Saturday, Sunday and public holidays with guided tours of inspection. School and tour groups by arrangement.

Admission: Adults $4, children $2, family$9.50. Entrance covers conducted tours of steam locomotives and vintage carriages.

Location: Geijera Place, off Cunningham Street
Kingston, near the Canberra Railway Station.

Public Transport: ACTION bus 370 (Saturdays), set down from Wentworth Avenue at Cunningham Street and walk up to Museum (700 metres). Sundays take 352 or 358 services to Kingston shops, walk down Kennedy Street to Cunningham Street.

Contact: c/- ARHS (ACT Division)
PO Box 112, Civic Square ACT 2608

Phone: (02) 6239 6707 or 6295 7909 for details

Facsimile: (02) 6284 2791

Internet: http://arhs.netsite1.net.au

Yass Railway Museum
Australian Railway Historical Society (ACT Division)

Local History Museum
1435mm gauge

In 1892 a 4.6km line, known as the Yass Tramway, was opened connecting Yass Town to the main line at Yass Junction. For most of its life, the Yass Tramway was operated by 4-4-2T 13-class locomotives that hauled mixed trains over the line. The Yass Town station has been restored as a railway museum to represent the period 1892 to 1920.

Displays: Renovated and repainted roadside station buildings feature Australia's shortest platform, with a comprehensive historical and photographic display of the Yass Tramway. A static display of rolling stock includes the remains of a P127 0-6-0T locomotive which worked the tramway between 1892 and 1910 and X200-class locomotive X203 which operated the tramway from 1964 to 1972. There is a consist of typical 4-wheel freight wagons, including a HG brakevan, synonymous with the Yass Tramway for many years and an Arnotts' biscuit van.

Opening Times: Friday to Monday, 1000-1600. Operations over a portion of the tramway with 6-seat track inspection cars is sheduled to commence in early 2000.

Location: Lead Street, Yass. Accessible by *Countrylink* and *V/Line* coach services to Yass (Phone 12 22 32) or *Countrylink* trains to Yass Junction and taxi (5km). Transborder coaches provide a Canberra-Yass service five times daily (twice on weekends), phone (02) 6226 3788.

Contact: Bob Hall, Yass Railway Museum
Lead Street, Yass NSW 2582

Phone: (02) 6226 2169; (02) 6259 0884 (AH).

Old Canberra Tram Company
Canberra Tradesmen's Union Club

Static Display (Trams)

The Tram Company restores and refurbishes tramcars from various Australian cities as an integral part of the Club's historical preservation activities. The trams are on display within the club premises.

Trams: Ten restored trams from Melbourne, Sydney, Adelaide and Brisbane are open to inspection every day. Pride of place is given to a 1920 Melbourne cable car located in the Tram House Family Bistro.

Open: 24 hours, 7 days a week. Members and guests and interstate visitors always welcome. No admission charge.

Location: Canberra Tradesmen's Union Club
2 Badham Street, Dickson

Public Transport: Action buses 380, 381 or 382 from City.

Contact: Annemarie Driver, Public Relations Officer
Phone (02) 6248-0999

Michelago Tourist Railway
Australian Railway Historical Society (ACT Division)

Tourist Railway (Steam)
1435mm gauge

DAVE OLIVER

Steam locomotive 3016 with a tourist from Canberra arriving at Queanbeyan railway station as railmotor CPH 37 from Royalla stands by in a siding.

The tourist train operates south from Queanbeyan as far as the picturesque village of Michelago. The railway is one of the most scenic in the state, with a 1 in 40 climb from Queanbeyan, fine views over the Tuggeranong and Melrose Valleys and typical rural countryside. Former NSWGR steam locomotives 1210 and 3016 (see Canberra Railway Museum), rail motors and diesel locomotives operate the line to a regular time-table.

Operations: A range of services operate throughout the year, generally on the first and third Sunday of each month, with additional services in holiday times as follows:

Boundary Rider Picnic Train: Steam or diesel-hauled trains from Canberra to Michelago and return, with a picnic included;
Tin Hare Express: Morning (0915) and afternoon (1330) trains operated by CPH rail motors to Michelago and return;
Spirit of Tuggeranong: Steam or diesel-hauled trains from Canberra to Royalla and return, with departures at 0915 and 1330.
Railroad Restaurant: Evening dinner train from Canberra to Royalla with 3-course meal served on the train;
Dinner/Dance Trains: Steam of diesel-hauled trains to Royalla and Michelago or Bungendore and Tarago with 3-course meal and dancing in a local hall, followed by supper.

Steam locomotives are used wherever possible. Charter trips are also operated.

Location: The Michelago Tourist Railway operates from Canberra railway station via Queanbeyan. The line runs parallel to the Monaro Highway for 50km to the terminus at Michelago.

Bookings:	ARHS Tours, c/-ARHS (ACT Division) PO Box 112, Civic Square ACT 2608; or PO Box 1615, Queanbeyan NSW 2620
Phone:	(02) 6239 6707 or 6295 7909 for details
Facsimile:	(02) 6284 2791
Internet:	http://arhs.netsite1.net.au

Cooma-Monaro Railway
Cooma Monaro Railway Inc

Tourist Line (Rail Motor)
1435mm gauge

COOMA MONARO RAILWAY INC

Restored railmotors with CPH 6 in the lead stand at Cooma railway station.

The railway from Queanbeyan to Cooma opened in 1887. For generations, overnight trains provided holiday-makers with access to the Skifields, but with declining traffic, the line closed in 1989. The Cooma Monaro Railway (CMR) was formed in 1992 to preserve the railway heritage of Cooma and the Southern Monaro following closure of the line. The group leases the heritage-listed 1889 railway station, yard and other railway buildings at Cooma and is developing the area as a historic precinct.

Features: The Cooma railway precinct is one of the best examples of a rural railway depot in NSW, retaining most of its original buildings including the State's last locomotive straight shed.

Rolling Stock: CPH railmotors Nos 6, 8 and 22, together with trailer No 55.

Operations: Rail motors provide heritage operations over the line between Cooma and Bunyan and Chakola on Saturdays, Sundays and public holiday (no Saturday service in June to October). Trains for Bunyan leave every hour on the hour from 1000 to 1600 (1100-1500 in Winter), with connecting services to Chakola subject to demand and train availability. The return trip to Bunyan takes about 45 minutes. Additional services run at other times.

Check at Cooma Visitors Centre, (02) 6450 1742 or 1800 636 525.

Return fares per section (Cooma-Bunyan; Bunyan-Chakola): Adult $7, concession $5, child $4, family $15. Special charter trains are also operated, check with CMR below.

Location: 114km south of Canberra on the Monaro Highway. Bus services operate from Canberra Jolimont Centre.

Information: Cooma Monaro Railway Inc
PO Box 1327, Cooma NSW 2630
Phone: 1800 636 525

 RNE

Skitube, Bullocks Flat
Perisher Blue Pty Limited

Tourist Railway (Electric Rack,
1435mm gauge

This railway serving ski resorts in the Kosciusko National Park opened in 1987 as Australia's first electric mountain rac railway. It links Perisher Valley and Blue Cow Mountain resorts to the road access at Bullock Flat. The 8.4km line has grade of 1 in 8 and 6.2km of the route is located in tunnel. It is the longest tunnel through solid rock in the Southern Hemisphere the highest railway in Australia (1900m) and the fastest rack-rail train in the world (40kph). Each of the three terminals ha a range of facilities including restaurants, ski hire shops, and bars.

Operations: Winter timetable (June-October): 24 hours/day operation (but closed 0200-0500 Mon-Thursday) with 20 minute departures 0700-1100 and 1500-1800.
                   Summer timetable: Call for departure times.
Fares: Adult return $25; $14 children.

Location: At Bullocks Flat 20km from Jindabyne, 471km south of Sydney. Take the Alpine Way 85km from Cooma - till you see the Skitube sign - to Bullocks Flat Terminal.

Public Transport: Regular coach services from Canberra an Cooma.

Contact: Grahame Linkenbagh, Operations Manager
                 Skitube, Bullocks Flat, Alpine Way NSW 2624
Phone: (02) 6456 2010

HERITAGE SITES (Register of the National Estate)

Goulburn Railway Station: Goulburn railway station, completed in 1869, is important as a relatively early station in New South Wales. The station, with its various Classical design elements, juxtaposed with the Gothic-inspired station master's residence, forms a building group of significant architectural interest in the city. The railway station has been restored and upgraded by *Countrylink*. The Signals and Communications Display Centre features a range of signals and communication equipment used by the railways, with hands-on levers, lights and railway yard diagrams.

Queanbeyan Railway Station: The station group, dating from 1887, is significant for the range of substantially intact railway

structures it encompasses. The station was one of only four 'firs class' structures erected in New South Wales between 1884 an 1890.

Yass Junction Railway Station: Opened in 1876 and expanded 1892 when a connecting line to Yass Town was opened. With it. two station buildings of very different styles, passenger overbridge signal box and other elements, the station represents a rich collectior of cultural features. The two-storey station and residence building on the down line is one of only two such buildings on the southerr line. The brick station building on the up line is a particularly gooc example of such a building.

MURRIMBIDGEE / MURRAY REGIONS

The rich agricultural and pastoral lands of the Riverina attracted settlers in the early nineteenth century. In response to competition from South Australia and Victoria, NSW adopted a policy in 1876 to push railways as rapidly as possible to the south-west of the colony. The railway was extended from Yass Junction to Wagga Wagga in 1879 and onto Albury in 1881, with a branch from Junee to Narrandera and Hay opening in 1882. A network of branch railway lines was constructed to service the agricultural industries of the region. The railway stations erected at Junee, Wagga Wagga, Albury and Hay were built to a grand scale: symbols not only of the taming of the frontier, but also of the rivalry between the colonies and Sydney's determination to extend its commercial domination of the country.

Albury-Wodonga (population 80,000) Albury's role as a break-of-gauge transfer station between the NSW and Victorian railway systems established its initial importance. The twin towns of Albury and Wodonga on each side of the River Murray are located strategically in the geographic epicentre of south-eastern Australia. Since it was identified as a regional growth centre in 1973, the combined city has grown rapidly as an industrial, educational and tourist centre.

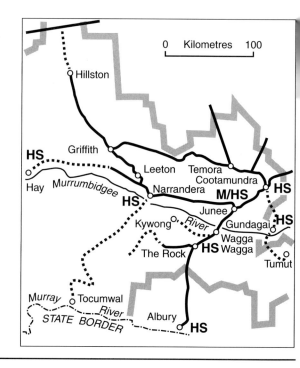

agga Wagga (population 58,000) has grown to become the
ate's major inland city with art galleries, live theatre and a uni-
rsity. The railway station has been restored under the *Countrylink*
pgrading program. There is a small museum collection of vehicles
d equipment used by railway fettlers on the station. A miniature
ilway operates in the Botanical Gardens and features an authentic
ation and booking office.

ootamundra (population 6500), was established in 1861 and
ew as a railway centre with the opening of the main southern line
1876. It remains an important rail junction and the historic rail-
ay station has been restored as a rail-coach interchange and tourist
formation centre.

ourist Information: Phone (02) 6942 4212.

nee (population 4500) is one of Australia's classic railway towns
hich developed around the needs of the steam locomotive. The
ritage railway station, built in 1883, includes a hotel and exten-
ve railway refreshment rooms (RRR) which served the needs of
ssengers in the heyday of railway travel. The buildings lining
e main street complement the station precinct.

Classic Australian country hotels offer an outstanding
vantagepoint to watch the passing railway action from their ornate
first floor verandahs. The almost completely intact mechanical yard
with a fine array of semaphore signals attracts visitors from Australia and overseas.

Tocumwal: Located on the Murray River, Tocumwal was a former
break-of-gauge station which saw frenzied activity during the War
years.

Getting There: The region is served by twice daily *CountryLink*
XPT services to Albury, plus a weekly service to Griffith, via Junee.
Phone (02) 6922 0488.

AUSTRAC: This regional freight operator, based in Junee, provides
regular services from regional centres to Port Botany (Sydney),
Port Kembla and Melbourne. Its distinctively liveried locomotives
add variety to railway operations on the Main Southern line and
branches to Griffith and Cowra.

ERITAGE SITES (Register of the National Estate)

lbury Railway Station: The large and lavishly decorated Vic-
rian Italianate station building was built in 1881 under the
rection of NSWGR Chief Engineer, John Whitton. As the major
reak-of-gauge transhipment point between the NSW and Victorian
ailways, the station came to symbolise the cost of early colonial
valry. The 455 metre length platform is the longest in NSW. The
ation has recently been restored to its original splendour.

lbury Railway Bridge: Placed in service in 1884, the bridge
as two main lattice truss spans each of 48.5m. It is one of a series
f twelve related bridges built between 1871 and 1887. The Bridge
Albury was the first to carry a double track and is the only two-
ack bridge of the series to remain in service under railway traffic.

ethungra Rail Spiral. This railway-engineering feature, located
0km north of Junee, spirals the main railway line around Bethungra
ill, crossing itself and the south line while transversing some of
e deepest cuttings in Australia. The spiral was constructed between
941 and 1946 and upgraded in 1993-94 for National Rail
perations.

ootamundra railway station: The 1887 building is
rchitecturally significant, its design being flavoured by Victorian
ustic Gothic style. Additionally, the platform roof is a very well
rafted structure, and the building is distinctive for its unusual
ctagonal tower.

Gundagai Railway Bridge. Completed in 1903, this 1km long
timber bridge over the Murrumbidgee flood plain is the longest
timber truss bridge ever constructed in Australia. The northern Approach consists of 72 timber truss spans, with a further five similar
truss spans on the south side, totalling 819m. The main span of the
bridge has a 61m main truss span with pinned joints and was supplied by Roberts of Pennsylvania. The bridge and railway precinct
are being restored by the local community.

Hay Railway Station: A grand and very decorative design, styled
in Victorian Free Classical architecture and built in 1882. The building has been restored and houses the Hay Employment Training
Centre and a rolling stock display is being established.

Junee Railway Station: The present station building was erected
in 1883. A large refreshment room and railway hotel were subsequently added. This building represents the ultimate example of
overseas stylistic influences in New South Wales in the 19th century. The former refreshment room now operates as a café.

Narrandera railway station: The station and stationmaster's
residence, dating from the early 1880s, represent an example of a
late Victorian railway complex in a New South Wales rural centre.

Wagga Wagga Railway Station: Dating from 1879, the station
is historically significant for its association with the extension of
the NSW railway network during the second half of the nineteenth
century. The grand railway station building has been restored by
Countrylink.

Junee Roundhouse Museum
Regional Heritage Transport Association, Junee Inc

Heritage Site/Museum

A H ROBINSON

Steam crane 1080 standing on the turntable at Junee Roundhouse Museum.

Australia's largest and most modern 360° roundhouse with 42 roads and a 100-foot diameter turntable opened at Junee in 1947. It represents the pinnacle of steam locomotive depot development. Following closure of the depot in 1993, the RHTA Junee has established a museum to preserve the history of the locomotive roundhouse and the role of transport in the distric

Features: The roundhouse forms the centrepiece of the museum and continues to operate as a working locomotive depot. There is a display of railway memorabilia and trikes. The east block of the roundhouse is used by AUSTRAC Ready Power as a base for re-building and maintaining locomotives for various clients. A HO-gauge model railway based on the Cootamundra/Parkes area of NSW will be operating from late 1999.

Rolling Stock: SRA diesel locomotives 4403 and 4807, restored Junee breakdown train featuring Brownhoist 50-ton steam crane No 1080 (built for US Army 1944), TPO mail van and a complete 12-car passenger carriage set. The locomotives and steam accident crane are in working condition.

Opening Times: Guided tours on Tuesdays and Thursdays at 1430 Saturdays, Sundays and public holidays at 1030 and 1430 (exce Christmas and Easter). Souvenirs and drinks available; mornin teas can be arranged.
Admission: Adults $4, children $2. Group concessions available

Location: Harold Street, Junee, 2km south of town centre (follo tourist signs off Olympic Highway)

Information: PO Box 271
                    Junee NSW 2663
Phone: (02) 6924 52909 or 6924 3239 (Secretary)
                    Fax (02) 6924 3762

BLUE MOUNTAINS

The Blue Mountains to the west of Sydney presented a natural barrier to the early railway builders: one which was overcome by building Zig Zags which were regarded as great engineering feats of the day. In 1867 the railway was extended west from Penrith, climbing 200 metres by the Lapstone Zig-Zag. Between Valley Heights and Katoomba the line climbs 700 metres in a distance of 30km. The railway reached Mount Victoria in 1868, when a small sandstone station was erected. The highest point (1115 metres) was reached at Clarence Siding, from where the railway descended 110 metres into the Lithgow Valley by the Great Zig Zag.

City of the Blue Mountains (population 64,000), comprising 26 towns and villages, is a popular tourist venue because of its clean fresh air, unique network of bushwalks, unrivalled vistas and close proximity to Sydney. The rail journey by *CityRail* double-deck, air-conditioned electric trains offers spectacular vistas.
Tourist Information Centre: Echo Point, Katoomba NSW 2780
Phone:　(02) 4739 6266

City of Lithgow (population 15,000), 153km west of Sydney, developed as a coal mining and industrial centre with the opening of the Great Zig Zag Railway in 1869. Coal mines were initially established to supply the needs of the railway. One of Australia's pioneer iron and steel works operated at Lithgow from 1875. The first (open-hearth) steel was produced here in 1900 and a blast furnace opened in 1907. An industrial railway system serviced the complex until the steel works were transferred to Port Kembla in 1928. The railway from Sydney to Lithgow was electrified in 1957 and the locomotive depot has become the base for *FreightCorp's* electric locomotive fleet.

　　Lithgow has become a major centre of industrial archaeology and railway heritage. The Great Zig Zag is now home to one of

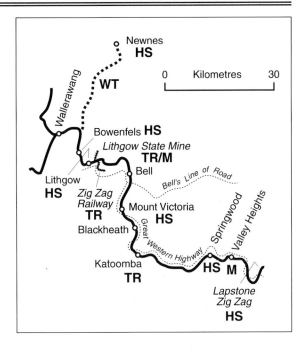

Australia's premier tourist railways while the former Lithgow State Mine has been developed as an industrial tourist railway and mining museum. An underground diesel mine locomotive and man-car are on static display in Rotary Park, Main Street. Lithgow is a convenient base for walking tours to the Wolgan Valley Railway.

Getting There: Lithgow (100km west of Sydney) is the terminus of regular *CityRail* electric commuter services. Trains depart Sydney Terminal station from 0600 daily, with hourly departures from 0819 during the week, less regularly on weekends and public holidays.

Katoomba Scenic Railway
Katoomba Scenic Railway Pty Limited

Tourist Railway (Funicular)

The incline railway is located near the site of abandoned coalmines. It was built in 1879 to service a coal mine in the Jamieson Valley. In 1948 it was purchased by Mr Harry Hammon and restored for tourist operations. Today the Scenic Railway provides visitors with access to self-guided walking tours in the Jamieson Valley. The History Tour depicts the mining era of the valley.

Features: The line is the world's steepest incline railway. It provides a unique ride through a tunnel and descends 415 metres with a maximum grade of 52° through an ancient rainforest in the Jamieson Valley. Due to increasing demand, a third car entered service in 1993, increasing seating capacity from 56 to 84 for each trip. On site, a bucket from the former shale ropeway and a 610mm gauge wooden railway truck provide a link to the incline railway's former industrial heritage. Also on site is an aerial cable car travelling 340 metres across a gorge 300 metres deep. The complex has a revolving licensed restaurant, snack bar and souvenir shop.

Operations: Trains operate at 10-minute intervals from 0900 until 1650 every day of the year.
Return fare: Adults $4.50, children $2.

Location: 110km west of Sydney on the main Western railway line and Great Western Highway. Take Cliff Drive and follow tourist signs to the scenic railway.

Public Transport: *CityRail* trains to Katoomba. Buses leave from opposite the Carrington Hotel in Katoomba Street, with *The Explorer* bus departing from Katoomba station on Saturday, Sunday and public holidays.

Contact:　Scenic Railway
　　　　　　1 Violet Street, Katoomba NSW 2780
Phone:　(02) 4782 2699; facsimile (02) 4782 5675

Valley Heights Locomotive Depot Heritage Museum
NSW Rail Transport Museum (Blue Mountains Division)
Steam Tram and Railway Preservation Society

Museum
1435mm gauge

DEREK ROGERS

The Valley Heights Loco Depot Museum with steam locomotives 1022 and 5461, electric locomotive 4601 and carriages on display.

During the steam era Valley Heights was the staging point for banking engines on the steeply graded Western line to Katoomba. The locomotive depot opened in 1913 and provided steam locomotives for assistance duties until electrification in 1957. Following closure of the depot in 1988, the roundhouse and associated buildings were preserved as a railway museum. The Steam Tram and Railway Preservation (Co-op) Society Ltd was formed to preserve and operate steam tram and light railway equipment. Following a fire, which destroyed the Society's former depot in Parramatta Park in 1993, the Society has relocated its operations to the Valley Heights Museum.

Features: The depot at Valley Heights consisted of a locomotive yard, 10 bay roundhouse, 18 metre (60ft) turntable, an elevated coal stage, water tanks and columns and provided pilot (assistant) engines for trains travelling to Katoomba and beyond. With electrification in 1956, Valley Heights depot became a base for the 46-class electric locomotives until 1996.

Locomotives: Standard goods 2-8-0 locomotive 5461 (Clyde 210/1916) of the type used for banking purposes from Valley Heights and 46-class electric locomotive 4601. Steam locomotives include 0-6-0ST *Stepho* (RS 2994/1899), ex-Commonwealth Portland Cement and ex-NSWGR 0-4-0ST 1022 (Vulcan 2505/1916).

Steam Trams: The centrepiece of the Steam Tram Society's collection is Sydney steam tram motor No 103A, built by Baldwin in 1891. The tram motor was fully restored for its centenary by the Rail Transport Museum at Thirlmere and has been rebuilt following the 1993 fire. 103A is one of only two Baldwin steam tram motors known to be operating in the world.

Rolling Stock: Comprises examples of typical stock used over the Blue Mountains during the 1950's, including the stainless steel inter urban cars which were introduced with electric traction during the late 1950's and a TAM sleeping carriage. Goods rolling stock comprising mainly of the 4-wheel type which played such an

important role in moving goods to and from the western regions of the State. Former N-class electric tram bodies 619 and 685 have been converted to steam tram trailers.

Displays: Rail heritage displays interpret the development and progress of the railways on the Western Line, with particular emphasis on the Blue Mountains Region. Memorabilia and artefacts including signalling equipment, signs, seating and photographs are displayed in the former administrative building. The main external features of the Museum provide grassed family barbecue and picnic areas: a Devonshire tea room, sales and information office and restoration areas for exhibits.

Opening Times: Sundays and public holidays, including Christmas

Location: On the Great Western Highway and Railway, 77km west of Sydney. Regular *CityRail* electric train services.

Address: The Secretary, Blue Mountains Division
NSW Rail Transport Museum
PO Box 484, Springwood NSW 2777
Phone: (02) 4751 4638 (weekends)
Steam Tram and Railway Preservation (Co-op) Society
PO Box 3179, Parramatta NSW 2124

ig Zag Railway
ig Zag Railway Co-op Ltd

Tourist Railway (Steam/Railmotor)
1067 mm gauge

MICHAEL FORBES

The guard gives the "green flag" as ex-QGR DD17-class 4-6-4T steam locomotive hauls a set of stainless steel carriages at the Bottom Points Signal Box.

he 7.5km tourist railway operates over the Great Zig Zag near Lithgow. Built between 1866 and 1869 to allow trains to egotiate the steep western face of the Blue Mountains, the Great Zig Zag was acclaimed as one of the engineering wonders of the 19th century. It has three levels each with a falling grade of 1 in 42 towards Lithgow, 3 viaducts and 2 tunnels. The Zig Zag was replaced in 1910 by a 10-tunnel, double track deviation opened and the original line fell into disuse. It has been evived as a tourist railway. Operations commenced along the "Middle Road" in October 1975, with the extension from Top oints to Clarence completed in October 1988.

Heritage Significance: The Great Zig Zag is regarded as the greatest engineering achievement in railway construction in Australia. At the time of building, 1866-1869, the Zig Zag was regarded worldwide as an engineering marvel. The three main viaducts are significant technical accomplishments, particularly when regard is given to the difficulty of their sites. They are in excellent condition. The provision of the railway in the period 1869-1910 assisted the major development of western New South Wales.

Features: The rail journey over the viaducts offers spectacular scenery and the opportunity to relive the steam train journey over the 19th century engineering wonder. From Clarence station the line climbs to 1115 metres, the highest point on the Western Railway, then enters the 492 metre Clarence tunnel. At the "Top Points", passengers have the opportunity to take in views over the Lithgow suburb of Oakey Park while the locomotive runs around the train for the descent down the "Middle Road".

Locomotives: 8 steam locomotives from Queensland and South Australia. Operating steam locomotives are: DD17-class 4-6-4T Nos 1047 and 1049 (built Ipswich 1951); BB18¼-class 4-6-2 No 1072, *City of Lithgow* (Walkers 540/1956); and C17-class 4-8-0 No 934 (Clyde 501/1949). Diesel locomotives include V13 0-6-0DM, ex-TGR and Mt Lyell Railway and ex-colliery locos.

Rolling Stock: 11 ex-QR vintage Evans Cars, 7 ex-QR stainless steel suburban cars and 4 ex-SAR *Long Tom* carriages, together with 6 ex-QGR 2000-class railcars. Various goods stock and gangers trolleys.

Operations: 7-days a week, with steam trains on Saturdays, Sundays, public holidays, and NSW school holidays (except the week before Christmas), and railcars on other days. Weekend departures from Clarence terminal at 1030, 1215, 1400 and 1545, the round trip taking 1 hour 25 minutes. Dual steam train/railmotor timetables on Sundays enable visitors to experience steam one way and a guided trip with photo stops the other. Weekday trains depart Clarence terminal at 1100, 1300 and 1500. There are more frequent trains at Easter and some school holiday weekends.

Fares: Adults $13, child $6.50, concession $10.50 (1999).

Location: Clarence Terminal station is beside the Richmond-Lithgow road 150km W of Sydney; 10km east of Lithgow.

Public Transport: *CityRail* trains to Zig Zag station (Bottom Points) stop on request. The 0820 ex-Sydney Terminal weekdays or 0802/ 0902 trains weekends and public holidays connect with Zig Zag services.

Contact: Michael Forbes, General Manager, Zig Zag Railway
PO Box 187, Lithgow NSW 2790

Phone: (02) 6353 1795. Recorded information (02) 6351 4826

RNE

State Mine Railway Heritage Park & Railway
City of Greater Lithgow Mining Museum Inc

Tourist Railway (Steam)/Museum
1435mm gauge

BOB McKILLOP

Restored workshop building and 2-6-2T locomotive 2605 at State Mine Railway Heritage Park, Lilthgow.

The heritage railway and mining museum has been established to restore and retain one of the great industrial heritage site of Australia. The State Mine Colliery and the former Lithgow Power Station were linked to the NSWGR by a 2.5km branch line which opened in 1920. The line has been restored as an operating heritage railway, which links the key sites of Lithgow' industrial heritage.

Displays: The museum has a display of coal and oil-shale mining equipment and memorabilia. Steam equipment and rolling stock are also on display. The remains of the steel works in Blast Furnace Park (off Inch Street) provide a tribute to the former era. Current development will extend the railway line to Eskbank Station - thus linking the historic Eskbank railway precinct, Eskbank House, Blast Furnace Park, Lake Pillans Wetland and the State Mine museum. Further plans involve the recreation of the original 1869 Lithgow Locomotive Depot.

Locomotives: Ex-NSWGR and Portland Cement Works 2-6-2ST 2605 (Dubs 2794/1892), ex-BHP industrial diesel D23 from the Port Kembla steelworks, ex-NSWGR 45-class diesel, 4514 (stored on behalf of M&S Gaut) and DM Railcars 661/761and 668/768, Ex-NSWGR 46 class electric locomotive 4615 is stored on behalf of the Sydney Electric Train Society. In addition, a range of underground locomotives, including two Glen Davis tram locos, Jenbach 4wDM and man-riding cars are included in the museum display.

Rolling Stock: A range of former NSWGR passenger cars,including six end-platform carriages, together with 4-wheel S-trucks, cement hoppers and refrigerator cars. A range of mine skips and transports is being restored.

Steam Equipment: Ex-NSW Tramways Clayton & Shuttleworth steam roller, steam pumps and equipment from the floating crane *Titan*, and various stationary and portable steam engines.

Operations: The Museum is open weekends, public and school holidays from 0900-1600 Summer and 1000-1600 Winter, with regular conducted tours. Other times by appointment. Train operations from Blast Furnace Park to the Museum on first Sunday of the month and public holidays.

Location: Trains operate from adjacent to Blast Furnace Park in Lithgow, 160km west of Sydney on Great Western Highway.
Public Transport: Lithgow is the terminus of regular *CityRail* electric commuter services.

Contact: Greater Lithgow Mining Museum
              PO Box 617, Lithgow NSW 2790
Phone: (02) 6353 1513, fax (02) 6353 1185

         RNE

HERITAGE SITES (Register of the National Estate)

Blast Furnace Park, Lithgow. The ruins of Australia's first steel works provide a monument to Lithgow's industrial history. It was here that the first iron and the first steel in Australia were cast. William Sandford established the blast furnace in 1886 and it continued production until 1928 when the entire industry was moved to Port Kembla. The site has now been developed as a park around the remains of the pump house and the foundations of the furnace. Industrial sidings are being reestablished on original alignments for State Mine Railway trains.

Bowenfels Railway Station: The historic Bowenfels railway station and adjacent station master's cottage, opened in October 1869, are regarded as some of the finest examples of railway architecture of their period. Their steeply sloping slate roofs, attractive verandahs and intricate work in both stone and joinery are unusual in NSWGR architecture. The railway station has been restored and is the home of the **Greater Lithgow Visitors Centre** providing tourist information, souvenirs, maps and brochures of local attractions and with displays of local art, pottery and crafts and historic photographs of Lithgow's industrial heritage.

Open: 0900-1700 7 days a week.
Address: 1 Cooerwull Road (off the Great Western Highway)
PO Box 682, Lithgow NSW 2790
Phone: (02) 6353 1859; Fax (02) 6353 1851
Web Page: http://llsp.com.au/~lithtour/

Caddies Restaurant, Bowenfels: The Station Master's residence is designed in Victorian Rustic Gothic style and like the station building is also constructed of coursed, random stone. It houses a popular licensed restaurant with a railway theme, including trikes, photographs and memorabilia. Dining 1830-2130, Wednesday to Saturday. Caddies Carriage Restaurant, housed in a 1949 railway carriage, is open for lunches and light refreshments from 1100-1600, Wednesday to Sunday.
Hosts: Matt and Lyn Warburton, Phone (02) 6353 1666

Eskbank Railway Station/Goods Shed/Locomotive Depot: Eskbank railway station, the first in the area, and goods shed have been restored as a base for the State Mine Railway Heritage Park Group. The foundations of the former locomotive depot and turntable pit have been excavated and a replica depot is under construction on the site.

Knapsack Viaduct: In the construction of the Great Western Railway from the Nepean River into the Blue Mountains, John Whitton constructed a zig zag at Lapstone in 1867. The sandstone viaduct over Knapsack Creek is one of Australia's most spectacular bridges. The bridge has seven arches, with the two central support arches being 38 metres above water level. The viaduct was converted to carry road traffic in 1938. Take marked exit from M4 Motorway at Emu Plains after crossing Nepean River.

Mount Victoria Railway Station. The whole of Mount Victoria village, including the outstanding sandstone station, is classified by the National Trust. The original section of the station was built in 1868 and extended in 1884, including railway refreshment rooms and hotel facilities. A local history museum, which includes railway memorabilia, is located in the station building.

Springwood Railway Station: The building features a high pitched iron roof formed behind high parapets having two Gothic gables to each side and central pediment carrying a date plaque.

Wolgan Valley Railway Display: The Wolgan Valley in the Blue Mountains north of Lithgow was the site of a large oil shale industry at Newnes from c.1906 to c.1932. It was served by a private, standard gauge, mountain railway that featured spectacular railway scenery through the enclosed Penrose Gorge and Wolgan River valleys. The line offered an outstanding example of early railway engineering and used Australia's largest Shay geared locomotives.

The line is of major heritage significance. It was a remarkable feat of civil engineering in that it was built in only 12 months over difficult terrain for a relatively low cost. Its remaining structures are a tribute to the skill of its builders, and the ambition of the men who conceived it. A static display of rolling stock and other items associated with the oil-shale industry has been established near the old Newnes Hotel, which now trades as a kiosk on weekends only.
Location: At Newnes 35km by car from the turnoff at Lidsdale, on the main Lithgow-Mudgee road. The turnoff is approx 1km north of Wallerawang power station. There is no public transport.
Contact: Alan Watson, Kerosene Shale Research
PO Box 126, Wallerawang NSW 2845

WALKING TRAILS

Glow Worm Tunnel: A walk to the Glow Worm Tunnel provides trekkers with the opportunity to follow the Wolgan Valley Railway formation through a 400m tunnel, now known for its glow worms, and tree fern gullies past spectacular rock formations. The Glow Worm Tunnel may be accessed from Newnes or from the southern end. This walk starts at Clarence on the Zig Zag Railway.

Newnes Historic Ruins Trail. The historic ruins at Newnes and walking trails along the railway formation are now tourist attractions. The track, which commences at the site of the former Newnes railway station is 5km and takes 4-5 hours. For walks, check with the Tourist Information Centre, Lithgow, or at the Newnes kiosk.

Lapstone Zig Zag Walking Track: The track follows the original cuttings of the zig zag to Lucasville station, providing views of the Knapsack Viaduct. Entry to the walking track is from the Great Western Highway at the Lapstone Hotel RAAF establishment. The walk, marked by signs, takes 1-2 hours. Phone (02) 4739 6266 for information.

EXPLORER COUNTRY
Central West and Orana Regions

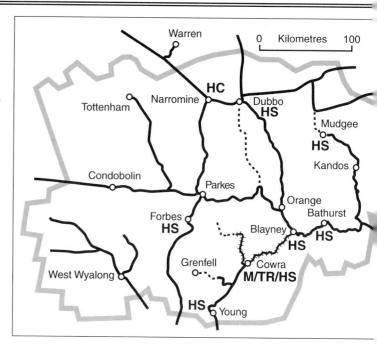

This vast "heartland" offers a wide range of tourist attractions based on the peacefulness and friendly nature of the local people. Its attractive rural scenery, agri-tourism, wildlife, history and heritage draw visitors from around the world. The region also serves as a gateway to the *Outback*.

The Great Western Railway was Australia's first railway built to the Inland. The main line between Lithgow and Blayney is particularly scenic with tortuous curves around rolling hills, including a horseshoe bend at Locksley, which offer outstanding railway photographic locations. The main rail route from Melbourne and Adelaide to Newcastle and Brisbane, via Parkes and Dubbo passes through the region.

Bathurst (population 28,000) 200km west of Sydney, was proclaimed a town in 1815 to become Australia's first inland settlement. Today it is an important education and industrial centre with railway workshops and the locomotive building plant of Clyde Engineering. History abounds in its fine buildings from the dramatic courthouse to restored workmen's cottages.

Orange (population 36,000) 276km west of Sydney on the main Western Railway line, is a commercial, educational and industrial city serving the Central West region of the state. Orange is an important railway junction for the main lines to Broken Hill (and Perth) and Cobar.
Information: Orange Visitors Centre, Civic Centre.
Phone (02) 6361 5226

Cowra (population 8,500) 300km west of Sydney in the Lachlan Valley is the service centre for a rich agricultural area and has recently emerged as a quality wine producing district. Cowra is located about half-way along the state's first cross-country railway between Harden and Blayney, opened in 1888.

Dubbo (population 38,000) is a rapidly growing regional city servicing the western districts of the state. Dubbo prospered as a major railway centre with lines to Wellington (and Sydney), Merrygoen (and on to Newcastle), Coonamble, Narromine and Yeoval (now closed). A top attraction is the Western Plains Zoo, one of the world's leading open-range zoos.
Daily XPT service to Sydney.
Phone: (02) 6881 2107

Mudgee railway station is a significant heritage item in the region.

Parkes (population 9,000) 365km west of Sydney, is at the cross roads of Australia's main transport corridors, including the ma Sydney-Perth and Melbourne-Brisbane railway lines. From th Parkes *Inland Port,* intermodal freight is assembled for forward ing, via Australia's national rail network, to the major cities ar ports. To mark the town's link with the railway, 4-6-0 steam loc motive No 3075 (built Eveleigh 1912) has been preserved at th Parkes Tourist Centre in Kelly Reserve, on the Newell Highway
Information: Parkes Tourist Centre, Newell Highway
(PO Box 532), Parkes NSW 2870
Phone: (02) 6862 4365/6862 1011

Getting There: There are coach connections from *CityRa* Lithgow services to a range of Central West towns. The dail *Central West XPT* train serves stations between Lithgow and Dubb with connecting coach services to towns in the region fron Bathurst, Orange and Dubbo. The region is linked to Sydney b the Great Western Highway and Bells Line of Road throug Windsor.

Lachlan Valley Railway, Cowra
Lachlan Valley Railway Co-op Society

Tourist Railway (Steam/Diesel)
1435 mm gauge

LAWRANCE RYAN

4701 arrives at Koorawatha on 21 February 1998 en-route from Young working SL61 passenger charter to convey patrons from Young to a pre-season Rugby League game at Cowra.

The former NSWGR steam locomotive depot at Cowra is home to the Society's collection of steam and diesel locomotives, rail motors and numerous items of historical rolling stock. LVR steam trains operate to Holmwood on the Cowra-Blayney railway and Koorawatha on the Cowra-Harden branch line. The LVR is accredited to operate mainline tours.

Features: An authentic locomotive depot from the days of steam, complete with original roundhouse (built 1923), turntable and timber-supported overhead water tanks. On display in the museum are the LVR's locomotives, rail motors and rolling stock.

Locomotives: Operating locomotives include ex-NSWGR 2-8-0 standard goods 5367 (Clyde 122/1914); 4701/16 Bo-Bo DE Goninan (1972); 4486 Co-Co main line de Goodwin (1967); and industrial de D9 ex-BHP Port Kembla (EE Aust 1956). Other steam locomotives ex-NSWGR are 4-6-0 3026T (BP 4469 of 1903); 2-8-2 5917, built by Baldwin in USA in 1952; 3237, one of the famous P-class 4-6-0 express locomotives of 1892; and 3013, a 4-6-4T suburban loco of 1903.

Rolling Stock: CPH and 900 Series DEB rail motors, 40 passenger cars and a variety of goods vehicles, a selection of which is on display, including TAM/EAM sleeping cars, HCX1187 side-loading passenger/baggage/guard car, Pullman car DEC26, end-platform cars, FS and RBS steel passenger, ABS dining car, RG1947 Greyhound car, EVA1501 TAFE classroom car and steam breakdown cranes.

Opening Times: Depot/Museum open 0930-1630 weekends and public holidays and on weekdays by special arrangement. LVR steam trains operate from Cowra Railway Station on the second full weekend of the month and long-weekends from March through to November.

Mainline trains are operated to other locations at irregular intervals. During days of high fire danger, railmotors or diesel-hauled trains will be substituted for steam. Visitors are advised to check with the LVR Booking Officer for up-to-date information. Phone (02) 6341 1052.

Location: The LVR Steam Locomotive Depot/Museum is in Campbell Street, Cowra, some 300km west of Sydney. Take the Mid-Western Highway to Cowra, then turn left into Fitzsimmons Street (near BP service station) and follow to "Give Way" sign at Brougham Street. Turn left into Brougham and across level crossing and take first right (Campbell Street) and proceed to LVR depot and car park at end of street. Trains operate from Cowra railway station.

Public Transport: coordinated rail-coach service to Cowra by State Rail and private bus operators.

Address: The Secretary, LVR Co-op Society
      PO Box 2794, Cowra NSW 2794
Bookings: Phone (02) 6341-1052; fax (02) 6341 3599
Infoline: 0413 455 367
Home Page: www.ozemail.com.au/~lvrcowra

Narromine Railway Heritage Precinct
Unlimited Narrromine Inc / Narromine Community Skills Project Inc

Heritage Centre

Narromine railway station has been restored to its original condition by the local community and serves as the focal point of the Narromine Railway Heritage Precinct. The station serves as a tourist promotion centre and provides facilities for *Countrylink* passengers and features interpretative displays of the role of the station in the community in the 1920s.

Heritage Significance: The town of Narromine was created by the opening of the railway in 1882 and the station and associated Station Master's cottage (completed 1883) were the first permanent buildings. The restored station is listed on the RNE and the pedestrian overbridge is listed on the State Rail Heritage Register.

Features: The station has been restored to its original condition of the early 1900s and serves *Countrylink* coach passengers with waiting areas, booking facilities and light refreshments. A collection of artifacts is being developed as a display to interpret the core functions of the station. Audio presentations will tell the story of the mail trains and branchline services.

Landscaped grounds, heritage display and train are under development and a future stage will include a Heritage Education Centre. This will interpret the history of railways in Orana Region. Craft manufacture will also be demonstrated. The Station Shop sells gift packs of Macquarie Valley produce, souvenirs and historic reproductions.
Opening Times: 1000-1600 daily.
Location: 40km west of Dubbo on Mitchell Highway.
Address: Unlimited Narromine Inc
         PO Box 377, Narromine NSW 2821

 RNE

OTHER HERITAGE SITES (Register of the National Estate)

Bathurst Railway Bridge: The bridge over the Macquarie River at Bathurst, opened for service in 1876, has three main lattice truss spans, each of 48.5m. It is the oldest of this type remaining in NSW and longest remaining metal truss bridge of its age in Australia.

Bathurst Railway Station: Opened in March 1876, the station building was regarded as one of the finest in the State at this time. With its curvilinear gables, it is a good example of Victorian Tudor architecture. The station has recently been restored to its former elegance with a modern *Countrylink* booking office and bus interchange. Clyde Engineering has restored pioneer Commonwealth Railways pioneer diesel-electric locomotive GM3 to its original condition for shunting operations at its Kelso plant.

Blayney Railway Station: This 1876 building is significant for its high level of intactness and its inherent interest in being one of the few stations in the state to have a residence/station building on an island platform. The opening of the railway was a watershed in the town's history, bringing with it marked prosperity.

Cowra Railway Bridge: Placed in service in 1887, the bridge over the Lachlan River at Cowra is the last of a series of 12 related bridges designed by Sir John Fowler built between 1871 and 1887. The Cowra bridge it has three main lattice truss spans, each of 48.5m and four additional minor approaches and high cast iron piers.

Dubbo Rail Bridge: Completed in 1884, the bridge over the Macquarie River at Dubbo is one of a series of twelve related bridges built between 1871 and 1887 of which eleven remain. It has three main lattice truss spans, each of 48.5 metres. The approaches previously included 39 timber girder spans each of 7.9m length, but these have been replaced in concrete.

Dubbo Railway Station built in 1881 together with the two storey sandstone station master's residence. The SM's residence classified by the National Trust and now serves as an administrative centre. The station has recently been renovated as a major *Countrylink* Travel Centre and rail-bus interchange for the Western Region.

Forbes Railway Station (1893) with its gabled form, symmetry and flanking wings, is significant for being a good example of late nineteenth century railway station in a New South Wales country centre. The station is one of a number of buildings in the town that helps to reflect Forbes' development from a gold town into a thriving pastoral and agricultural centre during the later part of last century.

Lithgow-Sodwalls Railway: Although this stretch of railway has been extensively rebuilt since its opening in 1869-71, the original structures and buildings are mostly still intact which represent a unique set of heritage items.

Mudgee Railway Station: This single storey Victorian Italianate railway station is listed on the Register of the National Estate as an excellent example of a late Victorian country railway station that survives relatively in its original condition. It is one of the few buildings of this type to retain unpainted exterior masonry walls and marks an important phase of country development following the rushes to the western NSW Goldfields.

THE LIVING OUTBACK

The Great Western Railway was Australia's first railway built in the Inland. It sought to open up the agricultural lands west of the Great Dividing Range and to tap the wool trade on the Murray-Darling River system back to Sydney. Beyond Dubbo, the railway created its own frontier. The first train ran through to Bourke on 3 September 1885. In the process, it crossed flat plains on what was then the longest stretch of straight track in the world, some 116 miles (187km) in length.

Further west, rich silver, lead and zinc lodes in the Barrier Ranges led to the development of Broken Hill as one of the world's great mining centres in the 1880s. To enable the development of the mines, a narrow-gauge railway opened in 1887 to connect Broken Hill with Port Pirie. To complete the link from Broken Hill to Port Pirie, the 56km gap from Broken Hill to the South Australian border was bridged by the **Silverton Tramway Company** (STC) which opened in January 1888. The STC remains an active short line and shunting operator and shunts mineral sidings in the Broken Hill area. The standard gauge link to the NSW system was not completed until 1927.

Broken Hill (population 24,500), once the richest lode of silver, lead and zinc in the world, is also a base for touring the *Outback*, the rugged heartland of Australia. The National Trust has classified the historic streetscape of Arthur Street. Detailed guides to walking and driving tours of the city's heritage are available from the **Tourist Information Centre**,
> corner of Blende and Bromide Streets, (PO Box 286)
> Broken Hill NSW 2880
> Phone: (02) 8087 6077

Silverton. This ghost town, 25km north-west of Broken Hill, was once a thriving mining settlement of 3000 people. Tourists now visit its art galleries, the Gaol museum, the Silverton Hotel (the scene of some Australian movies) and Penrose Park.

Cobar (population 4,000) is an important mining town. Copper was discovered in 1869 and the Great Cobar Mine was established in 1876. Following the opening of the railway in 1894, the Great Cobar became one of the largest mines in the country until its closure in 1919. A standard gauge electric industrial railway was constructed in 1908 to served the smelting works. The Cornish Scottish & Australian mine, 12km from Cobar, was reopened in 1965, while the Elura mine (47km west) followed in 1983 to exploit silver-lead ore. These mines generate significant rail traffic from Cobar.

Great Cobar Outback Heritage Centre
Council of the Shire of Cobar

Local History Museum

Located on the site of the Great Cobar copper mine, this museum portrays the social, pastoral and mining history of the district. It is housed in the Federation-style administrative office of the Great Cobar Mine built in 1910.

Exhibits: Royal Far West Health Scheme railway carriage No 3 LBK 86 built 1907 and converted in 1934) and Great Cobar Mine electric locomotive of 1908, the first electric locomotive in NSW. A 4w BE locomotive and ore trucks from the New Occidental Mine feature in the simulated underground mine.

Facilities: Souvenir shop, tourist information centre and free electric barbecues. Interpretative signs outside guide visitors through the grounds and an amazing collection of mining and transport artefacts, and on to the surrounding heritage areas.
Opening Times: 0800-1700 weekdays;
1000-1700 weekends and public holidays.

Admission: Adults $5, children $2, families $8.

Location: Barrier Highway, Cobar, 712km north-west of Sydney.
Public Transport: *Central West XPT* train to Dubbo, thence daily coach service. Daily coach services from Adelaide.

Contact:	Kay Palmer, Curator
	Box 341, Cobar NSW 2
Phone:	(02) 6836 2448; fax (02) 6836 1194

RNE

The Story of Nyngan
Bogan Shire Council

Local History Museum

Nyngan developed as a railway town around a steam locomotive depot. Located in the restored Nyngan railway station, this museum provides a social and economic history of the town titled *Nyngan, Our Inside Story.*

Exhibits: Life of the district's pioneers, including an interpretative display of the role of the railway in the development of Nyngan, including a simulated carriage setting and the original railway manual telephone exchange. A mining display is housed in another section of the station.

Opening Times: 1000-1600 daily.
Admission: Adults $2.

Location:	On Mitchell Highway, 599km north-west of Sydney.
Contact:	Glad Eldridge
	97 Cobar Street, Nyngan NSW 2825
Phone:	(02) 6832 1052

Broken Hill Railway, Mineral & Train Museum

Railway Museum
1067mm gauge

JOHN R NEWLAND

Sulphide Street Museum, once the Silverton Tramway Company's passenger station.

The museum is based in the former Sulphide Street passenger terminal of the Silverton Tramway Company (STC). The railway station was built in 1905 from sandstone quarried locally. The museum features railway and mining history, with particular emphasis on the locomotives and rolling stock of the STC.

Heritage significance: Considered a showpiece in its day, the station was for 30 years the only passenger terminal of the Silverton Tramway Company. It is now one of the few physical reminders of the early boom days of the Company. Architecturally it is an excellent unaltered example of its type while its location in the centre of the town makes it an important townscape element.

Displays: The museum features numerous items of signalling, track maintenance and workshop equipment used on the Silverton railway, together with Company documents and photographs.
Locomotives: STC locomotives 2-6-0 Y1 (built Beyer Peacock 1888), 4-8-2 W 24 (built Beyer Peacock 1951) and 0-6-0DH of 1953; ex-SAR T-class 4-8-0 locomotive No 181.
Rolling Stock: Former STC carriages and wagons, including an ex-SAR Dodge inspection car of 1938, 4-wheel GX ore wagon and SAR passenger cars 304 (1st class) and 409 (2nd class). The pioneer NSWGR standard gauge *Silver City Comet* diesel train set

headed by B-B DH DP 101 of 1937 is displayed in the former railway yard.
Opening Times:
The museum is open daily from 1000 to 1500 hours.
Admission: Adults $2, child/concession $1.50, family $5.
Location: at the former Sulphide Street Station of the Silverton Tramway Company opposite the Tourist Information Centre. Broken Hill is located 1120km west of Sydney.
Public Transport: Transcontinental *Indian Pacific* train, a weekly *Countrylink* train service from Orange and daily *Countrylink* road services connecting with the *Central-West XPT* at Dubbo.

Contact: PO Box 530
       Broken Hill NSW 2880

     ♿ 📖 **RNE**

HERITAGE ITEMS

Cobar Railway Station: Opened at the height of the 1890s depression, the station was built in brick to symbolise its importance as a terminus. From 1900 to 1914, the station was one of the busiest in the State. The station building has been restored and is managed by a local committee as a centre for community-based activities, including a cyber café, radio station and crafts.
Contact: Cobar Community Station Inc
       PO Box 634, Cobar NSW 2835

Silverton. The former Silverton railway station, locomotive water tank and a short length of line have been preserved. STC 2-6-0

locomotive Y11 (BP 3535/1893) is on static display in Penrose Park. At the Silverton Gaol and Museum, a battery-electric locomotive is on display.

Tarrowingee Railway, north of Broken Hill, was purchased by the NSW Government from the STC in 1901 to convey limestone to Broken Hill for flux in the smelters. The stone platform at Tarrowingee and also earthworks and structures of the former 1067mm railway can still be seen.

DAVID JOHNSON

The line between Normanton and Croydon in Far North Queensland has been in existence for a century. The Gulflander *comprising the railmotor and trailer has become a most popular tourist train which is seen here crossing one of the numerous bridge which regularly flood during the wet season.*

BRIAN WEBBE

The QR preserved BB18˘-class steam locomotive No 1079 shunts across a street in the town of Laidley, Queensland on 27 May 1999.

BOB SAMPSON

The 457mm gauge 2-4-0 steam locomotive Bill *stands on the turntable at the Semaphore and Fort Glanville Tourist Railway in Adelaide, SA.*

Top: The ex-QGR PB15-class steam locomotive No 738 is nearing Kunkala with a Rosewood Railway tourist passenger on Sunday, 27 July 1997.

Bottom: The first mainline steam for 1998 and the last Perth steam ever. Steam locomotive W 903 leads the MRWA and SO "under the wires" near Meltham, bound for Tooday on 3 May 1998.

Activities by the NSW Rail Transport Museum: a tourist train hauled by 5910 near Bylong on the Ulan line in the late afternoon of 8 Ju 1998 (above); volunteers shovelling coal into the firebox on a steam tourist excursion during July 1999 (lower left); cutting rivets from t tender of locomotive 2705 at Thirlmere in April 1995 during restoration (lower right). *All photos:Lindsay Luca.*

HUNTER REGION

The Hunter River was explored in 1797 and ship captains began collecting coal the following year. Settlement dates from 1801, when convicts were put to work mining coal, thus establishing the industry that was to shape the settlement of the lower river valley.

Colliery horse-drawn railways date from 1831 and the government's **Great Northern Railway** (GNR) opened from Newcastle to East Maitland in 1857.

The extensive railway networks that were developed to serve the collieries from the 1860s provide the basis for the region's significant railway heritage. The **South Maitland Railways** Pty Limited with 40km of railways served collieries in the district. Its famous 10-class 2-8-2T locomotives, based on the NSWGR 2-8-0 standard goods design, hauled trains over the SMR until 10 June 1983. All 14 of the 10-class locomotives have been heritage protected and are preserved by various museum groups. A number of museum and tourist railway projects have been established to promote this heritage in recent years. The region is also famous for its wines and water sporting facilities.

Newcastle (population 274,000), 168km north of Sydney, is Australia's second oldest city with an outstanding collection of heritage buildings. It is a major coal export port and has been an important steel producing centre. BHP's Newcastle steelworks, which played a dominant role in Australian industry from 1916, closed in 1999, although rod and bar processing activities will continue. The Newcastle waterfront has undergone stunning changes in recent times with the Honeysuckle Heritage Project and foreshore redevelopment scheme providing the colourful cosmopolitan facilities of Queen's Wharf. The coal export loading facility Port Waratah is the terminus for most coal trains in the Hunter region.

CityRail Hunter operates train passenger services in the region. Regular electric Inter-City services operate to the Central Coast and Sydney with local services to Morriset. Diesel railcars operate in the Maitland corridor to Telarah, with additional services to Scone and Dungog.

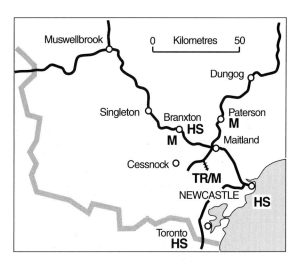

Info Line 131 500 during the hours 0600-2200 daily.
STA bus services operate in Newcastle City.
Information: The Tourist Information Centre is located in the fully restored Old Stationmaster's Cottage,
92 Scott Street, Newcastle NSW 2300
Phone: (02) 4929 9299

Maitland (population 50,000) was founded in 1804 and the city's many heritage buildings date from 1820. Maitland's High Street Station, opened in 1878, is categorised as a first class building and is listed by the National Trust. A steam tramway operated in Maitland between 1909 and 1926. High Street, with its sympathetic blend of historic buildings, handsomely restored facades and modern shopping conveniences has been developed as a Heritage Mall.

Hunter Valley Steamfest: The feature event of Maitland's Heritage Month each April, the Steamfest offers steam train rides from Maitland Station and open days with steam operations at the local railway museums.

Rail Motor Museum, Paterson
The Rail Motor Museum Society Inc

The Society was formed in 1984 to restore, maintain and operate members of a fleet of the Rail Motors that once served the New South Wales Government Railways. The best known of these were the 42ft CPH-class Rail Motors introduced in 1923 and popularly known as *Tin Hares*. The Society has obtained full accreditation under the NSW *Rail Safety Act* and operates rail motors to locations throughout the State.

The Depot: A three-road depot has been established adjacent to the North Coast Railway at Paterson. The former Station Master's Cottage has been restored to provide meeting and reading rooms, bookshop and other facilities.

Rail Motors: 5 of the famous *Tin Hare* CPH rail motors, which operated in NSW country areas from 1923 - Nos 1 and 7 are operational, with No 3 due to return to service in late 1999 – a 400 class railcar HPC 402 (built 1938), on lease to the SRA; 500-class trailer CT 501; and 600 class railcars 602, 606 and trailer 707 (non-operational). Several ex-NSWGR stores vans are also in the collection.

Operations: Rail motor tours are run on a regular basis and are available for charter: contact Mr B Agland (02-4933 8000). Details of tours on Home Page. Inspections of the depot can be organised by contacting the Secretary.
Location: The running depot is located on Webbers Creek Road at Paterson, 45km north of Newcastle on the North Coast line.
Public Transport: 5 daily *CityRail* services, Mon-Fri;
3 services Sat-Sun.
Address: Geoff Murray, Secretary
PO Box 445, Charlestown NSW 2290
Phone: (02) 4945 3677
Internet: www.railmotorsociety.org.au

Richmond Vale Railway, Kurri Kurri
Richmond Vale Preservation Cooperative Society Ltd

Tourist Railway/Museum (Steam)
1435mm gauge

RICHMOND VALE PRESERVATION SOCIETY

Richmond Vale Preservation Society's 2-8-2 locomotive SMR 25 at the former Richmond Vale colliery with a tour train.

This preservation group was formed to acquire and return to operating condition Australia's last commercial steam railway, the Richmond Vale Railway between Richmond Main Colliery and Hexham, a former shipping point on the Hunter River. The railway was built by J&A Brown from 1856 to transport coal for export. It was Australia's last steam-operated railway, the last steam locomotives being withdrawn in 1987. The complex is being developed as a mining museum and tourist railway.

Features: The Richmond Main Historic Park is heritage-protected. Mining equipment and colliery buildings and mining are featured, including the Heritage Workshop, which is fully restored and operating as in the 1920s. The Richmond Vale Preservation Society has rebuilt the railway between Richmond Main and Pelaw Main (4km) and further rebuilding is underway to Weston. Steam trains operate over the 4km direct passenger line, constructed between Richmond Main and Pelaw Main collieries in 1922, which offers spectacular working up 1 in 22 grades.

Locomotives: 16 locomotives: some static, some operational; some diesel but mostly steam and some cranes. Steam locomotives include an ex-J&A Brown No 23 - the last Robinson-designed ROD 2-8-0 (Great Central 1918) in service in the world - two former Richmond Vale Railway 2-8-2T locomotives (Kitson 4567/1908 and 4798/1911), two industrial tank locos and four ex-South Maitland Railways 10-class 2-8-2T locomotives. A 10-class locomotive(s) and 0-4-0ST *Marjorie* (Clyde 462/1938) are kept in operating condition.

Rolling Stock: Over 150 pieces of rolling stock representing types once frequent on the coalfields. Passenger rolling stock includes ex-Inter-City stainless steel carriages. A collection of 4-wheel non-air coal hoppers is on display, together with a range of specialist industrial rolling stock from the BHP steelworks at Newcastle.

Operation: First three Sundays of each month, from 1000-1700. Steam trains operations between Richmond Main and Pelaw Main collieries hourly from 1030 (last train at 1530). The return journey takes about 40 minutes.

Admission: Adults $10, concession/child $5. Fees allow rides or train trips all day.

Location: At the Richmond Main Colliery, 4km south of Kurri Kurri on Main Road 135, 30km west of Newcastle. From Sydney take F3 Freeway to Freemans Waterhole exit, turn left onto Main Road 135 and proceed for approximately 20km. There is no public transport.

Contact: Membership enquires and group bookings:
Richmond Vale Railway Museum
PO Box 224, Kurri Kurri NSW 2327
Phone: (02) 4936 4357
(02) 4937 5344 on operating days only.

☕ 📖 📷 🎋 RNE

Hunter Valley Tourist Railway, North Rothbury
Hunter Valley Railway Trust

Museum (Steam/Diesel)
1435mm gauge

This museum is located at the former Airfield Colliery (originally known as the Rothbury Colliery) and is connected to the Great Northern Railway at Branxton by a 5km privately-owned branch line. The colliery and branch line have been acquired privately and the Trust plans to operate steam-hauled trains over the line.

Features: As the scene of Australia's most serious industrial violence, the Rothbury Colliery site has major historical significance. The colliery ruins on site provide interest in industrial archaeology. **Branxton railway station** No 1 platform building, built in 1863, is the oldest surviving railway building on the northern line. The Museum locomotive shed has been built in an authentic heritage style.

Locomotives: Seven ex-SMR 10-class 2-8-2T locomotives and 8 ex-SRA diesel locomotives. Operational locomotives are 10-class Nos 17 and 23, 7350 and 4488.

Rolling Stock: The Museum specialises in passenger carriages and plans to recreate whole trains as they ran in service, e.g., a complete *Newcastle Flyer* set, an original mail train, a 1920-style *Caves Express* and a suburban end-platform car set. There are over 90 ex-NSWGR carriages in the collection and over 20 goods vehicles and associated railway cranes, including a 30-ton Cowan & Sheldon heavy-lift accident crane. Four interurban carriages are being restored for mainline traffic.

Operations: Open days are held during major heritage events, such as the *Maitland Steamfest* and approx quarterly. The Trust has an extensive collection of trikes, which are used on open days. Other times by request.

Location: Branxton is 10km west of Maitland on the Great Northern Railway and is served by regular *CityRail* services to Newcastle. The site is 5km from the New England Highway and is located in the heart of the main vineyard area of the Hunter Valley. At Branxton, turn left into Cessnock Road (also known as Branxton Road or Main Road 220). The Rothbury Riot memorial is at the Museum entrance on the right-hand side of the road.

Contact:	C A Richards, Executive Trustee
	Hunter Valley Railway Trust
	PO Box 37, Branxton NSW 2335
Phone:	(02) 4933 1923; Fax: (02) 4933 9923
	Mobile 019 459 313
E-mail:	hvrtmuseum@hotmail.com

    ♿ ⛩ RNE

HERITAGE SITES (Register of the National Estate)

Newcastle/Civic Heritage Precinct. Six former GNR locomotive workshop buildings are heritage listed and have been restored for use as a vibrant cultural and commercial centre. They comprise the 1886 locomotive boiler workshop (now a multi-function exhibition centre), the 1874 machine shop, 1880 blacksmith's and wheel shop (proposed for use as produce markets) and 1882 permanent way store (the Hunter Valley Wine Centre). The 1881 Divisional Engineer's office in Victorian domestic architectural style and the 1920 new erecting shop (now a visual arts centre) provide contrasting styles to the classic Romanesque. A Craven Brothers 16-ton overhead rope crane, built in 1886 for the locomotive boiler workshop, is fully restored to operating condition. It is the last of its type to survive in its original rope drive configuration in Australia.

Newcastle Railway Station: Completed in 1878, the station complex reflects its position as the headquarters of the former Great Northern Railway. There have been numerous additions and the building is flanked on the west by a typical country Railway Refreshment Room (1896) which, like the main building, is styled in Italianate architectural features. Two additional storeys were added to the RRR in 1923. The station is served by regular *CityRail* electric trains from Sydney.

Port Waratah Coal Export Facility. Ex-SMR 2-8-2T locomotive No 19 is displayed here with heritage coal hopper wagons and brake van.

Toronto Railway Station: The railway station (opened 1911) was terminus of the former Fassifern-Toronto line. Lake Macquarie & District Historical Society operates a museum which commemorates the early pioneers of the Lake Macquarie district. The museum is located in Victory Parade, Toronto, and is open Wednesday, Sunday and public holidays, 1300-1600.
Contact: PO Box 239, Toronto NSW 2283

NEW ENGLAND - NORTH WEST

The Main Northern Railway followed the routes taken by early European settlers to reach Tamworth in 1878, Armidale in 1883 and Tenterfield in 1886. The first railway link to Brisbane was established in 1888 when the line was extended to the Queensland system at Wallangarra. Railway traffic declined in the 1970s and the line closed beyond Dumaresq. The region has a rich agricultural base with vertically integrated industries servicing international markets.

Armidale (population 23,000) is an education centre and home to the University of New England, the first in Australia to be established outside the capital cities. The railway reached Armidale in 1883 and a locomotive depot was established. With through working of diesels between Werris Creek and the border in the 1960s the depot declined in importance. The railway station, station master's residence and gatekeeper's cottage are among the 35 buildings in Armidale classified by the National Trust.

Tamworth (population 35,000) is the nerve centre of the northwest and best know as Australia's country music centre. The Power station museum celebrates Tamworth's place as Australia's first city with electric lighting. Railway facilities include a regional freight centre.
Countrylink Travel Centre (02) 6766 2357

Dumaresq, the current northern terminus of rail services has its 1884 station fully restored by local enthusiasts. Historical photographs and graphics tell the story of the station and its role in the locality's development.

Tenterfield (population 3500) was the venue for Henry Parkes' famous federation speech of 1889 which led to the establishment of the Australian Commonwealth in 1901. The railway station (built 1886) is no longer served by trains, but remains one of the town's finest heritage buildings.

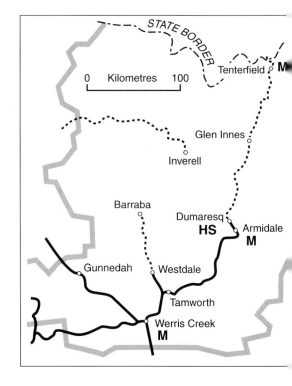

Getting There: *CountryLink* Northern Xplorer trains daily Armidale.

Werris Creek Railway Precinct and Museum

Heritage Site

Werris Creek, situated at the junction for the Main Northern and north-west lines, is a classic railway town with employme and economic opportunities revolving around the railway.

Heritage Sites: The large 19th century railway station building dominates the town which features classic country hotels. It comprises three linked main brick buildings with platforms both sides. The station is significant for its dominant effect on the streetscape and character of the town, for its elaborate detail and for its architectural quality. The 80 year old railway powerhouse is located opposite the northwest platform.

Displays: branch-line diesel locomotive 4705 on static display in the railway park, while mainline Alco DE locomotive 4465 is under restoration in the railway yard. A railway museum has been established in the old guards' barracks cottage. It houses a grow-

ing collection of railway photographs and memorabilia and serv as a Tourist Information Centre.

Opening Times: 1000-1200 Tuesday and Saturday.
Admission by donation.

Location: On Tourist Drive off New England Highway betwee Willow Tree and Tamworth.

Contact: Bruce Giffery, Caretaker
Phone (02) 6768 7273

Railway Station Museum, Tenterfield
Tenterfield Railway Station Preservation Society

Railway Museum
1435mm gauge

TENTERFIELD RAILWAY STATION PRESERVATION SOCIETY

Tenterfield railway station with MHO van as a static exhibit at left.

This group has restored the historical railway station at Tenterfield (opened 1886) and operates a museum devoted to railway artifacts and railway life.

Features: The railway station is an excellent example of Victorian Gothic architecture and was built in 1886 as the terminal station of the Great Northern Railway. Although no longer served by trains, the building remains one of the town's finest heritage structures. Internally, the building retains its features as they existed on the last day of train operations in the 1980s.

Exhibits: Displays are presented in all station rooms. Included are lamps, photographs, tools, record books, a vintage chainsaw used in sleeper cutting, railway reminiscences and much more. Recently restored passenger brake/luggage van, MHO 2609, also houses exhibits. The Museum has 7 perway trikes spanning 80 years of railway use. An Art & Crafts market is held in the station forecourt on the first Saturday of February, April, June, August and December.

Opening Times: 1000 - 1600 Wednesday - Saturday,
1200 - 1600 Sunday, and
daily during NSW/Queensland school holidays.

The museum can be opened at other times, with trike operations, for groups of 6 or more. Guided tours are available with advanced bookings.

Admission: Adults $2, child 50 cents.

Trike Operation: The Society has access to 10km of the line between Tenterfield and Bluff Rock. Motorised trolleys offer public rides of various lengths every Saturday.
Trike rides: Adult $2, child $1.
Location: On the New England Highway, 700km north of Sydney.
Contact: Tenterfield Railway Preservation Society Inc
PO Box 172, Tenterfield NSW 2372
Phone: (02) 6726 2223. Also,
Tenterfield Visitors Centre, Phone (02) 6736 1082

 RNE

Armidale Bicentennial Railway Museum

Railway Museum

The Armidale Bicentennial Railway Museum was established at the station in 1988 and became an annex of the Armidale Folk Museum in 1993.

Displays: The museum features the human input of men and women in the construction, maintenance and running of the railway in New England. It has a range of locally-based rail relics and memorabilia, including a one-eighth scale model of a wooden Queen Post bridge and 13 trikes and quadricycles.

Opening Times: Mon, Wed and Friday 0830-1000;
Mon-Friday 1000-1600 during school holidays;
or by prior arrangement. Free admission.

Location: Brown Street, Armidale, adjacent to railway station.

Contact: Peter Chambers, Curator
PO Box 75A, Armidale NSW 2350
Phone: (02) 6770 3536 or 6772 8666

HOLIDAY COAST

The mid-north coast, from the Manning River at Taree to Coffs Harbour in the north, has historically been an important timber-producing region. A number of logging railways worked in the rich forests of the region earlier this century. Today the rainforests, National Parks, beaches, rural vistas and sub-tropical climate of the region help to make it an increasingly popular holiday destination.

Coffs Harbour (population 25,000) is the main commercial cen■ for the region. It developed as a shipping port for timber produc■ and became Australia's main banana producing district. The c■ has subsequently developed as a manufacturing and tourist cent■ based on the Solitary Islands Marine Reserve and the rainforest the World Heritage listed Dorrigo National Park.
Getting There: Daily *Countrylink* Brisbane and Murwillumb■ XPT rail services.

Timbertown, Wauchope
Timbertown Community Enterprises Ltd.

Tourist Park Railway (Steam
610mm gauge

Timbertown is the recreation of an 1880s sawmilling operation on the mid-north coast of NSW. It presents a timber getter■ village built around a tough and hardy bush spirit, bush ingenuity and steam power. Timbertown is being redeveloped as■ base for local tourist enterprise.

Features: A 2.4km, 610mm gauge railway operates at the complex and represents the role played by railways in the success of the timber industry in the 1880s. There is a working steam sawmill, steam engines and a host of crafts people displaying the skills and trades of the era.
Locomotives: 0-6-0 (H/Clarke 1862/1953) ex-Macknade mill No 6; 0-4-2T (JF 17881/1929) ex-South Johnstone Mill No 10; and 4wDM (Motor Rail, 1929) ex-Harwood Mill.

Operations: 0930 to 1530 daily (except Christmas Day); norma■ six trains operate per day, with additional services in peak perioc
Location: In former State Forest on the Oxley Highway, Wauchop■ 8km west of the Pacific Highway.
Public Transport: Wauchope is served by daily XPT services. bus service departs from Port Macquarie at 0920 Monday-Frida■

Dorrigo Railway Museum
Dorrigo Steam Railway & Museum Ltd

Museum (Steam/Diesel)
1435 mm gauge

The Dorrigo Steam Railway & Museum was formed in 1973 to authentically preserve all manner of items from the railwa■ of NSW. The Museum has assembled Australia's largest collection of locomotives and rolling stock.

Locomotives: 18 ex-NSWGR steam locomotives, including 0-6-0 inside-cylinder goods 1904/1919/1923 (built 1877-79) and 2-8-0 standard goods 5069/5132/5353 which formerly operated the line, 2-6-0 Moguls 2408/2414/2535, 30-class 3028/3046/3090, 2-8-2 Baldwin 5920 and 263-tonne 60-class 4-8-4+4-8-4 Beyer Garratts 6039/6042.

11 ex-industrial steam locomotives, including ex-J&A Brown 0-6-0ST No 3 (Kitson 2236/1879) and ex-J&A Brown 2-8-0 20/24, built for the British War Department (ROD) in 1918 to the Great Central Railway "8K" class design.

20 diesel locomotives, including ex-SRA Co-Co de 4206 (built Clyde 1955) and Co-Co de 42102, ex-SRA Alcos 4420 and 4822, ex-BHP Newcastle centre-cab Bo-Bo DE 47 and 52 (Goninan 1960/ 1961).

Rolling Stock: 6 CPH Tin Hare rail motors, 2 HPC 400 rail moto■ and trailers and an extensive collection of NSWGR carriages, goo■ wagons and industrial rolling stock.

Operations: The museum is scheduled to open to the public 2000.
Location: Tallowood Street, Dorrigo. From Coffs Harbour ■ Waterfall Way, take Hosanal Street to North Dorrigo. Tallowo■ Street is first right over railway line.

Address: Dorrigo Steam Railway & Museum Limited
PO Box 200, Dorrigo NSW 2453
Phone: (02) 6657 2176
Homepage: www.ozemail.com.au/~drsm

Glenreagh Mountain Railway Museum
Glenreagh Mountain Railway Inc

Railway Museum
1435 mm gauge

The GMR was established to operate a tourist railway on the picturesque Glenreagh-Dorrigo line. GMR is restoring th■ Glenreagh to Lowanna section (32km) of the line. Initially ganger trolley rides are available from Glenreagh, with publ■ services using rail motors scheduled to commence by 2001.

Locomotives and Rolling Stock: Ex-NSWGR 0-6-0 goods locomotive 1919 (built 1878), together with goods and other rolling stock.
Opening Times: Trike operations between Glenreagh West and Tallawudjah Creek (2km) on weekends, public holidays and school holidays. Rail motor operation planned from 2001.

Location:
Address: PO Box 412
Glenreagh NSW 2450
Phone: (02) 6654 1282 or 6649 2189; Fax (02) 6652 6948
Homepage: www.gmr.org.au/

NORTHERN RIVERS

The rich soils of the Clarence, Richmond and Tweed Rivers provided the basis for the early development of the Australian sugar and dairy industries. While sugar remains the main agricultural base of the region, there has been significant expansion of horticultural crops, including macadamias, pecan nuts, tea tree and coffee. The climate and attractive scenery of the region has turned it into a rapidly growing area. The region is served by the main *National Rail* line between Sydney and Brisbane, with an important branch line from Casino to Murwillumbah.

Lismore (population), located on the Richmond River, is the commercial and educational centre of the region. The Norco Co-operative dairy factory is an important industry and the city is home to the Southern Cross University.

Casino (population 11,000) is an important railway town at the junction for the Brisbane and Murwillumbah lines which retains the last coal stage in the state and steam locomotive facilities. The massive vertical *Harmon* coal loader is one of the most significant steam-age memorials remaining in New South Wales.

Northern Rivers Railroad: This company, based at the former Casino locomotive depot, is a rail freight operator north of Grafton to the Queensland border and Murwillumbah. Its ex-SRA 421-class Co-Co DE locomotives are a distinctive element of the Region in their unusual livery.

Ritz Rail Tourist Train
Northern Rivers Railroad Pty Ltd

Tourist Train (Diesel)
1435 mm gauge

JAMIE FISHER

The Brunswick Car of the Ritz Rail Tourist Train at Casino on 28 May 1999.

A regular tourist train operation on the scenic branch line to Murwillumbah and Byron Bay was introduced in 1999. The authentically restored train recreates the art deco style and ambience of the 1930s. Themed dinner party excursions and special trains are also operated to a variety of destinations.

Locomotives: 4 ex-SRA 421-class Co-Co DE locomotives (Clyde/EM 1966).
Rolling Stock: 8 ex-SAR steel carriages and 1940s, 8 ex-VR carriages (restored for *Southern Cross Express* luxury train in 1980s) and ex-NSWGR air-conditioned carriages. Carriages feature French-polished timber, brass and chrome fittings, carpets and curtains. There are two dining cars offering quality meals to passengers.
Operations: The Byron Bay Experience departs Murwillumbah each Sunday at 1000 and arrives Byron Bay at 1110 with the return journey departing at 1500 and arriving Murwillumbah at 1615.

Special dinner party services generally operate on Saturday nights from Murwillumbah and special tourist trains operate to northern NSW sporting events.

Fares:	First Class	$38
	Tourist class	$32
	Concession	$22

Phone: 1300 655 808 for special trains and fares.
Contact: Warren Judd, Northern Rivers Railroad
9 Armada Crescent, Currumbin Waters QLD 4223
Phone: (07) 5598 6144; fax (07) 5598 6088

Melaleuca Station, Chinderah
Melaleuca Station

Tourist Park Railway (Steam
610 mm gauge

This tea tree plantation (a native *Melaleuca* species) has established a 1.5km of 610mm gauge steam-operated railway f[
tourists to view various aspects of their operations. The main tourist centre has been built as a recreated 1920's Victoria[
railway station.

Features: An 0-6-2T steam locomotive (Perry 2601.1.51 of 1951) formerly used at the Marian Sugar Mill at Mackay has been restored to operating condition and hauls two bogie carriages through the Tea Tree plantation to a tea tree distillation and processing factory. The *Red Rattler Restaurant* has been established in four ex-Melbourne swing-door suburban carriages at the station. Giftware and souvenir outlets.

Operations: Open 1000-1700 daily.

Admission: Free; train rides - Adults $5, children $2.50.

Location: Adjacent to Pacific Highway between Murwillumb[and Tweed Heads.

Contact: Melaleuca Station
            Pacific Highway, Chinderah NSW 2487
Phone: (02) 6674 3777; fax (02) 6674 4100

HERITAGE ITEMS (Register of the National Estate)

Casino locomotive depot: The depot includes an 8-road roundhouse built in 1933 to a 1915 design, turntable and storage roads. The heritage-listed *Harmon* coal loader, opened in 1956 as "state-of-the-art" steam era technology is scheduled for restoration. The depot now serves as the operating base for the NRR.

Grafton Bridges: The bridge over the Clarence River was designed by J W Roberts and was brought into service in 1932. Its opening completed the standard-gauge railway between Sydney and Brisbane. This bridge is unique in Australia, being the only double-deck bascule bridge. The bascule span operates by the Rall

(USA) system which involves a double movement, raising the ope[ing span and retracting it shorewards so as to clear the passagewa[

The 1915 timber viaduct south of the station has been replace[by a modern structure, but a section of the original viaduct h[been retained for display purposes.

Lismore railway station: The timber railway station and asso[iated locomotive and carriage sheds are listed on the Register [the National Estate. They are significant as a particularly inta[and elegant 19th century railway station set back from the ro[behind a car park.

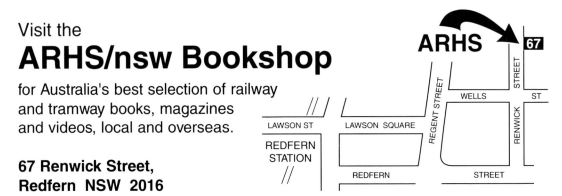

VICTORIA

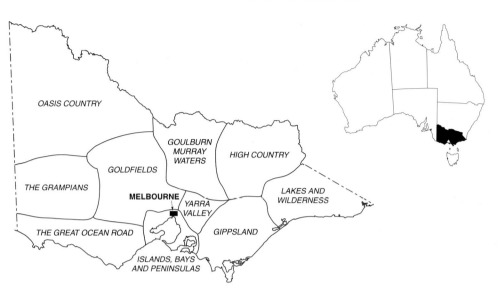

VICTORIA offers some of Australia's best known rail heritage sites. The wealth of Victoria's railway heritage and the compact nature of the State have resulted in a ch, varied and accessible range of heritage railways and amways compared with elsewhere in Australia.

The world famous **Puffing Billy Railway** on the outskirts f Melbourne is a must on all itineraries. Trains operate every ay of the year and the journey provides spectacular views of e cool fern gullies and forest country of the Dandenong .anges. For the steam enthusiast there are also regular mainline urs operated by **Steamrail**, the Seymour Railway Heritage entre and a steam-hauled train each Saturday over the **West oast Railway** to Warnambool, plus a number of tourist ilways around the State which operate on week-ends.

Victoria's economic prosperity was generated in its oldfields from the 1850s. Ballarat was the major city of the oldfields and it is notable for its fine buildings from the boom mes of the 1880s. The Ballarat East Locomotive Depot istorical Railway Complex brings together the railway eritage of the city, while **Ballarat Vintage Tramway** reserves its unique tramway heritage. The locomotive depot open on Saturdays and the tramway operates Saturday, unday and public holidays. To the north, Bendigo rivals allarat for its gold-generated opulence. The **Bendigo Vintage ramway** operates daily and offers the ideal way to explore e historic city. Nearby, the **Victorian Goldfields Railway** perates steam-hauled trains from Maldon on Sundays and ost public holidays. Another Sunday operator is the **Central ighlands Tourist Railway** at Daylesford, which operates ilmotors over a 9km line.

Other broad gauge tourist railways include the **Mornington eninsula Railway** (steam trains on first Sunday of the month), e **Yarra Valley Railway** and the **South Gippsland Railway**, hich operates every Sunday.

The Great Ocean Road is a leading tourist attraction. Visitors to this region can experience steam train rides over the 1067mm gauge **Bellarine Peninsula Railway** from Queenscliff on Sundays and public holidays, with additional services during school holidays.

Victoria's narrow gauge heritage is also preserved through the scenic **Walhalla Goldfields Railway** (Saturday, Sunday and public holidays), the **Coal Creek Bush Tramway** (daily operations), the **Alexandra Timber Tramway** (second Sunday of the month and public holidays) and the **Red Cliffs Historic Steam Railway** near Mildura (first Sunday of the month).

Melbourne's extensive tramway system has become an international symbol of the city. A number of heritage trams operate on the free City Circle service, and also to offer the ultimate dining experience of the **Colonial Tramcar Restaurant**. Others operate at the **Bylands Electric Tramway Museum** on Sundays. Also recommended is a visit to the **Railway Museum** at North Williamstown (open Saturday, Sunday and public holidays).

The **Association of Tourist Railways Inc** is the peak body for the Tourist Railway Industry primarily in the State of Victoria. Among many other activities, the Association represents its members collectively or individually in matters that affect the interests of its members. As part of the Association's purposes, it provides services regarding training standards, medical standards, railway operating standards and systems.

The Association may be contacted on telephone
(03) 9848 2236
or by writing to the Secretary at the registered address of
8 Tristania Street
Doncaster East Victoria 3109

MAINLINE TOURS

Steamrail Victoria Limited

1600mm gauge

As the steam era faded in Victoria, a committee was established in September 1965 to preserve historical carriages and ru them as steam-hauled trains. **Steamrail Victoria** was formed in 1975 and now operates a number of steam locomotives t haul the *Vintage Train* to various locations in Victoria. A division of Steamrail has been established at Ballarat (see Centr. Highlands). The operating base for Steamrail is at Newport Workshops where seven bays of the historic West block hav been developed as a heritage train depot.

Locomotives: Operating locomotives include 4-6-4 express R-class 761 and 766 (privately owned), mixed traffic 4-6-0 D^3 639 (Newport 1903), and K-class 2-8-0s of 1940-46 vintage, Nos 183 and 190. The *DieselRail* division has restored ex-VR diesel-electric locomotives S313, T356, T364 and T395 to operating condition. 0-6-0 DH M.231/2 serve as depot shunters.

Locomotives currently being restored include 2-8-0 K153, 4-6-0 A^2 986 and B-class diesel-electric B72.

Operations: Day tours on the first Sunday of the month between May and December, with additional services over Easter. Regular destinations include Castlemaine, Albury and Bendigo. Standard gauge tours available from 1997. Details and bookings direct to Steamrail (as below).

Location: Tours operate from Spencer Street Station, Melbourne. Steamrail (Ballarat) trains usually depart from Ballarat station, 119km north-west of Melbourne.

Contact: Steam Rail Victoria
PO Box 125, Newport VIC 3015
Information Service: (03) 9397 1953 or Fax (03) 9397 1041
Steamrail Ballarat, PO Box 499, Ballarat VIC 3353
Home Page: www.srv.org.au

DAVID JOHNSC

Steam locomotives K190/K183 on a Steamrail *tour to Leongath.*

Elecrail

Mainline Tours (Electric)

This Division of Steamrail Victoria has preserved historic electric multiple-unit rolling stock and locomotives.

Rolling Stock: Operational celestory-roofed multiple units include swing-door electric motor cars 111-year old 107M restored in 1916 brown with gold lining, and 1907-built 137M. Tait red sliding-door centre-aisle cars dating back to 1910 are 327M, 341T (trailer), 470M and the 4-car Victorian 150th Anniversary Commemorative Train 317M, 208T, 230D (driving trailer), and 381M. Electric mainline locomotive L.1162 (built 1953) was recommissioned in 1998, while electric locomotive E.1109 (built 1928) is undergoing major restoration.

Operations: Restored rolling stock and locomotives are used on special tours throughout the Melbourne electrified system.

Location: Restoration work is carried out on Saturdays at th National Trust classified Newport Workshops, West Block, Champion Road, Newport.

Groups and individuals welcome by prior arrangement. Neare station is Newport (15 minutes walk or taxi).

Enquiries, Tours & Visits: Please write at least a month in advanc to Elecrail, PO Box 125, Newport VIC 3015; or
Internet: www.srv.org.au

Seven-O-Seven Operations Inc

Mainline Tours (Steam)
1600mm gauge

R-class 4-6-4 locomotive No 707 was withdrawn from service on 21 May 1974. In 1980, a group of railwaymen, the Plan "R Group, commenced restoration of the locomotive. Seven-O-Seven Operations Inc was established as a non-profit organisa tion to maintain and operate the locomotive.

Locomotive: Restored R707 4-6-4 Hudson locomotive, City of Melbourne, built by North British in 1951, was returned to service on 20 July 1985. Sister locomotive R753 is currently being restored. The Group also has diesel-electric locomotives F 208 and Y 168.

Operations: R 707 is available for hire and charter to locations served by the 1600mm gauge Victorian Railways.

Tour Bookings: (03) 9670 7461

Contact: The Marketing Manager
Seven O Seven Operations Inc
Box 14174, Mail Centre
Melbourne VIC 8001

West Coast Railway

See Great Ocean Road Region for details of the WCR Warrnambool steam-hauled trains.

MELBOURNE-YARRA VALLEY REGION

Melbourne is renowned for its wide streets, century-old public buildings, iron-lace terrace houses, cosmopolitan life-style, extensive parklands and its trams. To the east, the attractions of the Dandenong Ranges and the Yarra Valley provide a strong tourism base.

By 1865, Melbourne had become Australia's largest city with a 26km suburban railway network operated by the Melbourne & Hobsons Bay United Railway Company. During the 1880s the fabulous wealth of the Victorian goldfields resulted in flamboyant architecture. Inner Melbourne is the focus of arts, culture, entertainment, tourism and recreation facilities. It is the focus of the State's rail system and the largest container port. Greater Melbourne is Australia's second city with a population of 3.2 million.

Melbourne's northern and western region is the heart of Australia's biggest manufacturing metropolitan area. Its railway heritage is focused on the historic workshops at Newport and the Williamstown line, which saw the birth of the Victorian Railways in 1859.

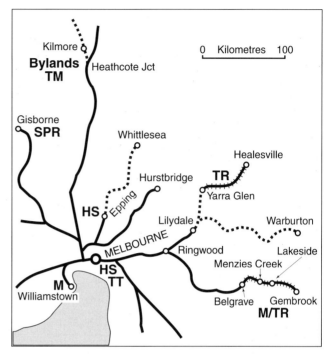

Public Transport: The Metropolitan transport region is divided into three fare zones, with an integrated ticketing system, which enables easy transfer between transport modes. Automatic ticketing systems are in operation.

Melbourne's tramway system is the largest in the southern hemisphere with street tramway and modern light rail operations. Cable trams were introduced in 1885 and operated until 1940, with a peak of 65 route km in 1891. By 1920 there were seven prominent operators of tramways in Melbourne, two cable and five electric. The Melbourne and Metropolitan Tramways Board and took over the tramway operations, with the exception of the Victorian Railways lines at St Kilda and Sandringham from February 1920. Most of the cable lines were replaced by electric trams, the last in October 1940. The system has been expanded in recent years and modern articulated light rail vehicles introduced. Older 'W' class trams have become the most identifiable symbol of Melbourne and have been classified by the National Trust. The W trams operate on selected routes from Malvern and Southbank Depots.

Swanston Trams: Serves 17 routes (214 route km) in the north-western and south-eastern suburbs, as well as the CBD.

Yarra Trams: Serves 10 routes (129 route km) in the north-eastern and south-western suburbs, including the popular City Circle Tram.

Bayside Trains: Operate on nine lines (237 route km) in Melbourne's northern, western and south-eastern suburbs.

Hillside Trains: Operates on six lines (129 route km) in the eastern and north-eastern suburbs.

Public Transport Information Phone: (03) 131 638.

Vintage Tram Services

Tourist Tramway (Electric)

A major tourist feature in Melbourne is the *City Circle* tram line opened in 1994. Refurbished W-class heritage trams in a special burgundy and cream livery offer a free service around the *City Circle*.

Trams: 10 W-class operate the City Circle service. A fleet of vintage Melbourne trams has been retained at Hawthorn Depot and Preston Workshops and are used for special working.

Operations: *City Circle* trams operate between 1000 and 1800 daily on a 10-minute headway.

Fares: The *City Circle* is a free service.

Location: Loop line around the Melbourne CBD.

Contact: Public Transport Information Phone: (03) 13 1638

Colonial Tramcar Restaurant

Tram Restaurant (Electric)

The tramcar restaurant operates three Melbourne trams. Since its inception in 1983, the Restaurant has become a star attractic and a tourist symbol of Melbourne. Patrons dine in lavish style aboard as they cruise the scenic streets of Melbourne to vie its classic public buildings, Victorian terraces, fashionable shopping areas and extensive parklands.

Trams: Three air-conditioned W-class trams, dating from 1927, refurbished in *Pullman-style* which features lush burgundy velvet and teak bench seats. Gold etched mirrors, scalloped drapes and brass lamps with tussled vintaged shades enhance the character of 1920s opulence.

Operations: The trams travel through the streets of the City and suburbs, including South Melbourne, South Yarra, St Kilda Toorak, Malvern, Balaclava and Caulfield. Regular services offer lunch and dinner. Tours are extremely popular and advance bookings are necessary. The trams are also available for promotions, group outings,

weddings, anniversaries and social functions.

Price Schedule: Lunch or dinner tours $55-90 per head all inclusiv

Location: Depart from Tram Stop 125,
cnr. Clarendon St. and Normanby Road,
Southbank, opposite Crown Casino.

Bookings: The Colonial Tramcar Company Pty Ltd
566 City Road (PO Box 372)
South Melbourne VIC 3205

Phone: (03) 9696 4000; Fax (03) 9696 3787

Railway Museum, North Williamstown
ARHS (Victorian Division)

Rail Museum
900/1067/1600mm gauge

The Victorian Railway Museum opened in 1962 and has an extensive range of Victorian locomotives, a VR tram and variou carriages, wagons and trolleys. In addition, there is a replica of an 1887 Victorian railway station, photographs and variou railway items on display.

Locomotives: 19 steam, 9 diesel and 3 electric locomotives, including H220 4-8-4 Australia's largest conventional steam locomotive, R704 express passenger 4-6-4 of 1951; the only remaining 4-8-2+2-8-4 Australian Standard Garratt locomotive, G33; A² class express passenger 4-6-0 995 of 1916; Y108, a classic inside-cylinder 0-6-0 of 1888; F176, a 2-4-2T motor, built in 1880; T94, freight 0-6-0 of 1884; and a Bo-Bo electric locomotive from the SECV 900mm gauge industrial railway at Yallourn.

Rolling Stock: Classic Victorian carriages and rolling stock, including VR Commissioner car *NORMAN* (built 1890), joint VR/SAR sleeping car, *TORRENS* (built 1909) and swing-door suburban electric motor coach (originally built 1888) and Walker diesel rail car of 1948.

Location: Champion Road, North Williamstown. By road take th Williamstown turnoff from Westgate Bridge and proceed dow Melbourne Road.

Public Transport: Williamstown line trains: the museum is appro 300m to the west of North Williamstown Station.

Contact: Railway Museum
GPO Box 5177AA, Melbourne VIC 3001

Phone: Museum (03) 9397 7412

Bookings and further information from ARHS, Victorian Divisior
(03) 9596 3249

Opening Times: Saturdays, Sundays and public holidays (except Christmas Day and Good Friday) from 1200-1700 - daily from 26 December to 26 January, and Wednesdays during school holidays from 1200-1600. Open by appointment for group bookings during weekdays. A buffet carriage is available for hire for birthday parties, etc.

Admission: Adults $5; child/concession $2.50.

Part of the Williamstown Railway Museum showing preserved steam locomotives on static display, a station, signal box and station name signs.

WILLIAMSTOWN RAILWAY MUSEUM

Puffing Billy Railway, Belgrave
Emerald Tourist Railway Board

Tourist Railway (Steam)
762mm gauge

MAL AUSTIN

NA-class locomotives of the Puffing Billy Society Nos 14A and 12A double-head a tourist train through the rainforest on its way to Gembrook.

Puffing Billy is Australia's premier preserved steam railway. The 25km line is the only surviving example of the four 2ft 6in (762mm) gauge lines built in Victoria around the turn of the century and it was the first Government railway to be saved for preservation. Following closure of the line in 1953, the preservation group was formed and reopened the line between Belgrave and Menzies Creek (6.3km) in 1962, Emerald (9.5km) in 1965 and to Lakeside (6.7km) in 1975. The final restoration of the line to Gembrook (25km) opened in 1998. The Society aims to maintain the historic integrity of the railway. Visual aspects and operating practices represent the period 1910-1930.

Features: The railway, built in 1899-1900, is listed on the Register of the National Estate. It is significant as one of the last remaining operating narrow gauge railways in Australia and is a major historical and tourist attraction carrying some 250,000 passengers per year. The journey provides spectacular views of the cool fern gullies as well as rolling hills and the Warburton Ranges on the new section of track towards Gembrook.

Locomotives: Six 2-6-2T NA-Class (Built Newport 1905-1914) one of which is awaiting restoration; B-class *Climax* geared logging locomotive (B/No 1694/1928); industrial 0-4-0ST ex-West Melbourne Gasworks (Peckett 1711/1926); two Decauville locomotives (43/1886 and 90/1890) and three diesel locomotives are in service. A 2-6-0+0-6-2 Garratt locomotive G42 is undergoing restoration (planned completion in 2000), and ex-South African Railways NGG-16 class 2-6-2+2-6-2 Beyer Garratt No 129 is awaiting restoration.

Rolling Stock: Ex-VR narrow gauge tourist carriages and ex-Mt Lyell Railway First Class carriages.

Operations: Trains operate every day except Christmas Day. There is a minimum of three trains per day. On most days, the first train departs Belgrave at 1030), with 4 to 6 departures per day on weekends and in holiday periods.

A *Luncheon Train* with luxury NAL carriages conveying passengers at first-class fares with a range of meal option departs Belgrave at 1200 on weekdays (excluding public and school holidays).

A *Night Train* operates on most Fridays and Saturdays, with pre-dinner drinks, three-course meal and wines. It is available for individuals and group bookings.

Commissioners Tours, which provide a guided tour of the railway operate at certain times throughout the year. Santa special trains operate on the three Saturdays prior to Christmas.

Fares (1999/2000): Belgrave-Menzies Ck $11.50 return;
Belgrave-Lakeside $19 return;
Belgrave-Gembrook $26 return.
Check for special trains.

Location: Trains operate from Belgrave, 40km from Melbourne CBD. By road take routes 22 or 26 to Upper Ferntree Gully, then 26 to Belgrave (Burwood Highway).

Public Transport: Hillside trains to Belgrave (outer suburban station), then follow signs to Puffing Billy station.

Contact:	Larry James, Secretary
	Puffing Billy Preservation Society
	PO Box 451, Belgrave VIC 3160
Phone:	(03) 9754 6800; Fax (03) 9754 2513
E-mail:`	pbr@pbr.org.au
Web Page:	http://www.com.au/pbr

 RNE

Menzies Creek Steam Museum
Puffing Billy Preservation Society

Railway Museum
610/762/1067mm gauge

The Puffing Billy Preservation Society's steam museum houses a collection of early steam locomotives from narrow gaug and industrial railways of the southern hemisphere, together with steam engines and machinery.

Locomotives: 13 locomotives, including 4 ex-Queensland sugar mills 610mm gauge locomotives, Beyer Garratt 2-6-0+0-6-2 ex-Australian Portland Cement (1938), a Shay geared locomotive (ex-Taiwan) and ex-Mt Lyell Abt-rack locomotive (NBL 24418/ 1938). A 0-6-2T Perry-built locomotive (7967.50.4 of 1950) and Malcolm Moore 4wDM locos have been restored to operating condition.
Location: At Menzies Creek, a station on the Puffing Billy Railway.

Opening Times: Saturday, Sundays and public holidays from 100 to 1700, or other days by special arrangement. Luncheon Tra passengers are provided with a guided tour of the Museum.
Contact: Larry James, Publicity Officer
        Puffing Billy Preservation Society
        PO Box 451, Belgrave VIC 3160
Phone: (03) 9754 6800

Yarra Valley Railway
Yarra Valley Tourist Railway Society Inc

Tourist Railway (Steam/Diese
1600mm gauge

This tourist railway group was formed in 1985 to preserve the railway line from Yarra Glen to Healesville, which was close in December 1980. The line served the Yarra Valley for nearly 100 years. The Healesville line had a frequent passenge service provided by rail motors connecting at Lilydale with suburban electric trains.

Features: The 18km line, originally opened in March 1889, is noted for its scenic attractions, particularly long trestle bridges at Yarra Glen, a tunnel and splendid views of the surrounding countryside. The historic Healesville railway station is being restored and the public are invited to inspect this work on running days.

Locomotives: Ex-VR diesel locomotives T341 and 0-6-0DH W250, with 2-8-0 steam locomotives J516 and J541 currently being restored to service.

Rolling Stock: Ex-VR vintage rolling stock, including early Victorian wooden carriages with exquisite craftsmanship and diesel-electric rail motor No 62.

Operations: Rail trolley rides operate every half-hour from 1100-1700 between Healesville and Tunnel Hill block post each Sunday

and public holidays. The trip offers scenic views over the Yarr Valley. The journey is available for special charter services. Tra services will commence once restoration of the line is complete.

Fares: Adults $5, pensioners and children $2, family $13.

Location: Current operations are at Healesville station, off th Maroondah Highway.

Public Transport: MET bus service (McKenzies) betwee Lilydale, Yarra Glen and Healesville.
Contact: Secretary, Yarra Valley Tourist Railway Society
        PO Box 30, Healesville VIC 3777

 RNE

Bylands Electric Tramway
Tramway Museum Society of Victoria

Tram Museum (Electric/Cable)
1435mm gauge

The Society was founded in 1963, with the aim of preserving historic tramway and associated vehicles from the Victoria transport scene. The museum site is part of the former Heathcote Junction to Bendigo railway line, which closed in 1968. I 1981 the Society established a second operation nearby in Hudson Park, Kilmore. This was initially a horse-operated tram way, subsequently replaced with a replica cable tram and trailer set.

Exhibits: 30 electric trams, providing an extensive collection of Melbourne trams, together with representatives from the provincial tramways of Ballarat, Bendigo and Geelong. Historical vehicles include Ballarat single-truck trams 23 (1909) and 17 (1915), Geelong No 9 (1915), and Melbourne L101 (1921), 6 W2 class and single-truck X467 (1927). Replica Melbourne cable tramway grip car No 593 and trailer No 171 operate in Hudson Park, Kilmore. A collection of historical private and ex-government buses are also available for inspection.

Operations: The museum is open on Sundays (public holidays excepted) between 1000 and 1700 hours. Cable tram operations at Kilmore have the same hours. The museum can be available for

inspection outside these hours upon request and with prio arrangement.
Location: Museum site and electric tramway at Bylands, 52kn north of Melbourne, just off Northern Highway (2.5km past Prett Sally). The cable tramline is in Hudson Park, Kilmore, 57km nort of Melbourne on Northern Highway. The museum site is not read ily accessible by public transport.

Contact: G Jordan, Secretary
        PO Box 27, Malvern VIC 3144
Phone/Fax: (03) 9798 6035

 RNE

Gisborne Steam Park
The Gisborne Vintage Machinery Society Inc

Steam Park Railway
610mm gauge

This steam park, nestled in the foothills of the Macedon Ranges, features narrow-gauge and miniature railways.

Locomotive/Exhibits: Restored 0-4-2T locomotive (Perry 9337.45/ of 1945), ex-Millaquin Sugar Mill No 9, operates over a 610mm gauge loop railway. The locomotive, a 1926 Fowler steam roller and Ruston Hornsby portable steam engine are housed in the Ratcliffe Pavillion. vintage machinery, 1920's farmer's workshop museum and vintage cars and trucks.

Operations: 1100-1600 first Sunday of each month, September to May, with narrow gauge and miniature (177mm gauge) train rides. An annual Steam and Vintage Engine Rally is held on the third Sunday in May.

Admission: Free to park, with charges for train rides. The Steam Park and railways are available for hire.

Location: Webb Crescent, New Gisborne (Melways 197F4), take New Gisborne exits from Melbourne-Bendigo Freeway to Station Road. No public transport.

Information: Barry Thomas, Secretary
Gisborne Vintage Machinery Society
PO Box 99, Gisborne VIC 3437
Phone: (03) 5428 7047

HERITAGE SITES

Flinders Street Railway Station is one of Melbourne's best known landmarks. The imposing Federation Free Classical building opened in 1910 with 11 through platforms. For generations of Melburnians, "meeting under the clocks" has made Flinders Street station a landmark of cultural significance through collective associations. The external fabric was upgraded in 1985 and the customer service facilities have been modernised in recent years. Each day 1450 train movements are made into and out of the station.

Former Victorian Railways Administrative Building, 67-67 Spencer Street:
Built in 1888-93 in Italianate style. As the largest office building to have been erected in Melbourne in the nineteenth century, it expressed the importance of the railways administration in Victoria in the late nineteenth and twentieth century. The building has recently been restored as the Grand Hotel and apartments.

Footscray Railway Station: Built in the classical late Victorian style during 1899-1908, this complex serves the Bendigo line (opened 1859) the mainline to Geelong (opened 1857) The main building is significant as an architectural *tour de force*, rare in stations of this size.

Hawthorn Railway Station: The weatherboard main station building and attached timber platform verandah date from 1890. The large canopy on the Island platform rests on large curved iron angles supported by cast iron columns. This structure was relocated from the old Flinders street station in 1901.

Port Melbourne and St Kilda Railway Lines Urban Conservation Area:
The reservation extends from Flinders Street Station to Port Melbourne and St Kilda stations (now used by light railway lines). Its cultural significance resides in its association with the first passenger steam railway in Australia and its impact on Melbourne's form. The reservation is complete and the structures necessary to maintain the fixed rail link (bridges, etc) are structurally intact and serviceable.

Spencer Street No 1 Signal Box: Commissioned on 17 July 1887, this signal box was expanded to 196 lever frames in 1913. It is the largest mechanical frame in Australia and the third largest in the world. The signal box remains in operation, controlling all train movements at the Melbourne end of the Dudley Street Passenger Yard, and trains from the Spencer Street Yard to Moonee Ponds Creek Junction.

St Kilda Railway Station: was erected in time for the opening (on 13 may 1857) of the line at the termination of a Melbourne and Hobsons Bay Railway Company branch line. The place is important historically as the oldest station building in Victoria. The restrained Italianate building originally featured a semi-circular portico. The station is to be redeveloped for commercial use.

RAILTRAILS

Lilydale-Warburton Trail: This 36km stretch of Railtrail has been established on the formation of the former branch line that served Warburton from Lilydale. The trail runs over 13 timber bridges and serves the need of walkers, horse riders, cyclists and wheel-chairs. The Lilydale end of the trail can be found by following the Maroondah Highway east and uphill from the railway station for 1km. At 300m past McDonalds and on the right, is a signpost indicating the patch. The Warburton end of the trail is behind the Visitors Information Centre. An active Friends Group helps maintain the trail.
Phone (03) 5964 3468).

Upper Yarra Walking Trail: The Upper Yarra Track provides enjoyable walking through tall eucalypt forest country along old timber railway formations and vehicle tracks. Starting at Warburton (71km east of Melbourne), the eight sections of trail totalling 81.5km lead to the Alpine National Park (see Gippsland Region). Former timber railway formations include those of the Federal Timber Company at Big Pats Creek and the New Federal Mill, and the Victoria Hardwood Company lines to Ada No. 2 and New Ada sawmills.

GREAT OCEAN ROAD

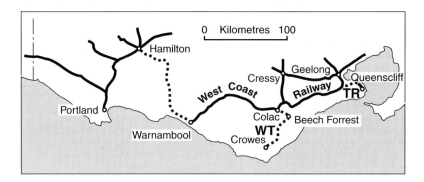

Victoria's Great Ocean Road offers one of the world's most spectacular and inspiring coastal experiences. From Geelong to Nelson, the region offers huge cliffs, roaring seas, safe surfing beaches, spectacular rainforests, historic shipwreck sites and the nature-sculptured Twelve Apostles. The historic settlements of the Bellarine Peninsula are also popular tourist attractions. With the opening of the Melbourne-Adelaide standard gauge railway via Geelong, the region is now integrated into the National Rail network.

Geelong (population 150,000) is Victoria's second largest city. It is a centre for the automotive industry, aluminium smelting, cement manufacture, oil refining and agricultural processing, while the Port of Geelong is Victoria's leading bulk grain export facility. The city is noted for its historical buildings. Australia's first country railway opened between Melbourne and Geelong 25 June 1857. An electric tramway system operated from 1912 to 1956.

Former Geelong Tramways tram No 40 of 1914 is preserved in Queens Park.

The seaside resort of **Queenscliff** (population 4000), with its 19th century fort, quaint cottages and grand hotels of last century, is a major tourist area.

Warrnambool (population 26,000) was established in the 1840s as a whaling and sealing port. Today it is a flourishing coastal resort with a fine legacy of 19th century provincial architecture. Its economy is based on the manufacture of processed dairy products and the textile clothing industry. The district is noted for its scenic coastal attractions.

Portland (population 12,000) has historic significance as Victoria's pioneer settlement: a whaling station established in 1829 and the Henty brothers established the first permanent European settlement in 1834.

The town has many fine bluestone buildings dating from the 1840s, including *Steam Packet Inn*, owned by the National Trust. There are more than 200 heritage buildings - both public and private - all lovingly restored. Portland now serves as an important deepwater port, shipping aluminium, grain and timber products from the surrounding regions.

Getting There:
V/Line Passenger Services: Trains operate between Melbourne and Geelong on an hourly basis for most of the day, with additional services at peak hours

For information, phone (03) 9619 1500

West Coast Railway: Operates public rail passenger service between Melbourne, Geelong and Warrnambool with connecting coach service to Port Fairy, Portland and Mt Gambier.
Four return services Mon-Fri, with reduced services Sat-Sun.

Steam locomotive R711 operates a Melbourne-Warrnambool service each Saturday outside Summer. The train departs Melbourne at 0843 each Saturday, and departs Warrnambool on the return journey at 1705. 1st class fare $47.80 single; $95.60 return.

Contact: West Coast Railway
Level 3, 75-77 Moorabool Street
Geelong VIC 3220
(PO Box 1936, Geelong VIC 3220)

Information & Bookings:
Phone: (03) 5226 6500; Fax (03) 5226 6520
Home Page: www.wcr.com.au/

Geelong Dinner Train
Supertrain Promotions

Railway Restaurant
1600mm gauge

A luxury dining experience is provided for patrons between Melbourne and Geelong return on a regular schedule using vintage dining cars.

Rolling Stock: Ex-VR dining cars *Avoca* (built 1927) and *Murray* built for the *Spirit of Progress* in 1937).
Operations: Friday evening return services depart Spencer Street Station at 1600 and 1917, returning at 1846 and 2210. Patrons are served champagne cocktails, entrée and main course between Melbourne and Geelong; followed by dessert, coffee and port on the return journey.
Bookings: (03) 9563 1270

Portland Tramway
Portland Cable Trams Inc

Tourist Tramway (modified Cable)
1435mm gauge

This tourist line is being established along the harbour foreshores with restored and replica cable trams from the Melbourne system which operated between 1885 and 1940.

Features: A 3.6km line, set in lawn, is scheduled to open in late 1999, runs from the Powerhouse Motor & Car Museum, past the Botanical Gardens and Maritime Discovery Centre, and follows the former railway alignment along spectacular cliff tops to the Water Tower Lookout. A heritage-listed goods shed is being restored as a depot, museum and display area. The Powerhouse Museum features veteran, vintage and classic motor cars, cycles, tractors and stationary engines.

Trams: Melbourne cable tram trailers Nos 95 (restored 1999) and 28; and a replica grip car (hydraulically driven; diesel powered). Trams on display at Powerhouse Museum and owned by the Portland Vintage Car Club include Melbourne cable tram trailer No 94, fully restored in 1994; a replica grip car (diesel powered)] and replica cable trailer 179 (based on an ex-Adelaide saloon body).

Operation: The tramway operated daily between 1000-1600 (commencing in 2000). Powerhouse Museum is open 1000-1700 weekends, school and public holidays; 1300-1700 weekdays.

Location: Depot/museum located in Henty Park
Bentinick Street, Portland

Contact: Phil Rudge, Secretary, Portland Cable Trams Inc
PO Box 126, Portland VIC 3305
Phone: (03) 5529 2590

HERITAGE ITEMS

Birregurra Railway Station and Water Tower: The station building (1877) is an important example of a smaller station design. The plan allowed for more logical and practical workspaces than previous railway station designs. The station was restored in 1996.

Bannockburn, Meredith and Moorabool Railway Stations: This notable group of stylistically similar railway station buildings on the Geelong-Ballarat line were built in 1862. The Meredith station is a finely proportioned and detailed Italianate composition with a distinctive timber bracketed verandah and an excellent illustration of country station architecture of the 1860s. It is constructed of locally quarried basalt.

Casterton Museum: This small farming settlement set amongst rolling hills and river redgums is located on the banks of the Glenelg River. The old Casterton railway station was redeveloped as a museum in 1971. There are five rooms displaying items of local historical interest.

Timboon Railway Trestle Bridge: The timber trestle bridge on the Camperdown-Timboon railway line at Curdies Siding was erected in 1892. It is one of few surviving railway structures of this type in Victoria.

RAILTRAILS

Old Beechy Line: The railway, which operated from 1902 to 1962, served timber industry communities. A display featuring a short length of track, a narrow-gauge flatcar (NQR87), replica station sign, crossing sign and milepost has also been established at the former Crowes station site. A 4km section of the narrow gauge (762mm) Beechy line that operated from Colac to Beech Forest and Crowes (71km) in the Otway forest has been opened to the public as a rails to trails walking track.

The track is located 16km south of Colac along Colac-Gellibrand Road. Look out for sign to Birnam Picnic Ground, location of former railway station. Follow signs for walks along former railway formation.

South Geelong to Drysdale Railtrail: This walking track follows the old VR branchline.

VICTORIAN GOLDFIELDS REGION
A Celebration of Living History

Victoria's Goldfields region is located just over an hour's travel to the north-west of Melbourne. From the 1850s, thousands of miners from around the world came to the diggings of the region to "find their fortune" and, later, some of the world's richest and deepest mines were established. The towns and cities of the region feature grand nineteenth century architecture that reflects the wealth of the period. The region offers divers economic, social and cultural services.

The wealth of the Bendigo goldfields led to the construction of a high-standard railway from Melbourne to Bendigo and to the Murray River at Echuca. The Melbourne, Mount Alexander and Murray River Railway Company was promulgated June of 1852 to build the railway but was unable to raise adequate capital and in 1856, the Government stepped in to build the line.

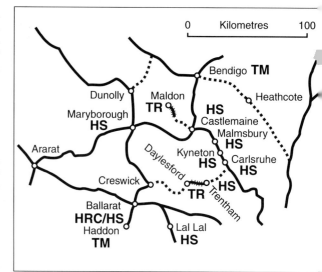

Ballarat (population 79,000) 119km north-west of Melbourne, was the scene of gold discoveries in 1851 and within 20 years the settlement was transformed into an elegant city. Today Ballarat has retained or restored much of its classic Victorian character and over 60 structures in the city are listed by the National Trust. The city is renowned for its parks and gardens, particularly the Botanic Gardens, adjacent to Lake Wendouree, the site for the 1956 Olympic Games rowing regatta. *V/Line* operates regular trains from Melbourne to Ballarat, from where coach services operate to other centres.
Tourist Information: Corner Sturt & Albert Streets.
Phone (03) 5332 2694

Bendigo (population 80,000) 162km north of Melbourne, was once the richest quartz reef mining area in the world. The wealth of the gold mines produced a building boom resulting in the city's magnificent Victorian buildings, which today, rank amongst the finest in Australia. The last gold mine closed in 1954, but the Central Deborah Gold Mine has been restored as a tourist operation by the Bendigo Trust.

Castlemaine (population 8000) was the centre of rich alluvial goldfields from 1852. The field only lasted for 20 years but many fine buildings were established during this period. The railway from Castlemaine to Maldon served the people of the district for 92 years until closure of the line in 1976. There are regular *V/Line* trains from Melbourne.

Maldon (population 1200), Australia's best preserved gold mining settlement, was declared a notable town in 1966. The town was surveyed in 1854 after the discovery of gold and the influx of 20,000 diggers. Deep quartz reef mining continued into the 1920s. Maldon is now a popular tourist destination with outstanding architecture and a restored gold mine. The Maldon Historic Reserve illustrates the evolution of the Victorian gold mining industry from primitive alluvial diggings through to capital intensive gold extraction and treatment processes. **Maldon Visitors Centre** (03) 5475 2569

Maryborough (population 8000) 70km north of Ballarat, was the site of a goldrush in 1854. The town is best known for its outstanding red brick railway station (see below). Public transport is by *V/Line* road coach from Castlemaine.

Daylesford (population 4000), a former gold mining town situated on the Great Dividing Range 650 metres above sea level, is now a tranquil mineral springs resort. The town was linked to the VR system by a branch line from Carlsruhe until closure in 1978.

Recently restored West Coast Railway locomotive R711 stands resplendently in its new WCR livery at Ballarat railway station prior to departure. This engine has been rebuilt using the latest steam locomotive technology and is also fitted with dual controls for remote diesel-electric operation.

WEST COAST RAILWAY

allarat Railway Precinct
allarat Rail Promotion Group
est Coast Railway/Steamrail Ballarat

e Ballarat historic railway precinct comprises the railway station, Ballarat East Locomotive Depot Historical Railway mplex, based on the former VR locomotive depot and stone goods shed, several classic Victorian railway industrial ildings and restored signal boxes. The Locomotive Depot is being developed as an operating base for tourist railway erations (West Coast Railway and Steamrail Ballarat). Steam locomotives and passenger rolling stock are restored and aintained at the depot. The Ballarat Rail Promotion Group coordinates the efforts of local societies to preserve and maintain e city's railway heritage.

eritage Significance: The nationally significant Ballarat railway ecinct was renowned for its grand station the complexity of its nalling operations. Ballarat Signal Box A was the largest echanical signal box in country Victoria, with 118 levers work-g 66 signals, 28 points and nine lockbars.

xhibits: Ballarat A and Ballarat East signal boxes have been urbishcd as a signalling and safeworking museum. The water comotive tank from Waubra have been relocated to the depot d the same is proposed for Ballarat C signal box.

comotives: Ex-VR classic inside-cylinder 0-6-0 locomotive 112 (Phoenix 238/1889) and 4-6-4 express locomotive R711 have en restored to operating condition at the depot, with several others aiting restoration. Y112 is available for charter work, while R711 uls regular WCR services from Melbourne to Warrambool.

olling Stock: Ex-VR DE railmotor RM56 being restored to oper-ing condition and historic V-class carriages.

Opening Times: Signal Box A open first Sunday of each month from 1030 to 1230.
Admission: Adults $2, children $1, family $5.
Other times for guided tours of the railway station and signal box A, or the Ballarat East Locomotive Depot can be made by appoint-ment (see below). Admission: Adults $5, child $2, family $10.
Open days are held to promote Ballarat's railway heritage at other times, including during the Ballarat Begonia Festival (March), Heritage Week (April) and the Heritage Festival (Novembr - December).
Location: 119km north-west of Melbourne.
Public Transport: Regular *V/Line* trains from Melbourne.

Contact: Hedley Thomson, Chairperson
Ballarat Rail Promotion Group
PO Box 1022, Ballarat Mail Centre VIC 3354
Phone: (03) 5320 5584 (W); (03) 5331 7831 (H)

RNE

endigo Vintage Tramways
endigo Trust

he Bendigo Trust operates the foremost vintage tramway in Victoria. Daily services transverse the historic city centre on an iginal route. The Bendigo tram system dates from 1890 when battery-powered trams were introduced. The system was nverted to steam operation in 1892 and electrified in 1903. The four route, 13.75km system closed in April 1972. Since ecember, 1972 a 3.9km portion of the system between the Central Deborah Gold Mine and the North Bendigo terminus has en maintained and operated as a vintage tramway. The trams are one of the city's major historical and tourist attractions.

eatures: The Bendigo Trust purchased all 23 electric tramcars sed by the SEC in 1972 and additional vehicles have since been quired for preservation and restoration. More than 20 trams are display at the tram barn/museum, together with historic photos d a souvenir shop. The tram barn (1903) is the oldest in Australia ill in use. The tram tracks run from the Central Deborah Gold ine through the city centre to the Museum/Depot, thence past the d Bendigo Gasworks to the North Bendigo Terminus.

rams: 32 vintage trams from Melbourne and Bendigo, most in orking condition, including five of the famous Birney cars 924/5), eight single-truck cars, double bogies and a crossbench ar (No 17) built in 1913. Many of these have been restored in their iginal colour schemes. A bogie SW6 tram has been converted to n air-conditioned mobile restaurant. One of the original battery ars (No 3) is under restoration.

perations: From 0930 every day except Christmas Day. Trams re normally boarded at the Central Deborah Gold Mine tram

terminus or the Fountain Stop. *Talking Trams* offer a recorded com-mentary highlighting 50 features along the 8km return route. The one hour tour includes a visit to the Museum/Depot. Trams may be booked for charter. The museum is open daily from 0800 to 1630. The restaurant tram runs services for morning tea, lunch, afternoon tea, dinner and special bookings.

Location: The Bendigo Vintage Tramways Museum and Depot is housed in the original carbarn at the corner of Tramways Avenue and Hargreaves Street.

Public Transport: Bendigo is serviced by regular *V/Line* Inter-City trains which take two hours for the journey from Melbourne.

Contact: Dennis Bell, Tramways Superintendent
1 Tramways Avenue, Bendigo VIC 3550
Phone: (03) 5442 2821 (depot) or
(03) 5443 8070 for charter bookings and tours.

Central Highlands Tourist Railway

Tourist Line (Rail Motors)
1600mm gauge

Volunteers have restored the 11km railway between Daylesford and Bullarto (the highest operating station in Victoria 747m). Restored vintage rail motors are operated over the scenic line. The railway is a key tourist feature in the district a attracts around 50,000 visitors a year.

Features: At the foot of Wombat Hill, one of the many extinct volcanoes of the district, is the Daylesford railway station, built in 1881 which is on the Register of the National Estate. The station (and lamp room on platform) is boom style, late Victorian architecture. The building plan is symmetrical about a central booking lobby and Station Master's office, flanked by a waiting room. This plan is believed to be the only one of its type built. The station, which is in the process of restoration, houses a display of railway memorabilia and a photo collection from the branch line. The CHTR operates the Daylesford Sunday Market, one of the largest outdoor markets in Victoria, every Sunday. Free entry to market and free parking.

Rolling Stock: 280 h.p. Walker railmotor (91RM) of 1951; diesel-electric railmotor of 1931 (63RM); DERM trailer of 1930 (26MT); and Tulloch railcar (DRC40) of 1971 have been restored to operating condition. Ex-VR railmotors 32RM/56MT (153 h.p. Walker and trailer), 53RM (Leyland) and RM74 Dodge Passenger Mail Motor are under restoration, while 82RM (280 h.p. Walker railmotor) awaits restoration. Tulloch-built railcar DRC40 has recently been purchased. Other items include diesel-electric locomotive Y159 (Clyde 1959), a small rail tractor, goods wagons, four restored workman's sleepers and several gangers trolleys, converted to use as passenger carrying vehicles.

Operation: Railmotors operate every Sunday at 1000, 1100, 1210, 1330 and 1445 from Daylesford to Musk (5km), with the 1100, 1210, 1330 and 1445 services continuing to Bullarto and return. Rail motors are available for charter.

Fares: Railmotor to Musk and return;
Adult $5, children $3, concession $4, family $16.
Bullarto and return;
Adult $7, child $5, family $20, concession $6.
Location: Railway Station, Raglan Street, Daylesford, 125k north-west of Melbourne.
Public Transport: *V/Line* road coach from Woodend with a retu day service from Melbourne, Monday to Saturday (Sunday servi evenings only).

Contact: David Smithwick, Marketing & Charters Manager
The Central Highland Tourist Railway
PO Box 93, Daylesford VIC 3460
Phone: (03) 5348 1759 (recorded information) and
(03) 5348 3503 (operating days)
Other enquiries   (03) 5348 3927
Facsimile (03) 5348 3927

Tulloch railcar DRC 40 pauses at Bullarto rail-way station prior to its return to Daylesford.

BARRY FEL

Haddon Tramway Museum
Melbourne Tramcar Preservation Association

Tram Museum (Electric)
1435mm gauge

The MTPA was incorporated in 1984 to preserve a selection of Victorian trams and buses. The museum has a modern ligh weight catenary electrical overhead system.

Exhibits: Victorian Railways tram No 41 from the St Kilda-Brighton electric tramway and Melbourne W2 trams Nos 357 and 407, W3 663, W4 670 and L103. All trams with the exception of L103 (under restoration) are operational.

Operations: The museum is not yet open to the public, although trams are operated for special tour groups.

Location: Sago Hill Road, Haddon, which is 12 km south west o Ballarat.

Enquires: The Secretary
Melbourne Tramcar Preservation Association
PO Box 324, Prahran VIC 3181

allarat Vintage Tramway
allarat Tramway Museum Inc

Tourist Tramway/Museum (Electric)
1435mm gauge

PETER WINSPUR

The Ballarat Tramway Museum's single-truck tram No 33 about to depart St Aidans Drive terminus.

he Ballarat tramway system opened in 1887 as a horse tramway and was electrified in 1905 with a fleet of 20 single-truck ectric cars. The system closed in 1971. The Ballarat Vintage Tramway was opened in 1974 to preserve part of this unique amway system as a working museum and tourist attraction. It operates along 1.3km of original track through the Botanical ardens on the western shore of Lake Wendouree. A study is assessing the viability to expand the vintage tram to link city urist attractions with the railway precinct.

xhibits: Eleven electric cars dating from 1912 to 1920 have been stored in the authentic colour schemes of the different eras in nich they operated. Nine Ballarat trams are of the "single truck pe". There are two rare classes of Melbourne trams from 1930/34, 3 661 and W4 671. Reconstruction has commenced of Electric pply Company tram No 12 of 1905. Horse tram No 1, which orked on the opening day of the local tramways on 21 December 87, has also been restored. A museum display of photographs d tramway artefacts is located in an unusual display area at the pot.

perations: Electric trams operate every Saturday, Sunday, pub-
holiday and school holiday, as well as every day from 25th
ecember to Australia Day between 1200 and 1700. Charters can
arranged at all times. No 1 horse tram operates approximately
nce per year (phone for information).

Special Events: Over the two March weekends of the *Ballarat Begonia Festival*, the tramway provides a park-and-ride transport service between neighbouring streets and the Gardens Reserve between 1000 and 1800 (special fares apply).
Fares: Adults $2, child $1, all day tickets $4.

Location: 3km west of the city centre. Take Western Highway, then turn right into Hamilton Avenue.
Public Transport: Take train to Ballarat, thence Sturt Street West bus (route 15) from near Post Office corner to Hamilton Ave, then short walk to tram terminus (only one bus service on Sundays) or taxi.

Contact: Peter Winspur, Secretary
                PO Box 632, Ballarat VIC 3353
Phone: (03) 5334 1580
Web Page: http://www.btm.org.au
E-mail: btm@netconnect.com.au

Victorian Goldfields Railway
Castlemaine & Maldon Railway Preservation Society

Tourist Railway (Steam)
1600 mm gauge

CASTLEMAINE AND MALDON RAILWAY

Restored Castlemaine and Maldon Railway steam locomotive J 549 crossing one of the timber bridges with a tour train.

The Society was formed in 1976 to restore and maintain the 16 km 1600 mm gauge line for operation as a tourist railway. 2km section of line was opened in 1986 and 7km of track is now in use.

Heritage Significance: Maldon railway station is listed on the Register of the National Estate because of the role it played in supporting the goldmining activities of the region and its significant contributions to the development and prosperity of this region. The station and its infrastructure, such as the water tower, tracks, early goods shed, turntable and houses for the railway employees strongly evoke that period when steam locomotives were the only way of moving people and goods around the country. The station is located in a historic setting amongst abandoned mining areas and other buildings of similar age. Maldon is the only country example of a Victorian Tudor style station building.

Features: The railway is a re-creation of Victorian Railways branch line history. Trains travel through picturesque forest. Maldon railway station, which is listed by the National Trust, has been restored as the Society's headquarters. Light refreshments and souvenirs are available from the kiosk at the station. At Castlemaine, the island platform and western side of the yard have been transferred to the CMRPS. The long term plan is for train operations from Maldon through to Castlemaine.

Locomotives: Five steam locomotives - 2-8-0 K 157 and 160, 2-8-0 J 549, 0-6-2T E 371 (Munro 13/1892) and 4-6-0 D³ 646, diesel-electric locomotive T333 and two shunting locomotives (F212 and DL-1), are owned by or are on loan to the Society. Ex-Victorian Railways 2-8-0 steam locomotives K 160 and J 549 have been restored to operating condition.

Rolling Stock: Ex-VR railmotors RM7 and 61RM and a large range of rolling stock are in service.

Operations: Trains operate from Maldon station on Sundays and most public holidays at 1130, 1300 and 1430, except during total fire bans. Steam trains also run on Wednesdays and every day from Boxing Day through to mid-January. A Heritage Weekend is held mid-year when a wide variety of trains are operated, including freight and mixed trains, together with night photography opportunities.

Fares: Adults $10 and children $6, family $29.

Location: At Maldon railway station. From Melbourne, via the Calder Highway to Elphinstone, through Castlemaine to Maldon. From Bendigo, via Lockwood.

Public Transport: There are regular *V/Line* trains to Castlemaine. There is limited public transport from Castlemaine to Maldon.

Contact: V Evans, Secretary, CMTR
c/- Railway Station
Hornsby Street, Maldon VIC 3463
Phone: (03) 5475 2598; fax (03) 5475 1427
On operating days phone (03) 5475 2966
Email: cmr@Castlemaine.net.au

RNE

HERITAGE SITES (Register of the National Estate)

Ballarat Railway Station: is a stuccoed complex comprising a platform shed built in 1862 and the entrance building dating from 1877-1889. The building is distinguished by its elevated pedimented portico, clock tower and arcade and by the enclosed platform shed. The railway station is an early surviving example of a very substantial railway station building. It has been restored to its former glory and recently had a modern train/bus interchange added.

Barkers Creek Railway Bridge, Harcourt: This substantial bridge was constructed of Harcourt granite in 1859 on the Melbourne-Bendigo railway. In three main spans of some 12.4m each, the structure is characterised by its deep arches and substantial abutments.

Carlsruhe Railway Station: The bluestone station building and residence structure is of a classical/mid-Victorian style. The original slate roof, cast iron gutters and bell cast verandah are retained. The location of Carlsruhe at the junction of the closed branch line to Daylesford, adds interest to the complex.

Castlemaine Railway Station: The buildings, in the Victorian free classical style, were opened in 1862. The long, face brick station building and polychrome brick goods shed with its imposing arches, along with the Midland Hotel just across the road, are key members of the Castlemaine central Conservation area. The cast iron water supply columns which survive at the ends of both platforms are strong reminders of the days of steam.

Creswick Creek Railway Bridge: Located on the Creswick Clunes line, the 1874 bridge is historically significant as an example of the work of The PHOENIX Foundry, the most important nineteenth century engineering manufactory in provincial Victoria. The bridge consists of wrought iron superstructure, supported on four groups of paired tubular cast iron stanchions across the Creek. The Bridge has three spans at 13.25m and two spans at 10.21m.

Stanford's Creek Railway Bridge: Erected in 1890 as part of the Wandong-Heathcote-Bendigo railway, the bridge is a notable example of timber trestle bridge construction. The railway was closed in 1968 and the bridge serves as a reminder of the line. Bridges of this type demonstrate a distinctive and now rarely used construction method that utilised the best qualities of the native ash timbers. Location: Northern Highway, 3.5km SSE of Pyalong.

Kyneton Railway Station Complex: The station (1862-3) is significant as an early and very substantial station complex on the first major country railway line constructed in Victoria. It is probably the largest bluestone railway station in the State. Also, the station complex contributes to the overall importance of the line which, in terms of its buildings and other structures (including two significant viaducts) is the most important in Victoria.

Lal Lal Railway Station and Water Tank: The bluestone station (1863) is in an Italianate-derived style composed to present a neo-picturesque composition. It is a notable example of a country railway station complex, distinctive architecturally for the design, detailing and stonemasonry of the two. The tank is a relic of the age of steam locomotion now lost.

Malmsbury Railway Bridge: Opened in October 1862 at location 101.6km as part of the fourth stage of the historic Melbourne to Bendigo railway. It has five 18.3m bluestone arch spans, with a total sum of spans of 91.5m and an overall length of 149m; the height from the riverbed to the rails is 22.6m. When completed it was the largest masonry bridge built in Australia.

Maryborough locomotive depot: was constructed as part of the development of Maryborough as a major rail terminal towards the end of the 1880's to service the far northern Mallee lines. It is one of the few built mostly of brick and is a striking example of the development of the rail network that played such a vital part in the settlement and prosperity of Victoria.

Maryborough Railway Station: The outstanding Federation Anglo-Dutch style railway station, built in 1892 is the dominant building in the town. It features stucco trimming, lengthy facade adorned by Flemish gables and a tall clock tower. The station is managed by the City Council which has restored the landmark to its former glory. An antique emporium, fine art gallery, café, tourist information centre and quarterly markets of old wares utilise the facility. Former VR 4-6-0 locomotive D³ 646 is on static display near the station.

Trentham Railway Station: The station was one of the two largest consignors on the Carlsruhe-Daylesford line during the second part of the 1880s when more than 20,000 tons of timber was railed from it each year. The station, with an attached station master's residence, goods shed, parcel shed, weigh-bridge and cabin, garden beds and associated hedge plantings, is of heritage significance. Trentham Railway & Agricultural Museum Society has undertaken restoration of the railway station. The Museum has assembled a collection of goods rolling stock, some from the late nineteenth and early twentieth century, including two ex-VR rail tractors (Nos 15RT and 40RT), and carriage 30AV which has been converted to a restaurant.

RAILTRAILS

Ballarat East to Eureka and Skipton: These two railtrails follow the old VR lines.

O'Keefe Trail: The City of Greater Bendigo Council has developed the O'Keefe Trail for walkers, cyclists and horse riders over 13.2km of the former Bendigo-Heathcote railway from Bendigo to Axedale.

OASIS COUNTRY AND THE GRAMPIANS
Sunraysia, Murray-Mallee and Wimmera Regions

This tourist area features the national parks and great rivers of inland Australia. The Wimmera is Victoria's main cereal cropping area. The variety of scenery and landscapes, particularly the Grampians National Park, provides a strong tourism base. The region is served by the main Melbourne-Adelaide railway line and a network of branch lines servicing wheat-producing districts. The region was opened up for agriculture after 1875, when the railway opened from Ballarat to Ararat. The completion of additional branch lines - to Portland in 1877, Avoca in 1890 and Gheringhap in 1913 - contributed to the growing importance of Ararat as a railway junction.

The Chaffey Brothers first developed the extensive irrigation areas of Sunraysia in the 1880s. The region has become the largest wine grape producing area in Australia and also produces citrus, dried fruits and vegetable crops.

Mildura (population 21,000) the main commercial and tourist centre for the region, is the fastest growing provincial city in Victoria. Mildura has a wide range of tourist features and accommodation. A number of paddleboats, including the famous paddle steamer *Melbourne,* operate from Mildura wharf.
Tourist Information: Alfred Deakin Centre, Deakin Avenue. Mildura for information: Phone (03) 5021 4424

Swan Hill (population 9000) developed as a river port from 18. With the opening of the railway from Bendigo in 1890, the distr was opened to closer settlement and built on its river heritage actively promote a local tourist industry.
V/Line trains operate to Swan Hill.

Horsham (population 17,000) is the main commercial centre the Wimmera. *V/Line* opened a regional freight centre in 1976.

Ararat was the site of an alluvial gold rush in 1857. The railw line from Melbourne, via Ballarat opened in 1875 which becar the main line to Adelaide. With the opening of lines to Maryborou and Portland, Ararat became a major railway centre with a lar locomotive depot. The railway complex developed as the ma regional rail junction in Western Victoria for passengers, freig maintenance of locomotives and rolling stock, and trains were ser iced with provisions and crews.

Koondrook Railway Station Museum

Local History
1600mm gauge

The 22km Kerang and Koondrook Tramway was built by the Shire of Kerang in 1889. The tramway was operated by th Shire until it was taken over by the VR in 1952. Koondrook is the only town in Victoria with a station situated in the ma street. Passenger services ceased in 1976 and the line closed in 1983.

Features: The ornate corugated iron Koondrook station, situated in a centre of the road garden setting, was restored in 1983 and is classified by the National Trust. It is supported by a static freight train display headed by a replica body of the 1929 *Sentinel* 4-wheel vertical boiler geared steam tank locomotive, which operated on the line with more conventional veterans purchased second and third hand. The Shire rebuilt Hinksons Siding, the main intermediate station. A separate Tramway display at the Kerang Museum includes an original wooden wagon, number plated and photographs of the line.

Museum Opening: The Kerang Museum is open Saturday and Sunday, 1300-1600.

Location: Atkinson Park, on the south side of the Murray Valley Highway, beside Kerang town, 340km north of Melbourne.

Public Transport: A day return on the Swan Hill train-bus-tra on Sundays allows 3½ hours to inspect the Kerang Museum and taxi visit to Koondrook station.
Contact: Kerang & Koondrook Tramway Association
2/51 Campbell Street, Heathmont VIC 3125

♿ **RNE**

A 1983-built replica of the 1929 Sentinel engine of the Kerang and Koondrook Tramway with a QR open wagon, L class sheep van and ZL brakevan in Main Street at Koondrook station.

DON POTT

ed Cliffs Historical Steam Railway Inc
unraysia Steam Preservation Society

Tourist Line (Steam)
610mm gauge

he Society was formed in 1994 to operate the restored Kerr Stuart 0-4-2T steam locomotive that formerly operated between d Cliffs railway station and the Red Cliffs pumping station. The locomotive, owned by the Rotary Club of Red Cliffs, was stored to working order by the Sunraysia Steam Preservation Society in 1987. A 2km section of the former 1600mm gauge d Cliffs-Morkalla branch line has been converted to 610mm gauge for tourist train operations.

comotive: Kerr Stuart 0-4-2T steam locomotive (B/N 742/1901) s been restored to operating condition. It operated at the Red ffs pumping station between 1924 and 1953.

lling Stock: Bogie passenger carriages, one with wheelchair cess.

en: Trains operate on the first Sunday of each month, 1300-00.

cation: At Red Cliffs, 10km from Mildura on the corner of Calder ghway and Werrimull Road, 2km from Red Cliffs township.

The station and facilities are located at the former point of divergence of the former Morkalla branch from the Melbourne to Mildura line.

Public Transport: *V/Line* rail services to Bendigo, thence coordinated road coach to Mildura.

Contact: Red Cliffs Historical Steam Railway Inc
PO Box 64, Red Cliffs VIC 3496
Phone: (03) 5024 2262
Sunraysia Tourist Information Centre: (03) 5021 4424

rarat Railway Heritage Association

Railway Museum

his group was formed to preserve the historic railway precinct at the important railway junction of Ararat and to establish a useum of railway memorabilia in the former Ararat A Signal Box.

atures: The railway station (built 1875) is a single-storey brick ilding in bi-chromatic Classical Revival style. The yards included range of other railway equipment and buildings, including a comotive turntable and engine shed, two water tanks in Gordon reet, the associated railway workers' cottages.

Museum: Ararat A Signal Box has been relocated to the up end of the station and houses a collection of railway memorabilia.
Opening Times: Check with local Tourist information centre.
Location: Birdwood Avenue, Ararat, 211km west of Melbourne on the Western Highway (from Ballarat) [directions to get there]

ERITAGE ITEMS

arriages Restaurant, Swan Hill: Two former *Tait* suburban ooden carriages form the centre attraction at this restaurant, located Pioneer Motor Inn, Swan Hill.

ildura: Former VR 2-8-0 locomotive K 175 is on static display a park near the river.

erviceton Historical Railway Station: This classified Station 888) was jointly built by Victoria and South Australia on the isputed Territory, resulting from an incorrect border survey of 847 and is the only railways customs post on the Victorian-South ustralian border. Victorian Railways architects designed this aracteristically-styled late Victorian era red brick building with central two storey position, flanking office wings, extensive nderground storage and service areas. The Station presents displays f local and railway memorabilia, together with a BYO restaurant.

Location: Elizabeth Street, Serviceton, Victoria.
Opening Times: Selected weekends or by appointment.
Admission: Adults $2, child $1.

Swan Hill Pioneer Settlement: Ex-VR D³-class 4-6-0 locomotive No 640 (Thompson 1/1914) is on static display.

RAILTRAILS

Grampians Railtrail: This track follows a section of the former VR line from Stawell to a stone quarry at the foot of Mt Difficult. The rail trail extends 3km from the heritage-listed quarry toward Stawell. The quarry is well provided with information signs and two 610mm gauge quarry wagons are on site.

GOULBURN VALLEY / NORTH-EAST
Goulburn-Murray Waters/Legends, Wine and High Country

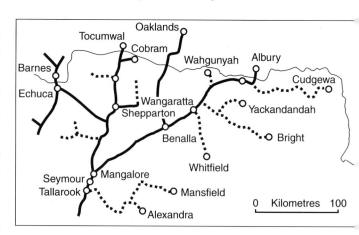

The north-east region is located on the main transportation and communication links between Melbourne and Sydney (Australia's two largest cities) and is pivotal to the south eastern Australia triangle including Adelaide. The region is home to some of Victoria's most interesting towns, great expanses of untouched bushlands and gateway to Victoria's high country. It features some of the State's most famous wine producing areas.

The Goulburn Valley is the fruit bowl of Victoria and food processing and canning operations in the Shepparton area generates significant freight traffic for *Freight Victoria*. Branch lines from Echuca serve the southern NSW centres of Deniliquin and Moulamein, while the Goulburn Valley branch extends to a freight centre at Tocumwal in NSW.

The Shire of Alexandra offers lake and mountain resorts within close reach of Melbourne. The rich forests of the area previously yielded timber for the rapid growth of Melbourne; today winter resorts entice the visitor.

Railway Services: *V/Line* trains operate to Seymour, Albury, Bendigo, Swan Hill and Echuca. Melbourne-Shepparton rail services are operated by Hoys Roadlines. They provide 26 train services per week on a non-reserved basis.

Greater Shepparton (population 60,000) is the main commercial centre and *solar city* capital of the region. It is a just two hours drive north from Melbourne, the State's capital city, and 40 minutes drive south of the Murray River. It is a country city in the middle the intensive agricultural areas of the Goulburn Valley.

Seymour (population 11,500) is located on the Goulburn River. With the opening of the railway in 1872, it became an important

locomotive depot for the north-eastern and Goulburn Valley lin. Its railway tradition has been preserved as a railway heritage cen.

Wangaratta (population 20,000), located on the junction of Ovens and King Rivers, is the service centre for the region and h a strong manufacturing base. Former VR 2-8-0 locomotive K 1 is on static display in a park south of the station.

Echuca-Moama (population 11,500) grew on the riverboat tra during the nineteenth century, becoming the major trans-shipme port from the paddle steamers to the railway serving Melbour. The railway line opened in 1864 and Echuca became a bustli port, but the river trade declined after 1880 as more railway lin were opened up. Local preservation projects focus on these tran port forms. The **Echuca Steam, Horse and Vintage Rally,** he over the long week-end of June, brings together one of Australi: biggest collections of steam-powered machinery, traction engin and model steam locomotives.

Bright (population 2000) since 1945, Bright has become important tourist centre for alpine resorts.

HERITAGE SITES

Benalla Locomotive Depot: The engine depot is a double gable-roofed, timber-framed, corrugated- iron clad dwelling. The depot is significant as an early representative example of iron railway building construction in Victoria. The depot was a service point for steam locomotive engines on the main line and the Yarrawonga branch line.

Echuca Engine Shed was erected 1864-5 by the Victorian railways department. The extensive red brick structure has a long gabled form. It is a fine example of railway architecture and was built during the greatest period of Victoria's expansion.

Echuca Road/Rail Bridge: The iron girder bridge which carried road and rail traffic over the Murray River from 1878. It is regarded as one of the four most significant metal girder bridges in

Australia. A new rail bridge opened in 1989 and the old brid now carries local road traffic.

Seymour Railway Station: Seymour railway station and R freshment Rooms have been fully restored. The Railway Refres ment Rooms are available for hire.

Yea Railway Station: The railway from Tallarook opened 1883 and closed in 1978. The heritage-listed railway station is r garded as the most intact example of a small group of standa Victorian Gothic-styled station buildings. It has been restored the Friends of Yea Railway Inc. Markets are held on the third Sa urday of each month, along with goods shed art displays. The Y Railtrail follows the old VR line for a short distance.

RAILTRAILS

Murray to Mountains Railtrail: Stage 1 of this railtrail is establishing a 94km track to link together all the existing sections of track between Myrtleford and Bright on the former VR branch line. The scenic Victorian Railways line from Wangaratta to Bright opened in 1890 and closed in 1983 with passenger services ceasing in 1952.

Stage 2 is a loop joining Wangaratta with Rutherford and Stage 3 follows the old narrow gauge King Valley line from Wangaratta to

Walking Trails

Whitfield. Remnants of the former railway include old station sign old louvre vans and the original engine shed at Whitefield.

Wodonga-Cudgewa: The right-of-way of the closed branch lir between Wodonga and Cudgewa is being developed as a touri walking and bike track. The old line was regarded as one of th most scenic in Australia.

eymour Railway Heritage Centre
eymour Railway Heritage Centre Inc

Heritage Railway Centre
1435/1600mm gauge

P FOOT

Steam locomotive J 515 of the Seymour Railway Heritage Centre is rapidly accelerating the bank at Mangalore with the down Yarrawonga Easter Special on 1 April 1999.

eymour Loco, the former VR steam locomotive depot that served the north-east region, is now the base for Victoria's largest ollection of operating locomotives and heritage carriages. The Centre is dedicated to preserving Victoria's railway heritage d operate tour trains over the *V/Line* system. The centre is also the base for V/Line's *Classic Carriages*, which have been stored for charter operations.

ocomotives: Two steam and eight diesel locomotives, including stored ex-VR 2-8-0 J515 (VF 6061/1954), the first T-class esel-electric locomotive (T320 of 1955), T357 and Y133, pioneer ainline diesel-electric B74 (of 1953) and ex-Commonwealth Railays diesel-electric GM.36. 2-8-0 loco J512 is under restoration.

olling Stock: Restored diesel-electric rail motor RM58, dieselydraulic railmotor DRC43 and 33 vintage carriages. Serviceable ock include 7 VR/SAR joint-stock and 7 VR 12-wheeler E-type ooden carriages, 4 ex-Spirit of Progress 1937 steel carriages, a burban Tait train, the classic parlor car *Yarra* (built for the *Sydney xpress* in 1904), State Car No.4 (the *Royal Carriage*), dining car d four 6-wheel vintage carriages dating from 1880. The Centre as also restored vintage 4-wheel freight rolling stock.

perations: Restored locomotives and vehicles are available for re and are also used for members outings and special events.

Visitors are welcome to inspect the depot on weekends and at other times by prior arrangement.

Opening Times: Tuesday, Thursday, Saturday and Sunday, 1000-1500. Admission by donation. Visitors must be escorted on site. Guided tours by arrangement - $50 per group, including barbecue.

Location: Victoria Street Extension, Seymour; 100km north of Melbourne.
Public Transport: *V/Line* trains, 9 services weekdays, 5 Saturday and 3 Sunday.

Contact: Seymour Railway Heritage Centre
PO Box 515, Seymour VIC 3661
Phone: (03) 5799 0515; Facsimile: (03) 5799 0556

Alexandra Timber Tramway
Alexandra Timber Tramway and Museum Inc

Industry Museum/Railway (Stea.
610mm gauge

PETER MEDLIN

On a wet December day, John Fowler 0-6-0 locomotive hauls its train at the Alexandra Timber Tramway.

This museum is based at the former Alexandra railway station which houses a collection of historical and railway intere
The Museum is developing a timber settlement, which is to include a steam-operated sawmill similar to those that operated
the Rubicon forest earlier this century. A 610mm gauge railway has been built around the site to provide visitors with t
experience of narrow-gauge operations. It is being extended through Alexandra township along the route of the form
Rubicon timber tramway.

Features: The Museum features logging, sawmill and tramway equipment from the timber industry. Working models of historic timber mill working life are exhibited. An extensive collection of memorabilia and photographs relating to the history of the region are also on display. The heritage railway station at Alexandra has been fully restored.

Locomotives: Three steam locomotives from the Queensland canefields - John Fowler 0-6-0T (11885/1909) and Hudswell Clarke 0-6-0s (1098/1915 and 1555/1925); a timber tramway tractor, and Australia's pioneer diesel locomotive built by Kelly & Lewis of Melbourne in 1935.

Operations: Steam-hauled trains operate on the second Sunday of each month and on most public holidays. Mid-week tours are welcome by prior arrangement.

Location: Alexandra is 130km north-east of Melbourne on ▮ Maroondah Highway. The museum is located in the form Alexandra Railway Station opposite the corner of Station Str▮ and Vickery Street.

Public Transport: A *V/Line* day return bus service is availab▮ from Melbourne on Sundays (depart Spencer Street 0945), w two hours available at Alexandra.

Contact: Alexandra Timber Tramway & Museum Inc,
              PO Box 288, Alexandra VIC 3714
Phone: 015 509988 or (03) 5772 2392

 RNE

Bright & District Historical Museum

Local History Museum

The Bright historical society has restored the 1900 station building as a local history museum with a section devoted to th
history of the Bright-Wangaratta railway.

Exhibits: Ex-Victorian Railways rolling stock - a 1917 BU passenger carriage, CE class luggage van (1907), ZL guards van and five goods wagons - are on display. The museum has numerous railway artifacts, signals and a collection of photographs taken along the Bright railway line over the years on display.

Opening Times: The museum is open on Sundays, September to May from 1400-1600; and during school holidays, on Tuesday, Thursday, and Sunday, or by appointment.

Admission: Adults $2, children 50c.
Location: Railway Avenue, Bright; 80km south-east of Wangara▮ on the Great Alpine Road.
Public Transport: *V/Line* coaches operate from Wangaratta dai▮
Address: Bright & District Historical Society
              PO Box 265, Bright VIC 3741
Phone: (03) 5755 1356

RNE

˙LANDS, BAYS & PENINSULAS

ˑe tourist centres around Port Phillip Bay and Western Port ˑe classified as the Islands, Bays and Peninsulas Region. ˑornington Peninsula, forming the eastern shore of Port ˑillip Bay is Victoria's oldest and most popular holiday ˑayground, but is now enjoying renewed fame as a major ˑliday destination only one hour from the State Capital. ˑe region was served by the Great Southern Railway from ˑelbourne to Port Albert which opened in 1892, together ˑth lines to the Mornington Peninsula.

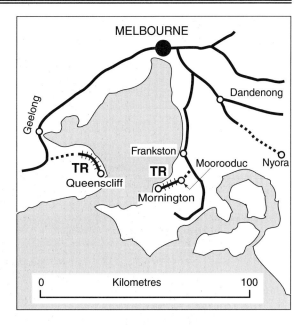

ˑankston (population 106,000) is the gateway to the Mornington ˑninsula and its largest shopping and service centre.

ˑetting There: Bayside electric train services operate from ˑndenong to Pakenham and Cranbourne, while the Mornington ˑninsula is serviced by Bayside electric trains to Frankston with ˑsel train connections to Stony Point.

ˑornington Tourist Railway
ˑornington Railway Preservation Society Inc

Tourist Line (Steam/Diesel)
1600 mm gauge

ˑe Mornington Railway Preservation Society, formed in 1984, has restored the section of the abandoned Baxter to Mornington ˑilway line from Moorooduc to Mornington (Yuilles Road). The Society operates vintage steam-hauled tourist trains over ˑis 6km section of the line.

ˑcomotives: Operational 2-8-0 steam locomotive K163, built ˑ41, diesel-electrics T334 and T411 and a *Track Chief* No 1 die-ˑl tractor. Non-operational Track Chief No 21diesel tractor and ˑam locomotive K 177 which is undergoing restoration. The Track ˑiefs are the only two of their kind in the world. They can operate ˑ road or rail.

ˑlling Stock: Six passenger cars dating from 1909 to 1943, a 95-ˑar old van fitted as a cafe and two 6-wheel guards vans are ˑerational. The Society also owns one ex-VR DE railmotor and ˑany other carriages and vans requiring restoration.

ˑperations: Steam-hauled passenger trains operate on first Sunday ˑ the month between 1100 and 1700. Departures are approximately ˑurly from Moorooduc to Mornington (Yuilles Road) and return ˑpprox. 50 minutes). Trains also operate on most public holidays ˑd on each Wednesday and Sunday during the Christmas/January ˑliday period.

Fares (1999/2000): Adult return $6; concession $4; child return $3.

The Society's train is available for charters, excursion or film work. For further information and membership details, contact the Society at the address below.

Location: Moorooduc railway station (Melway 105 K9) 60km south-east of Melbourne on the Mornington Peninsula. Enter from Mount Eliza Regional Park, off Two Bays Road from Moorooduc Highway (Route 11) and follow signs.
Public Transport: Bayside electric train to Frankston, thence bus to Mornington. Alight corner Nepean Highway and Pentecost Road and walk 300m to Yuilles Road station.
Address: Mornington Railway Preservation Society
PO Box 193, Mornington VIC 3931
Phone/fax: (03) 5975 3474 or (03) 9789 2087

Bellarine Peninsula Railway, Queenscliff
Geelong Steam Preservation Society

Tourist Railway (Steam
1067mm gauge

DAVID JACKS

Ex-TGR 4-6-2 steam locomotive M6 with a tourist train at the Bellarine Peninsula Railway on 16 May 1999.

The 16km Bellarine Peninsula Railway from Queenscliff to Drysdale operates over part of the original 1600mm gauge Queensc
to South Geelong railway.

Features: The Bellaring Peninsula Railway provides a unique opportunity to see examples of rolling stock from railway systems throughout Australia. Trains depart from the historic Queenscliff station and follow a scenic water route around the shores of Swan Bay to Laker's Siding (4.5km) then climb over the rolling Bellarine Peninsula hills for a further 11.5km to Drysdale.

Locomotives: Nine steam, two diesel-electric and two diesel-mechanical locomotives. Operating locomotives are ex-WAGR 2-8-2 V1209 (RSH 7778/1955), ex-SAR 4-8-0 T251 (Walkers 276/1917), ex-TGR 4-6-2 M6 (RSH 7429/1951), ex-QR 4-6-0 PB15 454 (Walkers 99/1909), ex-Aust. Portland Cement 0-4-2ST No 6 (Huds Clarke 646/1903), ex-TGR 0-6-0DM VA1 and V8, and ex-TGR diesel-electrics X3 and X20.

Rolling Stock: Three railmotors, 22 vintage passenger cars and 29 wagons/service vehicles. One carriage in regular use dates from 1888.

Operations: Trains operate every Sunday and public holiday (except Christmas Day and Anzac Day) and on Tuesday, Wednesday and Thursday during school holidays. Normal services depart Queenscliff at 1115 and 1430 to Drysdale, and at 1330 to Laker's Siding. Trains depart Drysdale at 1215 for a return trip.

Services also operate daily from 26 December until the seco Sunday in January, on every Saturday in January and over the Eas weekend. The railway operates the *Easter Steam & Railw Extravaganza* on Easter Saturday and Sunday. Diesel services place steam on days of total fire ban. Group bookings and tr hire welcome.

Fares: To Laker's Siding; adult return $6.
              To Drysdale; adult return $12.

Location: By road, 90 minutes from Melbourne via Geelong the Bellarine Highway. By vehicle and passenger ferry fr Sorrento to Queenscliff (year round) or summer passenger serv between Sorrento, Portsea and Queenscliff; Phone (03) 5258 32

Public Transport: By rail, to Geelong (information 136 196), th bus to Drysdale or Queenscliff (Phone 5223 2111).
Inquiries: Bellarine Peninsula Railway
              PO Box 166, Queenscliff VIC 3225
Phone: (03) 5258 2069; fax (03) 5258 4037
              Information: 1900 931 452

GIPPSLAND
Natural Discovery Region

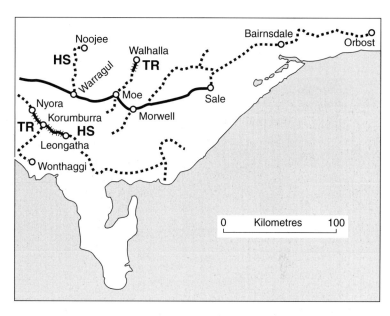

Historically the Gippsland region was Victoria's most inaccessible area with rugged and picturesque country. Even after the opening of the railway in the 1880s, many areas remained isolated until the twentieth century. Substantial growth came to the region with coal mining. Black coal was mined at Korumburra in the late nineteenth century and the State Mine at Wonthaggi provided coal for VR steam locomotives. Extensive brown coal deposits were first mined at Morwell in 1916 for the manufacture of briquettes. From the 1920s, thermal power stations were built on the fields and today the Latrobe Valley is the main source of Victoria's electricity. The region is Victoria's main producer of forest products and exports a wide range of agricultural produce.

Warragul and Traralgon (population 21,000) are the main commercial service centres for the region.

Moe (population 21,000) and Morwell (population 19,000) are mining and industrial towns in the Latrobe Valley.

Sale (population 15,000) is the service centre for an important agricultural district and the Bass Strait oil and gas fields.

Getting There: Bayside electric train services operate to Pakenham. V/Line Passenger operates daily *Gippslander* passenger trains to Sale and additional services to Traralgon.

South Gippsland Railway
South Gippsland Tourist Railway Inc

Tourist Railway (Steam/Rail Motor)
1600mm gauge

The South Gippsland Railway was established in 1993 to privately manage, maintain and operate a 40km (25 mile) section of the century-old former South Eastern Line (also known as the Great Southern Railway), a rural mainline of the Victorian Railways. At its peak, the South Eastern Line was one of the busiest in the State with locomotive depots at Koo-Wee-Rup, Nyora, Korumburra, Foster and Yarram. A branch line from Nyora served the State Coal Mines at Wonthaggi. Located just over an hour's drive from Melbourne, the SGR provides steam and diesel services on the former VR mainline between Nyora and Leongatha. The line is the steepest remaining mainline in Victoria as it transverses the Strezeleki Ranges and presents a challenge to steam locomotives. The railway is fully accredited and is operated predominantly by volunteers.

Features: The SGR is headquartered at Korumburra where the large station includes licensed dining and refreshment facilities, tourist information and an art gallery. It offers the only Driver Experience in Eastern Australia whereby participants are able to drive and fire steam or diesel locomotives and railcars at mainline speeds.
Locomotives: SGR operates Bo-Bo DE T 342 and 345, both restored in VR blue and gold.
Rolling Stock: *Redhen* 300- class and *SuperChook* railcars formerly used by *TransAdelaide* in South Australia. Ex-VR DE railmotor 55RM, on loan from the ARHS Railway Museum, has been fully restored in VR Blue/Gold. Ex-VR E-class carriages 19, and 36 BE are in use. Van 17CW is used as a public viewing carriage on locomotive-hauled trains.
Operations: Every Sunday departing Leongatha at 1100, 1415; Korumburra at 1030, 1130, 1330 and 1445; Nyora at 1230 and 1545.

Charter trains operate on a 7 days a week basis. Single journey approx. one hour duration. Saturday night and Summer Twilight Rail cruises feature food, drinks and entertainment. Licensed restaurant at Korumburra. Driver experience courses are provided as required.
Location: SGTR headquarters are at the heritage-listed Korumburra railway station, 120km south-east of Melbourne on the South Gippsland Highway.
Public Transport: *V/Line* road coaches operate daily from Spencer Street, Melbourne to all stations.
Contact: General manager, South Gippsland Tourist Railway
            PO Box 5, Korumburra VIC 3950
Phone: (03) 5658 1111; Fax (03) 5658 1511

Coal Creek Bush Tramway
Coal Creek Historical Village

Tourist Park Railway (Diesel)
610 mm gauge

COAL CREEK HERITAGE VILLAGE

Ex-Queensland sugar mill Bundaberg Fowler 0-6-2T Count Strzelecki *on its return to service at Coal Creek Heritage Village, Korumburra on 19 December 1997.*

The site of Victoria's first black coal mining at Coal Creek has been developed as a historical village to preserve the ear industrial era of the 1890s. The village, established in 1974, is an educational and entertainment complex that captures tradition of the early farming and coal mining era. Over 40 buildings have been moved to the site from locations in Sou Gippsland and faithfully restored. The 1.6km Coal Creek Bush Tramway serves the complex.

Displays: The Coal Creek railway station is being developed as a museum of railway memorabilia and the history of the Great Southern Railway. Several items of VR rolling stock are preserved on site, including 2-8-0 locomotive K169 of 1941. Industry in the village complex tells the story of early enterprises, including the original poppet head of the Coal Creek Proprietary Mine, a sawmill and blacksmith shop.

Locomotives: Ex-Queensland canefield 0-6-2T *Count Strzelecki* (Bundaberg Foundry 7/1952), plus Ruston & Hornsby 4wDM locomotives. 3 bogie carriages.

Operations: 1100-1600 daily – steam weekends and public holidays, diesel-hauled trains other days.

Fares: All day ticket; Adult $4, child $2, family $10. A special $10 cab ride ticket is also available.

Location: 117km south-east of Melbourne on the South Gippsla Highway.
Public Transport: *V/Line* daily coach services from Spencer Stre Melbourne, providing about four hours at Coal Creek.

Contact: Coal Creek Historical Village
South Gippsland Highway, Korumburra VIC 395
Phone: (03) 5655 1811

Walhalla Goldfields Railway

Walhalla Goldfields Railway Inc

Tourist Railway (Steam/Diesel)
762mm gauge

The Victorian Railways operated a 42km narrow-gauge (762 mm) railway from Moe on the Gippsland line, through rugged country to Walhalla between 1910 and 1944 (the Moe-Erica section closed in 1954). This volunteer preservation group is restoring the spectacular Stringers Creek Gorge to Walhalla section of the former VR narrow-gauge Moe-Walhalla Railway is a major tourist attraction for the region. Considered a masterpiece of engineering, this section of the line clings to a narrow ledge blasted along the southern side of the Gorge. A 3km section of the line from Thomson River to Happy Creek is currently in use.

Heritage Significance: The railway bridge over the Thomson River (1909) is heritage-listed as a key remnant structure of the Moe to Walhalla narrow gauge railway, which was associated with both the gold mining and timber industry eras of the region. It was thought of as an engineering marvel and achievement at the time of its construction. The bridge is one of the well known and most photographed landmarks in Gippsland.

Features: The line includes the 100 metre length Thomson River Bridge, which is on the Register of the National Estate. Phase II of the project will extend the line to Walhalla, requiring the rebuilding of six timber trestle bridges.

Locomotives: John Fowler 0-6-0DM No 14 from the SEC Yallourn railway and KASEY (Baldwin 4wDM) are operational. 0-6-0 H/Clarke (1553/1924) currently under restoration and regauging.

Rolling Stock: Three tourist passenger carriages.

Operations: From Thomson River each Saturday at 1130, 1300 and 1400; Sundays and public holidays at 1100, 1230, 1400 and 1530. Additional services operate to Sunday timetable during school holidays (check Info line). The return journey is approximately 45 minutes. Trains are available for charter.

Location: 44km north of Moe, via Erica; 2 hours drive east of Melbourne. There is no public transport.

Contact: Commercial Manager, Walhalla Goldfields Railway Inc c/- Post Office, Walhalla VIC 3825

Phone: (03) 5165 3442 (Thomson station, operating days only). Recorded Info (03) 9513 3969

Web Page: www.comu.net.au/wgr/

 RNE

HERITAGE ITEMS

Noojee Trestle Bridge: At Noojee (31km north of Warragul) an outstanding timber trestle bridge has been conserved as a symbol of the logging railways which enabled the sustainable harvesting of timber in the 1920s The bridge was rebuilt in 1939 after a bushfire. It is 103 metres long and 22 metres high and is one of the most substantial timber railway trestle bridges built in the State. Such timber bridges characterised the railways of Gippsland. The Noojee bridge is an important representative example of this bridge type and of the construction techniques using locally felled timber for these bridges.

Port Welshpool Museum: The local museum has a good wagon and other memorabilia from the Welshpool to Port Welshpool narrow gauge line.

Static Display Steam Locomotives: Ex-VR 2-8-0 locomotive K154 is on display at the Old Gippstown Folk Museum, Moe, while G50 is in Rotary Park, Latrobe Street, Warragul.

Stony Creek Bridge: This wooden trestle bridge, built in 1916 on the Bairnsdale-Orbost Government line, is one of the longest and tallest in the state. It is heritage listed on the Register of the National Estate.

Walhalla Historic Area. Walhalla was the site of Victoria's richest reef gold mines. The 15 mines which operated on Cohens Reef produced close to one and a half million ounces of gold, making it one of the richest gold bearing reefs in the world. The Long Tunnel Company at Walhalla was the most successful mining company in Australia in terms of yield per tonnes of ore crushed. The company built 43km of narrow-gauge railways to carry timber for their mining operations.

The Long Tunnel Extended Mine is now operated as a tourist mine. A 2500ha area surrounding the town was declared a Historic Area in 1983. Many of the old mining railways are now walking tracks. The best one to follow is from the western side of Walhalla to the original steel bridge that carried the tramway over the Thomson River.

Wonthaggi State Mine: The former black coal mine, which supplied coal for VR locomotives, has been restored as an operating tourist mine. Ex-VR 2-8-0 locomotive K192 is on static display at the mine site in Garden Street, Wonthaggi.

RAILTRAILS

Anderson-Wonthaggi Railtrail. The 16.5km section of the former railway line between Anderson and Wonthaggi is being developed as part of a State system of railtrails for the use of walkers, cyclists and horse riders. The railtrail links tourist attractions in the region which offer spectacular coastal scenery.

Bairnsdale-Orbost Rail Trail: Some 100km of the former railway line between Bairnsdale and Orbost is being developed as a rail trail. A highlight is the inclusion of the heritage-listed Stony Creek Bridge (see above). The recreational trail provides a link between the communities of Eastern Gippsland.

Collins Siding to Tyers Junction: This railtrail follows the route of the former Forestry Commission 2ft-6in gauge line.

Erica-Thomson River: This 5km railtrail follows the route of the closed narrow-gauge line from Erica to Thomson River. It is managed by the Walhalla Tourist Railway Committee and links with the WGR operation at Thomson River.

Great Southern Railtrail: Stage 1 of this railtrail from Leongatha to Koonwarra was opened in 1998. It takes in histor sites, has rural views, a wide variety of bushland communities an offers spectacular views of Bass Strait and Wilson's Promontry.

Contact: Friends of the Great Southern Railtrail
              60 Ellens Road, Mirboo North VIC 3871
Phone: (03) 5662 2607

Mirboo North-Boolarra Trail: This 13km recreational railtra is located on a section of the former Morwell-Mirboo branch lir The communities were founded by the railway and the railtrail aga forms a link between the communities. It features lush Sou Gippsland farmland with pockets of native vegetation and vie of the Strzlecki Ranges. An annual bike ride is held over the trail March from Boolarra with return over local roads.

Moe to Yallorn: This railtrail follows the old VR line formatio

Upper Yarra Walking Trail: The Upper Yarra Track provid enjoyable walking through tall eucalypt forest country along c logging railway formations and vehicle tracks. Starting at Warburt (see Melbourne Region), the eight sections of trail totalling 81.5k lead to the Alpine National Park.

BOB McKILLC

This trestle bridge near Noojee has been restored as a tribute to the "bush engineering" skills of the pioneer sawmillers who built logging railways to transport their product.

TASMANIA

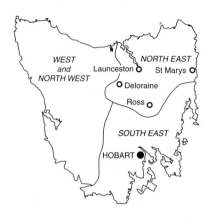

HOBART AND THE SOUTHEAST

Hobart (population 147,000) is the capital of Tasmania and is renowned for its fine nineteenth century buildings and magnificent harbour setting. Electric trams commenced operations in Hobart in 1893, the first successful electric tramway system in the Southern Hemisphere. The 1067mm gauge system operated by the Hobart Electric Tramway Company and then the City Council featured the most extensive use of double-deck trams in Australia. The system was extended to a maximum length of 27km in 1932, but closures commenced in 1945, with the last 9km line being closed on 24 October 1960. Several trams have been preserved and a heritage line using double-deck trams is under consideration.

Public Transport in Hobart is provided by *Metro Tasmania*. There are 297 route km of bus services radiating from the Metro City Bus Station at the GPO. Route information is provided at major interchanges at Metro City in Elizabeth Street, Glenorchy and at Rosny Park on the Eastern Shore.

For Metro timetable information, phone 13 2201 from anywhere in Tasmania.

Huon Peninsula: The forestry industry has dominated economic activity in the south. Several operators had logging railways to transport logs to their mills.

HERITAGE ITEMS

Margate Train. ex-TGR 4-6-2 locomotive MA3 (RSH 7426/1951) and railcar DP24 are on static display at the Puff 'n' Billy Market at Margate on the Channel Highway.

TGR Locomotives. Ex-TGR 4-6-2 locomotives MA1 and M1 are on static display in Rotary Park, Granton - at the junction of the Midland and Lyell Highways - and at Ross respectively.

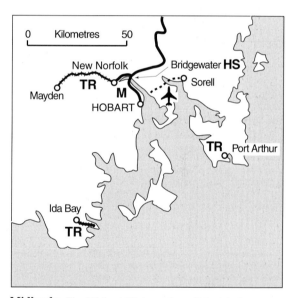

Midlands: The Midland Highway from Hobart to Launceston serves a number of historic towns which feature important items of their convict past.

Bridgewater bridge: This bridge is significant in the context of transport links between Launceston and Hobart, where bridge and railway crossings over the Derwent River at Bridgewater have been constructed and upgraded since the middle of the 19th century. The current bridge carrying road and rail, was completed in 1946 and is the fourth bridge constructed at Bridgewater since 1849. The 336m long, bridge has a centre lift span and two flanking trusses which support the lift span towers.

Tasmanian Transport Museum, Glenorchy
Tasmanian Transport Museum Society

Museum/Steam Centre
1067mm gauge

TASMANIAN TRANSPORT MUSEUM SOCIETY

Tasmanian Transport Museum Society's 4-6-2 locomotive and restored carriages for mainline operation.

The Society was established to preserve items of public transport and steam technology, including railway locomotives and rolling stock, trams and buses. The present museum site, adjacent to the *Tasrail* mainline railway, was obtained in 1972.

Features: The railway section of the museum includes the rebuilt New Town station (incorporating a display of artifacts), roundhouse, carriage/tram sheds, the relocated Botanical Gardens signal box and other railway items. The museum has a connection with the Tasrail system enabling transfer of locomotives and rolling stock for tours.

Locomotives: Seven 1067mm gauge ex-TGR and private railway steam locomotives. Two steam locomotives, 2-6-0 C22 built by Beyer Peacock (B/No 4414/1902) and M5 (Robt Stephenson Hawthorn 7425/1951), together with diesel-electric Y4, have been restored to operating condition. Other locomotives on display include ex-TGR 4-8-2 freight locomotives Q5 and H1; and a B-class Climax logging locomotive. X1, Australia's first main line diesel electric locomotive built in 1950, and former EZ Company/EBR Ruston 0-4-0DM are available for shunting duties. The Climax and a 0-4-0 vertical boilered locomotive built by Markham (c1892) and used on logging tramways are undergoing restoration.

Rolling Stock: TGR railcars DP15-PT4, DP26 and SP4, a former Sentinel steam railcar converted to carriage; 5 railway carriages, including a 4-wheel vehicle built in 1869 for the Launceston and Western Railway; and 5 goods wagons. Ex-TML 6-wheel carriage B+21 under restoration.

Electric Tramcars: Launceston tramcar 13 (1910), Hobart single truck double-deck tramcar 46 (1922) and Bo-Bo tram No 14 (1950); 2 trolley buses from the Hobart services.

Operation: Saturday, Sunday and public holidays from 1300-1630. A steam train operates passenger services over some 0.5km of track on the third Sunday of the month and a diesel railcar offers rides on the first Sunday. Museum opens at 1100 on steam train running days.

Admission: Adults $3 ($5 on steam running days), children $1.50 ($2 on steam running days).
Location: The Museum is located in Anfield Street, Glenorchy opposite the Northgate Shopping Centre.
Public Transport: Northern suburbs bus services from the city (Stop 33 on Main Road).
Contact: Secretary, Tasmanian Transport Museum Society
                 GPO Box 867J, Hobart Tas 7001
Phone: (03) 6272 7721
Internet: www.tased.edu.au/tasonline/railtas/ttms/ttms.htm

 RNE

Derwent Valley Railway
Derwent Valley Railway Preservation Society Inc.

Tourist Line (Steam/Diesel)
1067 mm gauge

DENNIS HEWITT

Derwent Valley Railway's diesel-electric X18 passes Goulds Lagoon wildlife sanctuary on a charter train.

The Derwent Valley railway is regarded as one of the most scenic branch lines in Australia. The Derwent Valley Preservation Society is a voluntary organisation that has restored this important piece of Tasmania's railway heritage and operates excursion trains between New Norfolk, Mount Field National Park and Mayadena on this line. Occasional steam- or diesel-hauled excursions are also run to destinations on the Main Line.

Locomotives: Ex-TGR 4-8-2 H 2 (VF 5950 of 1951), recently overhauled; pioneer Bo-Bo mainline diesel-electric locomotives X 10 and X 18 (VF 1805/1950 and 1818/1951); Bo-Bo DE Y 2 (TGR 1961); and diesel shunting locomotives U5 and V7 (awaiting restoration).

Rolling Stock: Three former *Tasman Limited* articulated carriages (ACS.2, 3 and 4) and two ex-Emu Bay Railway *West Coaster* carriages (ABL 1 and 2). A collection of old goods rolling stock is being restored for per-way and maintenance duties.

Operations: Various excursions and charter trips are operated over the Derwent Valley Railway and Main Line. Enquire at booking office for details of forthcoming operations. The train is available for charter groups and corporate functions. Art & craft staff are held at New Norfolk station.

Bookings and fares: Phone (03) 6234 6049 (Business hours);
fax (03) 6231 3752; or write to
Birch Travel, 45 Victoria Street, Hobart TAS 7000.

Location: The Society is based at the New Norfolk railway station, Station Street, New Norfolk, 38km northwest of Hobart via the Lyell Highway. Some excursions depart from the Hobart regatta grounds, near the CBD.

Public Transport: A regular Metro bus service operates within the Hobart metropolitan area. Between Hobart and New Norfolk, the bus opoeration is infrequent and a hire car is advisable.

Contact: Dennis Hewitt
Derwent Valley Railway Preservation Society Inc
PO Box 478, New Norfolk TAS 7140
Phone: (03) 6261 1946 (bh); (03) 6249 3250 (a/h); or
Fax: (03) 6261 5301
Email: able@netspace.net.au

Classic Rail Tours

Mainline tours (steam/diesel)

Classic Rail Tours is a company operating Tasmanian rail charters/tours and based at the Tasmanian Transport Museum. It specialises in smaller (up to 70 passengers), high quality tours and charters around the State's rail system.

Rolling stock: Ex-TGR railcars DP13 and DP14 (built 1939) have been immaculately restored by the Company. Tasmanian Transport Museum Society-owned 4-6-2 steam locomotive M5 and restored carriages AAL10 and SP4 are also used for tours.

Operations: Details of upcoming tours and charter quotations can be obtained from Classic Rail Tours. The booking agent for tours is RACT Travel.

Contact: Colin Wood
5 Oast Street, New Norfolk TAS 7140
Phone: (03) 6261 1171; fax (03) 6261 3872
E-mail: classicrailtours@bigpond.com

Bush Mill Railway, Port Arthur
Bush Mill Steam Railway and Settlement

Tourist Line (Steam)
381mm gauge

Located just 1km north of the Port Arthur Historic Site, the Bush Mill Steam Railway and Settlement features one o Australia's most unique narrow gauge railways, a steam timber mill and displays of early logging operations.

Features: The railway takes visitors on a 4km return trip through scenic bushland down a hillside track packed with features, including a switchback, the 70m long "Serpentine" trestle bridge and a series of sharp horseshoe bends, embankments and gradients up to 1 in 25.

The Bush Mill Settlement is an authentic reconstruction of a 100-year old steam sawmill and features innovative sound and light displays to tell the story of the early pioneers. A working blacksmith, the Bush Skills Theatrette and examples of early logging railways and equipment are just some of the many fascinating aspects of this award-winning attraction. A family restaurant, tree tops pavilion and craft and gift shop are included in the complex.

Locomotives: K3, a ½ scale replica of Tasmania's famous K-cla 0-4-0+0-4-0 Garratt locomotive, entered service in 1990. *Mou taineer*, a 0-4-0TT steam locomotive and a 4wDM locomotive a also in service.

Operations: Open daily from 1000-1700 (except Christmas Day Trains operate from Bush Mill at 1015, 1115, 1230, 1330, 143 1530 and 1615 and take 30 minutes for the round journey. An a ditional hour is recommended to visit the pioneer settlement.

Location: Arthur Highway, 1km before Port Arthur, 100km sou of Hobart on Highway A9. Adjacent to Fox & Hounds Resort an Port Arthur Caravan Park.

Public Transport: Tigerline or Experience da tours to Port Arthur from Hobart. Enthusias can arrange a longer stay at the Bush Mill wi coach drivers on the day.

Contact:	The Bush Mill
	Port Arthur TAS 7182
Phone:	(03) 6250 2221.
Home Page:	www.bushmill.com.au

The half-scale replica of the K-class 0-4-0+0 4-0 Garratt and 0-4-0TT Mountaineer *are b ing made ready at the loco shed at the Bush M Railway.*

BUSH MILL RAILWAY

Ida Bay Railway, Lune River
Trans-Derwent Ferry & Railway Company

Steam/Diesel Tourist Railway
610mm gauge

The Ida Bay Railway was built in the 1920s to carry limestone. It was originally steam worked, with Malcolm Moore petr locomotives being introduced after World War II. A 6.8km section of the line has been preserved and is operated as a touri attraction.

Features: The line is Tasmania's longest operating 610mm gauge railway. The line follows scenic water inlets and bays to The Deep Hole, passing through the original Ida Bay township, cemetery, bush and button grass plains. A full commentary takes passengers back into history of 100 years and more. Picnics and bushwalking facilities are available. Back packers-type cabins are available next to the station - ideal for railfan groups.

Locomotives: The 0-4-2T steam locomotive (Hunslet 1844/1936) from the original railway has been fully restored. Three original petrol and diesel industrial locomotives (Malcolm Moore 1943) and a replica 1910 box-cab tram motor.

Operation: Daily, Boxing Day to early March with trains at 1000, 1200, 1400 and 1600, plus extra trains on Sunday. Early March to Easter, Sundays only at 1030, 1200, 1400 and 1600. Same timetable daily, Easter Friday to Tuesday, with extra trains on Sunday and Monday. Easter to end of October, Sunday only at 1200, 1400

and 1600. November-December, Sunday only at 1030, 1200, 140 and 1600. Steam-hauled trains operate by arrangement Sundays for group bookings.

Fares: Adults $11, children $6, family $27. Group booking a available - Phone (03) 6298 3110.

Location: Situated 113km south of Hobart on the A6 Huon Hig way. The Ida Bay Railway is the most southerly in Australia.

Contact:	Ida Bay Railway
	128 Sandy Bay Road, Sandy Bay Hobart TAS 700
Phone:	(03) 6223 5893 (Hobart) or
	Lune River at (03) 6298 3110

NORTH EAST TASMANIA

North-east Tasmania features adventure tours, wilderness, internationally-acclaimed food and wine, historic villages, national parks, spectacular coastlines, arts crafts and country markets.

Launceston (population 68,000) developed as a 19th century river port with wharves, warehouses and a splendid customs house. The city has a historic ambience created by its distinctive architecture. Electric street trams commenced operations in Launceston in 1911, and the system reached 20km in length in 1937. The system closed in 1952 and public transport in the city is now provided by *Metro* buses.

Launceston has been the centre of Tasmanian railway operations since 1871 when the Invermay workshops were established as the home of the broad gauge Launceston and Western Railway and the workshops became the industrial linchpin of the Tasmanian railway system. New railway workshops have recently been constructed at East Tamar Junction to replace the old facilities. The heritage-listed Invermay site is being redeveloped as a commercial, community and parklands centre.

Tourist information: Tasmanian Travel & Information Centre
cnr St John and Paterson Street, Launceston.
Phone: (03) 6336 3122

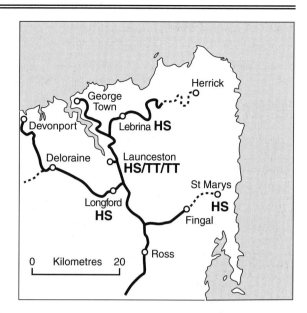

Deloraine was the terminus of the pioneer Launceston & Western Railway. Ex-TGR 4-6-0 locomotive E1 (Beyer Peacock 4967/1907) is on static display in Apex Park adjacent to the river bridge on the main road. It is the only surviving member of this class.

Invermay Railway Heritage Precinct, Launceston
Launceston Tramway Museum Society Inc
Queen Victoria Museum & Art Gallery

Tourist Tram
1067mm gauge

The former TGR workshops at Invermay are being conserved as a national cultural attraction. The historic integrity of the Railway Workshops has been conserved with building's providing storage and exhibition space for the Queen Victoria Museum's collection of heritage items. The Launceston Tramway Museum Society provides passenger transport services over a 2km line around the site, while the Don River Railway provides displays in the spring and operates several tourist trains.

Heritage Significance: The Launceston Railway Workshops demonstrate the development of railway policy, engineering and operations in Tasmania from 1875 to the 1950s. Adelaide engineer, E G Stone's use of reinforced concrete in the construction of the 1923 Main Workshop is indicative of a high level of technical innovation at the workshops. The construction of the Diesel Workshops was Australia's first facility for the conversion of railways to diesel power. The former Tramways Workshops group of buildings provide evidence of the operations of the Launceston Municipal Tramways Workshops.

Railway Collection: Queen Victoria Museum owns ex-TGR 4-4-0 express locomotive A4 (BP of 1891) which operated several Royal Trains in the 1920-30 period (currently at Don River); TGR/AN Bo-Bo DE locomotive Y3 (TGR Workshops 1962); and a 610 mm gauge 0-4-0WT locomotive (currently at Sheffield).

Contact: Elspeth Wishart
Queen Victoria Museum & Art Gallery
Wellington Street, Launceston TAS 7250
Phone: (03) 6323 3777; Fax (03) 6334 5230

Tramcars: Restored ex-Launceston Tramways Bo-Bo tramcar No 29, built LMT Invermay Workshops in 1930 (awaiting running gear); Launceston tram single truck tram No 8 (under restoration); with Nos 26 and 14 awaiting restoration. The Society has 4 ex-TGR gang motors and two tourist-type passenger cars.

Features: The present 2km line runs from a replica TGR station near the location of the old Launceston station northwards to the former roundhouse area. The Tramway Society operates from a section of the former Invermay Road Tram Depot, which served the Launceston tramways until 1932.

Operations: Gang motors and carriages operate around the Invermay site each Saturday, 1000-1600. Adults: $2, child 50c. Contact Tourist Information Centre, (03) 6336 3122, for details.

Location: Inveresk Railyards, Launceston.
Contact: Ralph Proctor (President) or Philip Archer, (Secretary)
PO Box 889, Launceston TAS 7250
Web Page: http://www.muse.com.au/tram/index2.html

 RNE

Penny Royal World Tram

Tourist complex with an operating tram which formerly served on the Launceston tramways.

Tram: Launceston tramways Car No16 restored to working order with Huon pine ceiling, blackwood fittings and original brass rails. It is powered by a diesel engine.

Operations: 1000-1630 daily. The tram operates a 10-minute service over 500 metres of track between the Penny Royal Watermill-

Windmill area and the Gunpowder Mill.

Location: 147 Paterson Street, Launceston TAS 7250
Phone: (03) 6331 6699

HERITAGE ITEMS (Register of the National Estate)

Conara Railway Station: The former railway station has survived to be a reminder of the redundant passenger rail system of Tasmania. The remarkable cantilevered awning is supported by steel rails in a most innovative manner.

Longford Railway Bridge: One of the most significant bridges in Tasmania, the Longford railway bridge, was constructed on the first Tasmanian railway line from Launceston to Deloraine, opened in 1871. A through-lattice truss, it represented the most advanced technology of the day and was designed by Irish-born railway engineer, W T Doyne.

Longford Viaduct: The viaduct, on the Launceston to Deloraine railway line, has five spans of 12 metres, which are supported on piers tapering slightly at the springing of the arches. It is historically significant as one of only two railway viaducts in Tasmania, erected on the State's first steam railway from Launceston to

Deloraine, opened in 1871. The viaduct has aesthetic significanc for its scenic interest at the approach to historic Longford Town

Lebrina Tunnel: Located on the North-East Railway, 3km sout west of Lebrina, the one kilometre long brick horseshoe arche single track railway tunnel is one of only three tunnels in curre use in Tasmania. It was the major engineering effort on the lin Each end is a brick retaining wall, neo-Egyptian in style with central low pediment above sloping brick walls.

St Marys railway station: This railway station, and that at Fing are both originally of identical plan. In so far as they have no pla form awning and with symmetrical facades front and rear, the represent an eloquent testimony to Tasmanian railways past. Marys railway station has been restored as a craft shop and Bo-B DE X30 is on static display.

WEST and NORTH - WEST TASMANIA
Touch the Wilderness

Tasmania's West North West tourism region includes the agricultural and forest areas of the North-West and the rugged beauty of the West Coast. The rich tin, silver and copper mining fields of the West Coast generated towns, mines and railways which offer fascinating insight into the heritage of an earlier era. Numerous narrow gauge railways were constructed to link the mines to port outlets and smelters. A horse tramway was built from the port of Emu Bay (now Burnie) to the mineral field at Waratah in 1878 and was upgraded to a 1067mm gauge railway in 1884.

The **Tasmanian Government Railways** served the North West with a main line from Devonport to Wynyard and numerous branches to serve agricultural districts. From Burnie, the **Emu Bay Railway Company** (EBR) constructed a railway from Burnie (Emu Bay) to Zeehan, where a connection was made with the TGR line from Strahan. The EBR was acquired by Tasrail in 1998 and now operates as part of the overall system. Other railways on the West Coast included the famous Abt rack railway of the **Mt Lyell Mining & Railway Company** from the port of Regatta Point to Queenstown and the rival line of the North Mt Lyell Company from Kelly Basin to Gormanston. There were also numerous 610 mm gauge railways.

Devonport (population 22,000) located on the Mersey River, is at the heart of Tasmania's beautiful, dramatic north-west coast. As the terminus for the Bass Strait vehicular ferry, the city is the gateway to the region. The railway was extended westward from Deloraine to Devonport in 1885.

Tourist information: *The Showcase*, 5 Best Street
Devonport TAS 7310
Phone: (03) 6424 8176

Burnie: (population 19,000) 50km west of Devonport, is a industrial city based on the forest and mineral wealth of the We Coast. The city is built around the shores of Emu Bay and is Aus ralia's fifth largest container port.

Zeehan was the centre of a silver and lead mining bonanza fro 1882 and large lead smelters were established in 1898. Extensiv narrow-gauge tramways were constructed to bring ore and firewoc from the Zeehan and adjacent Dundas fields to the furnaces.

Strahan located on Macquarie Harbour, was established as a po to service inland mining fields in 1883. It is a classified Histor Town, with many heritage buildings giving the town a distinc cultural charm. The picturesque quayside railway station at Regat Point served as the change-over point between the Mt Lyell Rai way and the Government line to Zeehan. The station has bee restored.

Queenstown (population 2600) was established in 1896 to serv ice the Mt Lyell mining field. The town was linked to the port c Strahan by the famous Mt Lyell Abt railway in 1899 until the rai way's closure in 1963. The Mt Lyell mine closed in Decembe 1994, but has been reopened under new owners.

Public Transport: Metro Tasmania operated 15 routes in th North West, primarily in Burnie, with services to Wynar Ulverstone and Penguin. Services operate Monday to Friday onl A similar public transport service is scheduled to commence i Devonport.

Redwater Creek Heritage Museum, Sheffield
Redwater Creek Steam & Heritage Society Inc

Tourist Railway (Steam)
610mm gauge

This steam, rail and heritage museum is located at Sheffield on the former TGR branch line from Railton to Roland. The museum provides a showcase of old machinery and skills. Stage 1 has established 1.4km of railway at the Sheffield site.

Heritage significance: The former Sheffield railway station (built 1913-14 and used as railway station until closure in 1957) has been relocated and restored at the site. There are two other heritage buildings and a locomotive shed.

Locomotives: Krauss 0-4-0WT steam locomotive (composite of B/N 5682 and 5800/1910). Ex-Mt Lyell Railway 0-4-0WT No 10 (Krauss 6067/1910), belonging to the Queen Victoria Museum is on lease to the railway.

Rolling Stock: Carriages include restored, first class passenger car built for the NE Dundas Tramway in 1898, 2nd class passenger car ex-Boulder Tramway, guards van and flat car.

Operations: Steam train rides on first weekend of each month, 1100-1600. An annual *Steamfest* is held over the March Labour Day weekend and features Tasmania's largest display of working steam-era machinery - including traction engines, steam rollers, a steam wagon and vintage machinery - and steam train rides. Inspection by appointment with the contact listed below.

Admission: Steam train rides; adult $3; *Steamfest* admission; adults $6, concession $4, children $2.

Location: At junction of Sheffield main road and the tourist road to Cradle Mountain. No public transport. Sheffield is 30km south of Devonport.

Contact: Peter Martin
  PO Box 143, Sheffield TAS 7306
Phone/fax: (03) 64 91 1613

Don River Railway, Devonport
Van Diemen Light Railway Society Inc

Museum/Steam Centre
1067mm gauge

The Society operates the 4km Don River Railway in northern Tasmania as a tourist railway and museum which features the largest collection on steam locomotives and passenger carriages in Tasmania. The branch line, originally constructed in 1915-16, closed in 1963 and was restored by the Society from 1973. Steam-hauled vintage trains are operated over the scenic line along the banks of the Don River to Coles Beach.

Display: The railway station houses a souvenir shop, refreshment facilities and a museum display of railway artifacts and photographs.

Locomotives: 11 steam locomotives from the TGR, Emu Bay Railway and Public Works Department. Four steam locomotives are operational: CCS-class 2-6-0 No 25, two M-class 4-6-2 Nos M4 and MA2, and Emu Bay 4-8-0 No 8 (Dubs 3855/1900). Pioneer TGR diesel-electric locomotive X4 and Bo-Bo diesel-electric Y6 is accredited for mainline use. Diesel-electric Co-Co locomotive 966 was the first ALCO Model DL531 to be preserved in Australia. The other four diesel locomotives are used for shunting duties at Don. The classic TGR 4-4-0 express locomotive A4 (built by Beyer Peacock in 1891), Fowler 0-6-0T and a carriage SP7, a former Sentinel steam railcar, are undergoing restoration.

Rolling Stock: 20 passenger carriages and two railcars. Classic carriages include B2 6-wheel side-door car built for the broad gauge Launceston & Western Railway in 1869 and converted to 1067 mm gauge in 1897 (restored to 1897 condition); BA49 an ex-North Mount Lyell end-platform car of 1899; AB+5, originally built as a 4-wheel carriage for the TML Railway in 1879 and rebuilt as bogie end-platform car in 1888; and EBR side-door carriage/van DB5. 1939 vintage railcar, DP22, and trailer PT3, operate mid-week services. Freight wagons from an extensive collection are being progressively restored.

Operations: 0900-1600 daily throughout the year, except Christmas Day and Good Friday. Trains operate from 1100 to 1500 each open day - steam Sundays and public holidays, diesel week-days. Trains depart Don on the hour, returning from Coles Beach at 20 past the hour. Special steam-hauled trains are operated over ATN Tasrail's mainlines on selected dates.

Location: The line runs from Don Village to Coles Beach, 3.5km W of Devonport along the route of the former Melrose branch line.
Contact: Harry Camplin,
  c/- PO Don TAS 7310
or contact local Tasmanian Visitor Information Network.
Phone: Don Museum site (03) 6424 6335; fax (03) 6423 6925

Restored ex-TGR 2-6-0 steam locomotive CCS 25 about to depart Coles Beach for return to Don River.

GREG COOPER

Wee Georgie Wood Railway, Tullah
Wee Georgie Wood Steam Railway Inc

Heritage Line (Steam)
610mm gauge

One of Tasmania's best known "little railways" was the Tullah Tramway from Farrell, on the Emu Bay Railway, to the silve[r] mining settlement of Tullah on the West Coast. The line was the only form of transport to Tullah from 1909 until the railwa[y] closed in 1964. The local group has restored 1.6km of line around Tullah. This is currently being extended to 5km of track[.]

Locomotives: The restored steam locomotive, *Wee Georgie Wood*, an 0-4-0WT built by John Fowler (B/No 16203 of 1924), from the Tullah Tramway, operates trains over the line. A second steam locomotive (Krauss 5988/1908) is undergoing restoration. Passenger carriages are from the Lake Margaret Tramway and Mt Lyell railway.

Operations: The steam season is from September to Easter on alternate Sundays between 1200 and 1600. Group tours can be arranged at other times.

Train fares: Adult $2, child $1, family $5. Facsimile Tullah Or[e] Treatment Ltd Farrell Junction to Tullah tickets are issued.

Contact: Anne Drake, Wee Georgie Wood Steam Railway In[c]
              PO Box 55, Rosebery TAS 7470
Phone: (03) 6473 2228; or
              contact the Tasmanian Visitor Information Network
              Cnr Elizabeth/Davey Streets, Hobart TAS
              Phone: (03) 6230 8233

West Coast Pioneers Memorial Museum, Zeehan
West Coast Heritage Authority Ltd

Museum
610/1067mm gauge

Zeehan on Tasmania's West Coast was a boom town serving numerous rich mines in the 1890s and early 1900s. The Wes[t] Coast Pioneers Museum, managed by West Coast Heritage Authority, features mining and railway history.

Displays: The railways and tramways on Tasmania's West Coast are a major feature of the museum's exhibits, with many photographs, locomotives and rolling stock. The photographic collection traces the whole history of the area from solid bush through the days of boom and bust, to the rebirth of modern mines.

Locomotives: ex-TGR C.1 (BP 2-6-0 of 1884) and a 4-8-0 steam locomotive (Dubs 3854/1900) from the Emu Bay Railway. 610mm gauge locomotives include ex-Mt Lyell 0-4-0T No 8 (Krauss 5480/1906), Renison Tin Mines 0-4-0T No 2 (Krauss 4087/1899), Lake Margret Tramway 4wPM (Romeo 770/1925) and two Mt Lyell underground electric locomotives.

Rolling Stock: A 1922 Daimler railmotor once used by the Genera[l] Manager of the Mt Lyell and Railway Company is the pride of th[e] railway section.

Open: 0830-1800 every day October-March and
                0830-1600 April-September.
Admission: Adults $3, concession $2, family $7.
Location: Located in Main Street, Zeehan 283km northwest o[f]
                Hobart on Tasmania's West Coast.
Contact: Christine Brown
                PO Box 70, Zeehan TAS
Phone: (03) 6471 6225; fax (03) 6471 6650

Mt Lyell Abt Railway

Tourist Railway (steam)
1067mm gauge

The 34km railway line built by the Mount Lyell Company in 1896-99 to link its mine at Queenstown with the port of Regatt[a] Point became famous for its Abt-rack locomotives hauling trains through rugged terrain. The line closed in 1963, but there wa[s] local support to reopen the line as a tourist railway. The Mt Lyell Abt Railway Society was formed in 1994 and cleared a sectio[n] of the formation as a heritage walk. In 1997, Tasmania obtained a $20.45 million Federal Government Grant to rebuild th[e] historic railway. The restored line is schedule to open in time for the Centenary of Federation in 2001.

The Journey: The 34km line will provide an extraordinary and diverse environmental experience during a 2 hour journey through rainforest and wild-flowing rivers/streams over 32 timber trestle bridges.

Locomotives/rolling stock. Two of the famous Mt Lyell Abt steam locomotives, Nos 1 and 3 (Dubs 3369/1896 and 3730/1899) have been dismantled for assessment prior to planned restoration. Release of Abt locos Nos 2 and 5 is under negotiation. New carriages are being constructed for the railway.

Display: The Galley Museum (cnr Driffield and Sticht Streets, Queenstown) has an extensive photographic display depicting the town's mining and railway past. Information signs and directions

regarding the Abt Project have been erected at Miners Siding an[d] other locations.

Operations: The tourist railway is due for opening in 2001. Pre[-] opening operation may occur on completed sections of track. A[n] independent private operator will be appointed to manage the rail[-] way. The Mt Lyell Abt Railway Society provides volunteers t[o] assist with operations and maintenance.

Contact: Information on the project through the Tasmanian Vis[i-] tor Information Network,
              Cnr Elizabeth & Davey Streets, Hobart TAS
Phone: (03) 6230 8233
Also,   the Secretary, Mt Lyell Abt Railway Society
              PO Box 269, Queenstown TAS 7467

HERITAGE WALKS

Mt Lyell Railway Heritage Walk. The Mt Lyell Abt Railway Society has cleared 17.5km of the formation of the famous Abt rack railway between Queenstown and Teepookana as a heritage walk. A third of the track from both Queenstown and Strahan is now easily accessible for walking. Regatta Point-Teepookana sections have been upgraded by Forestry Tasmania for car tourist access. Viewing platforms and information signs have been erected at Teepookana and Quarter-mile Bridge.

Former Zeehan Tramways. A section of the old tramway fo[r-] mation in Zeehan, including the Spray Tunnel, has been restore[d] as a tourist drive and walking track. The formation of the Comstoc[k] tram line from Trial Harbour Road to Zeehan provides an interes[t-] ing walk to explore the history of former mines and tramways. Map[s] of the former tramways are available from local outlets.

SOUTH AUSTRALIA

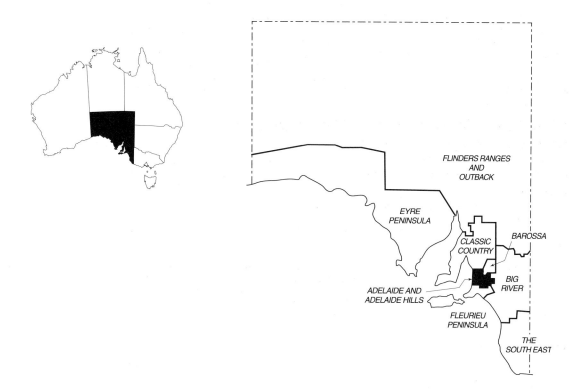

THE FIRST SOUTH AUSTRALIAN broad-gauge (1600mm) railway opened in 1856 and lines were constructed northward to serve copper mining areas. However, the cost of these early railways was considered excessive for the struggling colony and less expensive transport solutions were sought. A horse-worked narrow gauge (1067mm) railway was constructed between Hoyleton and Port Wakefield in 1870. Light steam-worked railways were subsequently constructed to this gauge to open up land for agriculture. As a consequence, numerous break-of-gauge stations were required and these generated significant social and economic costs.

South Australia has a wealth of railway heritage, particularly in its fine railway buildings, many of which were constructed in stone. Despite the difficulties of the State's economic base, some of Australia's most successful railway preservation groups have been established in South Australia.

The **Port Dock Station Railway Museum** remains Australia's outstanding railway museum and its setting in the State Heritage Area of Port Adelaide adds to its attraction. The **Tramway Museum at St Kilda** is noted for the quality of its restoration of Adelaide's electric trams and the tourist railways operated by *SteamRanger* and the **Pichi**

Richi Railway Preservation Society are among the premier lines in Australia. Railway preservation in South Australia is also notable for the variety of heritage maintained by smaller groups. **The Victor Harbor Horse Tramway** is the only seven-day a week horse-drawn public tramway in the works, while the nearby **Port Milang Historic Railway Museum**, the Murray Bridge Wharf Railway and the Port of Morgan Historic Museum tell the history of the interaction between river and rail transport. Recently, the **Barossa Wine Train** and **Limestone Coast Railway** have linked rail travel with the attractions of South Australia's famous wine-producing regions. The **Wallaroo-Kadina Tourist Railway** and **Steamtown Peterborough** also offer unique tourist train experiences. Narrow gauge operations at Moonta and Cobdogla enhance the appeal of museums devoted to copper mining and irrigation development respectively.

The main voluntary preservation groups in South Australia are members of the **Council of Historic Railways and Tramways in South Australia** (CHRTSA). CHRTSA provides a consultative and advisory service on behalf of its members and serves as an umbrella body promoting rail heritage as a tourist attraction.

ADELAIDE REGION

Laid out in 1836 by Colonel William Light on a square mile grid pattern encircled by a buffer zone of parkland, Adelaide (population 1.1 million) is one of the best planned cities in the world. Its attractive streetscapes are maintained through preservation of outstanding Victorian and Federation homes and public buildings. Adelaide plays host to a variety of festivals based around the arts, wine, sport and ethnic heritage.

The first steam railway was a suburban service between Adelaide and Port Adelaide, which opened in 1856, followed by the northern line to Gawler. Several private companies built suburban railways to Glenelg, Marino, Grange and Henley beach and this system forms the basis of today's suburban rail network.

Adelaide's flat terrain enabled the development of Australia's largest horse tramway system that shaped the patterns of urban development from the 1870s. By 1883 there were eleven companies operating horse trams. The lines were taken over by a municipal trust and electrified from 1908.

Tourist Information: South Australian Travel Centre
18 King William Street, Adelaide
Phone: (08) 8212 1644

TransAdelaide: Operates most rail, bus and tram public transport services within the Adelaide metropolitan area. The 123km rail network is based on a north-south axis from Gawler to Noarlunga with branches to Outer Harbor, Grange and Belair. Services are operated by air-conditioned diesel railcars. Tickets may be purchased from selected outlets, including the railway station and newsagents, or on buses or trams. Train tickets must be prepurchased.
Phone (08) 8210 1000 for information.

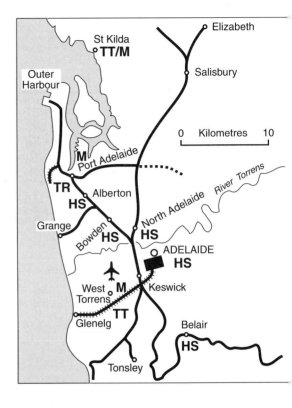

Keswick Terminal, located 2km west of the city centre, is the terminal for interstate passenger services. A minibus service operate to major hotels and the Adelaide Railway Station.

Glenelg Tramway
Heritage Tramway (Electric)

The former private railway to Glenelg was converted to an electric tramway in 1929. This 11km line remains in operation a a historic tramway operation serving commuters from the bayside suburb. In addition to its commuter function, the vintag tramway provides tourists with the attraction of a journey in genuinely historic trams to the beachside resort where the colon was originally founded.

Trams: 21 H-class tramcars, built in 1929, which have been refurbished to their original splendour.

Operations: 0600-2330 Monday-Saturday;
0930-2330 Sundays with services at 15-20 minute intervals.
Information: Phone 8210 1000.

Semaphore and Fort Glanville Tourist Railway
Tourist Line (Steam,
Port Dock Station Museum/Cities of Port Adelaide-Enfield & Charles Sturt
457mm gauge

This steam tourist railway operates over 2 km on the foreshore of the historic Semaphore precinct between the Jetty and For Glanville. Semaphore developed as a seaside resort with the opening of the railway in 1878 and an electric tram to Por Adelaide opened in 1917.

Locomotive: 2-4-0 *Bill* constructed by Willis Light Engineering of Western Australia in 1992.
Operations: Hourly between 1200-1600 each day SA during school holidays (Sept/Dec-Jan/April). Hourly 1200-1600 Sundays and public holiday from October-April inclusive. Hourly 1200-1600 Saturdays, February-April Inclusive.
Fares: Adults $4, children $2, family $10.

Location: Semaphore Jetty, 3km from Port Adelaide.
Public Transport: Bus 333 provides walking access to both termin
Contact: Port Dock Station Railway Museum
Phone (08) 8341 1690

Port Dock Station Railway Museum, Port Adelaide

Museum (Steam/Diesel)
457/1067/1435/1600 mm gauge

R SAMPSON

0-6-0T steam locomotive PERONNE *shunts carriages past the Woodville signal cabin at the Museum on 12 July 1998.*

Port Adelaide is the historic maritime heart of South Australia and is home to some of the finest heritage buildings in the state. Designated as the First State Heritage Area, the precinct offers an outstanding "walk through history" tour. The Port Dock Station Railway Museum is in the heart of the precinct. The complex, its outstanding railway collection, the heritage setting and interpretative presentations combine to create Australia's finest railway museum.

Features: The museum is located on the site of the first steam railway in South Australia which opened in 1856. Incorporated on the site is a 100 year old timber goods shed and a large pavilion which houses the South Australian Railways collection, including a break-of-gauge station with 1600mm and 1067mm gauge trains on either side. The former Woodville signal cabin is being rebuilt as a working cabin operating numerous signals and points on the Museum's 1067mm gauge trackwork. When completed in 2001, this SAR 'narrow gauge yard' with cabin, signals, crane, etc. will provide a "hands-on" interpretative "pre-computer" era display item. A new pavilion dedicated to the Commonwealth and Australian National Railways input to railways since 1901 is scheduled for completion in March 2001. It will display locomotives and rolling stock on a totally enclosed four-track multi-gauge display. Trains operate around the museum site and multi-gauge turnouts are a feature of the museum's trackage. There is a theatrette, special exhibition areas and museum bookshop.

Locomotives: 26 locomotives on three gauges, including SAR 4-6-0 Rx. 93 (Dubs 2142 of 1886); Silverton 2-6-0 Y12 (BP 3526/1893); BHP Whyalla 4-6-0 No 4 (BLW 41242/1914); SAR No 504, a 222 on 500-class 4-8-4 locomotive (A/Whitworth 637/1926) which ushered in the *big power* era in South Australia; SAR 4-6-2 No 624 (Islington 1937); SAR 4-8-4 No 523 (Islington 1943); SAR 1067mm gauge Beyer Garratt No 409 of 1953; and No 900 the pioneer SAR mainline diesel-electric locomotive (Islington 1951). Commonwealth Railways locos include 4-6-0 G1 of 1914, the first mainline locomotive on the Transcontinental Railway; pioneer diesel mainline loco GM4 and 6wDH shunter MDH.

Rolling Stock: 14 railcars and passenger carriages, including a Pullman dining car, Vice-Regal car, narrow-gauge sleeping car *BAROOTA*, CR Wegmann lounge, dining and sleeping cars, SAR Brill 75-class rail car of 1928, Bluebird railcar 257, Redhen suburban railcars 400/875/321 and CR Budd railcar CB1.

Operations: 1000-1700 daily. Group and school visits are catered for at reduced prices. Dining car *ADELAIDE* and former SAR buffet carriage can be hired for special functions. Further information is available from (08) 8341 1690.

Live Steam: 457mm gauge operates Sundays and school holidays. Ex-Broken Hill Associated Smelters 0-6-0T locomotive *PERONNE* (Andrew Barclay 1545/1919) operates the 1067mm gauge railway on special occasions. Broad gauge trains operate to the Museum on special occasions.

Admission: Adult $8, children $3, concession $6, family $19. Souvenir ticket and train ride included with admission.

Location: Lipson Street, Port Adelaide. A large public car park adjoins the site.

Public Transport: *TransAdelaide* suburban trains to Port Adelaide station (Outer Harbour line), then 10 minutes walk to the museum, or buses 153 to 157.

Contact: The Manager, Port Dock Station
PO Box 3153, Port Adelaide SA 5015

Phone: (08) 8341 1690; facsimile (08) 8341 1626

 RNE

Tramway Museum, St Kilda
Australian Electric Transport Museum (SA) Inc

Tramway Museum (Electric

AUSTRALIAN ELECTRIC TRANSPORT MUSEUM

A line-up of heritage trams Nos 264, 42 and 186 at the Museum.

Adelaide was the first Australian city to establish a permanent horse tramway system which eventually grew to 51 route mile (82km) of track. The horse tramways were converted to electric operation from 1909 to 1914. Adelaide tramway operation closed by November 1958 with the exception of the Glenelg line. The St Kilda Museum was established in 1957 to preserv and operate historic transport vehicles of all kinds, with special emphasis on electric trams and trolley buses that were built in Adelaide or operated there. Trams operate over a 2km track to the St Kilda beach, a round trip taking 20-25 minutes.

Features: Visitors can ride the splendidly restored trams to the Mangrove Trail and Adventure Playground at the beach. The modern display gallery features panels depicting Adelaide's tramway and social history, a continuous audio-visual display and bookshop. Street furniture from the tramway era is in use in the yard, while a cafeteria, toilet facilities and car park are provided.

Trams: 1 horse tram (Adelaide, Unley & Mitcham No.15 of 1880), 20 electric trams (13 of which are in passenger service), 4 trolleybuses and a 3-door diesel bus of the type which replaced most of the tram services. The Museum's Adelaide trams are Nos A1, the first electric tram of 1908, a (Bib & Bub) 14-15, B (toastrack) 42 of 1909, C (Desert Gold) 186 of 1918, D (enclosed bogie) 192 of 1912, E (semi-open bogie) 118 and E1 (saloon bogie) 111 of 1910, F (drop-centre) 244 of 1925, F1 (drop-centres) 264 and 282 of 1928, G (Birney) 303 of 1925, H (Glenelg) 355, 360 and 362 of 1929 and H1 (prototype) 381 of 1953, the last tram built. Other trams are Ballarat 21 and 34 and Melbourne W2 trams 294 and 354 (works car). Large models of an Adelaide *Stephenson* pattern double-deck horse tram and drop-centre tram are in display in the interpretative gallery.

Operations: 1300-1700 on Sundays and most public holidays (except Christmas Day and Good Friday), on the Wednesdays of th April, July and September-October school holiday vacations an every day from 26 December to the New Year holiday inclusive Four or five different trams are used on most days, and at leas eight trips are run. The museum also opens on extra days as adver tised in the local press. Charter groups can be accommodated.

Admission: Adults $5, concessions/children $3 (including all tram rides). Charter rates on application.
Location: St. Kilda, 27km North of Adelaide. Take Main Nort Road to Gepps Cross, then Port Wakefield Road to Waterloo Cor ner, then left along St Kilda Road to Museum site.
Public Transport: There is no direct public transport, but *TransAdelaide* train journey to Salisbury station can be followe by a taxi trip to St Kilda.

Contact: Colin Seymour, President,
            Tramway Museum St Kilda
            GPO Box 2012, Adelaide, SA, 500i
Phone: (08) 8280 8188, 8281 4390 or 8297 4447
Fax (08) 8280 8528

West Torrens Railway Signal/Telegraph & Aviation Museum
City of West Torrens

Located in the original West Torrens Council Chambers, this museum displays a variety of rarely seen historical railway signaling equipment. The display shows the changes over many decades. The railway display demonstrates the City of West Torrens' links with public transport, with street tramways, the Holdfast Bay Railway and the SAR Mile End goods yards being located within the city boundaries. The Aviation displays are linked to the Vickers Vimy aircraft at Adelaide International Airport, also within the city.

Exhibits: Working displays include "hands on" operation of manual and automatic staff instruments, party telephones. Level crossing equipment, Farrell's Flat signaling equipment and portion of an interlocking frame from Adelaide yard. There is an extensive collection of signal and safeworking equipment from the SAR and other Australian railway systems.

Opening Times: Sunday 1300-1630.
Other days for conducted tours by appointment.
Admission: Adults $2, concession $1.
Location: 112 Marion Road, Brooklyn Park 5032
Contact: Curator, Eric Kelly (08) 8443 7651 or
Don Temby (08) 8373 3554

HERITAGE ITEMS (Register of the National Estate)

Adelaide Railway Station: The imposing station building with its North American features opened in 1928. The building was extensively altered to become the Adelaide Casino in 1978. The station also serves as the terminus for *TransAdelaide* metropolitan rail services. The renovated building won the National Architecture Award for recycled buildings in 1986.

Alberton and Bowden Railway Stations: Dating from 1856, these are the oldest surviving railway buildings in Australia lay claim to being the oldest Government railway structures in the British colonies. Alberton Station is almost unaltered. It is a rare and unusually intact survival that has strong associations with the earliest period of South Australia's railway development. The design is of interest to architectural history. The austere rectangular gabled form, the economical way in which the platform verandah is incorporated into the main roof, and the unusual arrangement of doors (apparently for handling both passengers and goods through the same building), contrasts with most other station buildings of the later 19th century.

Belair Railway Station and Signal Box: The station, which is the eastern terminus of *TransAdelaide* suburban services, houses the original railway signal cabin, of weatherboard construction. Architecturally, the station buildings are a good example of 19th century timber, iron and steel design utilised for secondary stops along railway routes. The signal box has been restored as a museum.
Opening hours: Third Sunday of the month, 2pm-4pm winter, 2pm-5pm summer.
Contact: c/- Neil Stallard
39 Ashby Avenue, Blackwood SA 5051

Islington Railway Workshop: The complex was established in 1891 as the major railway workshops and training centre for apprentices in South Australia. The original workshop buildings were of dressed stone, with brick facings and a uniform architectural style. These buildings represented one of the most important industrial complexes in South Australia during the late nineteenth century, responsible for the manufacture and repair of South Australia's railway locomotives and rolling stock.

A major upgrade of equipment and processes in 1925-1927 resulted in the workshops being reinstated as one of South Australia's most significant industrial complexes, producing heavy locomotives and manufacturing large-scale products including freight cars, boilers, motor bodies and electric cranes.

Locomotive *Sandfly*: The diminutive pioneer 0-4-0ST locomotive *Sandfly* (Baldwin 7860/1886), the first locomotive to work in the Northern Territory, is preserved outside the waiting room on No1 platform of Keswick Railway Station.

North Adelaide Railway Station: Opened in 1857, this is the third oldest surviving railway station in Australia. The design combines a typical mid-Victorian four-room cottage under the same roof with the station's business functions, in a way that presents a symmetrical front to both portions. The building has been restored after a period of neglect.

BAROSSA MID NORTH REGION
Classic Country

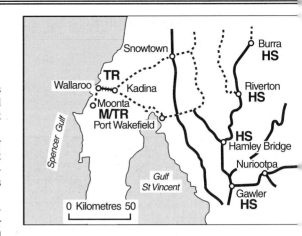

The Mid-North includes the heritage of South Australia's copper mining industry, the vineyards of the Barossa and Clare Valleys, and historic settlements with National Trust buildings.

Early development in the region was generated by copper mining at Kapunda and Burra, followed by larger deposits at Wallaroo, Moonta and Kadina (the *Copper Triangle*). Thousands of Cornish miners settled in the *Copper Triangle* towns and the area became known as *Little Cornwall*.

Copper mining provided the impetus for railway construction. The broad gauge railway from Adelaide to Gawler opened in 1857 and was extended to Kapunda in 1860 and reached the inland port of Morgan in 1878. A branch from Roseworth reached Burra in 1870. The broad gauge Midland system was extended to Terowie (1880), the Barossa Valley (1911), Clare (1918), Snowtown (1923) and Port Pirie (1937).

On the Yorke Peninsula, a 1067mm gauge horse tramway opened between Port Wakefield and Hoyleton in 1870. This provided the base for the SAR narrow-gauge Western System railways, which were converted to broad gauge in 1927. The Snowtown-Wallaroo line, converted to dual gauge in 1982, has been mothballed since 1990, but is under review for reopening by ASR.

Gawler (population 15,000) is the gateway to the region and railway junction for the Burra and Barossa lines. The agricultural and locomotive manufacturing firm of James Martin & Company established their works in Gawler in 1852. The firm gained their first contract to manufacture railway wagons in 1870 and the first locomotive was built in 1888. James Martin built 233 locomotives for railways in South Australia, Western Australia, New South Wales, Tasmania and Queensland by 1915, when the firm was taken over by Perry Engineering. The new owners continued to build locomotives at Gawler until 1927.

Port Pirie (population 15,000), on Spencer Gulf 224km north of Adelaide, developed as an industrial city based on the world's largest lead smelters which process ore transported from Broken Hill over the narrow gauge. Rail transport underpins the city's role as a major grain shipping port. The Regional Tourism & Arts Centre is located in the former Mary Elie Street railway station (1967-86) provides a central focus for tourist activities in the city. Phone (08) 8633 0439

Kadina (population 3700) the main commercial centre of the *Copper Triangle*, was established in 1861-62 as a supply town for the copper mines. It features several museums depicting the district's history.

Burra (population 1200) is a historic mining town established in 1846 by South Australia Mining Associates as Australia's first company town. Burra had become the state's largest town outside Adelaide by 1851. The railway opened in 1870, but the open cut mine closed in 1877. Many of the town's building have been restored by the National Trust including the powder magazine (1847) pump-houses, mine shafts, gaol, post & telegraph office and miner's cottages.

Moonta Museum & Tourist Railway
National Trust of SA (Moonta Branch)

Tourist Railway (Diesel)
610mm gauge

The National Trust has established a museum and history resource centre in the former Moonta Mines Model School of 1878. The museum features displays of the district's mining history and Cornish heritage. As part of the adjacent, Wheal Munta Mining Display, a 2km tourist railway provides tours through the State Heritage area. Moonta railway station has been restored and provides a photographic display of past railway and mining activities.

Locomotives and Rolling Stock: 2 industrial 4wDM locomotives. A range of mine trucks is on display. A broad-gauge double-deck horse tram which operated at Moonta until 1931, has been restored and is on display.

Operations: 1300-1500 Saturday, Sunday and public holidays with departures on the hour. Daily, 1100-1600 during school holidays. Trains take visitors on a 50 minute round trip past the reservoir and ore sorting floors, then through a tunnel in Ryan's tailing heap. It stops at the former precipitation works for a well-documented story of copper recovery and then onto the restored Moonta Railway station to begin the return journey. The station is adjacent to the National Trust Museum.

Fares: Adults $2.50, children $1. Museum admission $3 adults.

Location: 1.5km from Moonta on Verran Terrace. Moonta is 17km from Kadina.

Public Transport: Premier Roadlines offer services from Adelaide to Moonta.

Contact: Secretary, PO Box 23
   Moonta SA 5558
Phone/fax: (08) 8825 1944

 RNE

Barossa Tourist Rail Service
Barossa Wine Train

Mainline Tours (Railcar)
1600 mm gauge

AUSTRALIAN ELECTRIC TRANSPORT MUSEUM

The Barossa Wine Train passing through the rows of cultivated grape vines.

The Barossa Valley is Australia's best known wine area and the venue for popular one, two and three-day tours from Adelaide. The Barossa Wine Train provides the opportunity to enjoy the attractions of the district in a relaxed atmosphere.

Features: Tours are operated from Adelaide Railway Station by refurbished Bluebird railcars (Nos 251/2 and 101) to the towns of Tanunda in the Barossa Valley. The train offers the soft comfort of the way rail travel used to be, with reclining seats and large picture windows to view the scenery complimented by fascinating commentry. Snacks, beverages and superb South Australian wines are available from the carriage bars.

Operations: Tuesday, Thursday and Sunday, departing Adelaide at 0850 and arriving Tununda at 1020. The return service departs Tanunda at 1550 and arrives Adelaide at 1720.

Fares: Return Adelaide to Tununda $55 per adult. All-inclusive adult return $85 (including bus tour around Barossa and lunch). Other tour options are available on request.

Bookings:　Barossa Wine Train
　　　　　　　Lower Ground Floor, 18-20 Grenfell Street
　　　　　　　Adelaide SA 5000
Phone:　　(08) 8212 7888; fax (08) 8231 5771
E-mail:　　info@barossawinetrain.com.au
Home Page:　www.barossawinetrain.com.au

Wallaroo-Kadina Tourist Railway
Yorke Peninsula Rail Preservation Society

Tourist Railway (Diesel)
1600mm gauge

This broad gauge tourist railway operates over 10km of line linking Wallaroo and Kadina, the pioneer copper mining towns of the 1860s. Passengers have the opportunity for historic walks through Wallaroo and Kadina, together with spectacular views of Spencer Gulf and Wallaroo Bay from the train.

Train: Ex-VR diesel locomotive T387 is used to haul vintage ex-VR/SAR joint-stock passenger carriages over the line with a licensed dining car. Rolling stock includes classic E-type 12-wheel, wooden, celestory-roof carriages 16 BE, 18 BE, 24 BE and SAR brakevan converted to a kitchen car. Joint-stock sleeping car *Angas* is undergoing restoration.

Display: A small museum of historical railway photographs and memorabilia is located in the former Wallaroo goods shed.

Operations: Second Sunday of the month at 1300 from Wallaroo to Kadina and return. Additional trains on Easter Saturday and Sunday, Kernewek Saturday and Sunday, Christmas Eve Supper Train and New Years Eve Supper Train. Private hire and dinner trains are available most days.Extended journeys to Bute are sched-

uled to commence in late 1999.
Fares:　　Wallaroo - Kadina return
　　　　　　Adults $8, concession $6, children $4, family $20.
Location: at Wallaroo railway station, 10km west of Kadina.
Public transport: Premier Roadlines offer daily services from Adelaide to Kadina, Wallaroo and Moonta.

Contact:　Yorke Peninsula Rail Preservation Society
　　　　　　PO Box 502, Wallaroo SA 5556
Phone/fax: (08) 8823 3950

 　RNE

Ellen Street Railway Station, Port Pirie
National Trust Museum

Local History Museum

The Ellen Street Railway Station, built in 1902, was served by trains running down the main street of the city. The most unusual feature is the "pavilion type" Victorian architecture. The station has been classified by the National Trust. With the opening of the standard gauge railway to Broken Hill in 1967, the station was closed and converted to a museum depicting local and railway history.

Displays: Scale model and history of the Port Pirie smelters and exhibits of railways and shipping. The narrow-gauge 0-6-0T industrial shunting locomotive, *Port Pirie* (AB 1955/1928), is located as a static exhibit in the museum grounds.

Opening Times: Every day of the year except Christmas Day.
Monday to Saturday 1000-1600, Sunday 1300-1600.

Admission: Adults $2, children $1, family $5.
National Trust members free.

Location: Ellen Street, Port Pirie. Access is via road and rail from Adelaide, Alice Springs, Perth, and Sydney via Broken Hill.

Public Transport: Daily Stateliner and Greyhound buses from Adelaide. If visiting by rail (*Indian Pacific*), transport needs to be arranged in advance from the Coonamia siding, 3km out of Port Pirie, to the city.

Address: The Secretary, National Trust Museum
c/- 184 Balmoral Road, Port Pirie SA 5540

Phone: (08) 8632 2272 or 8632 1080

 RNE

HERITAGE ITEMS (Register of the National Estate)

Burra Railway Station: The attractive 1870 station building with repeating gables and unusual 'wave' form verandah, decorative chimneys and quoinsm contrasting features with dark stone walls is an important example of a country rail terminal in the Victorian style. The station has been restored for use as an art gallery.

Gawler Railway Station: The present bluestone station building was opened in 1879. A new goods shed had been built the previous year and a train shed too was built in the 1870s. Architecturally, the station displays rare structural techniques and ornamental masonry work. The SAR operated a horse tramway from the station to the town centre.

Hamley Bridge (68km north of Adelaide) is the junction of the branch line to Balaklava. The fine bluestone station building of 1880 has been restored as a private home following heritage principles.

Hoyleton Goods Shed: The classic goods shed, of solid stone construction was built in 1869. It marked the terminus of the Hoyles Plains-Port Wakefield horse-worked tramway, which was the first entirely agricultural line to be built in South Australia and the first south Australian 3ft 6in gauge line.

Kapunda Railway Station and Goods Shed: Built in 1860-61, the design and scale of the building testifies to the significance of Kapunda in the economy of South Australia at the time. It is one of South Australia's finest early colonial public buildings, incorporating a two-storey office and master's dwelling with single storey amenities and stores.

Moonta Railway Station: Architecturally, the railway station is an important example of the station design allocated to the large country centres of the State and is a delightful application of the Queen Anne style to a 'utilitarian' structure.

Riverton Railway Station: Riverton (96km north of Adelaide on Main North Road) was the junction of the Burra and the (now closed) Clare Valley railway lines. The outstanding railway station signal box and stone goods shed are historically significant as the largest, and most important railway station complex of the state's lower north. The station complex is important for the high quality of its architecture and for the technical achievement of its elaborately detailed and finished range of bluestone buildings. The precinct provides good examples of a once-common cast-iron railway water tank on stone tower and engine/goods shed. The 1860 station has been restored to provide al fresco dining on the platform, bed & breakfast accommodation, a café, art gallery and exhibition space. Former Adelaide *Red Hen* suburban railcars have been restored to provide accommodation.

Contact: Errol and Ruth Bain
PO Box 123, Riverton SA 5412

Phone: (08) 8847 2051

Tarlee Railway Station (76km north of Adelaide) serves as a reminder of the importance of this small railway centre as a loading point for stone from local quarries for the construction of major public buildings in Adelaide.

RAIL TRAILS

Riesling Trail: Sections of the former Clare Valley railway from Riverton (1918-1984) are being developed as a linear park for outdoor recreational activities. Currently the 12km section Watervale and Sevenhill in the Clare Valley wine area is open.

Eventually the full 80km of the former line will be developed as the *Riesling Trail*.

FLEURIEU PENINSULA / ADELAIDE HILLS

The Fleurieu Peninsula offers a range of tourist attractions. Victor Harbor and Goolwa are important resort towns while the McLaren Vale, Langhorne Creek and Currency Creek areas are some of the top quality wine growing areas in the State.

Australia's first public railway, the horse-operated line from Goolwa on the Murray River to Port Elliot, began operating in 1854 to provide an outlet for goods transported on the inland waterway to Goolwa. Up to 300 paddle-wheel riverboats competed to transport cargoes from inland ports to Goolwa and Port Milang.

The railway from Mount Barker and Strathalbyn to Victor Harbor was opened in 1885. Since 1986 the area has been served by Steam Ranger tourist trains. The *Cockle Train* between Goolwa and Victor Harbor operates in holiday periods.

Mount Barker (population 15,000), a growing commuter area in the Adelaide Hills, is the base for the Victor Harbor Tourist Railway. The restored Mount Barker station is used by VHTR and the local Tourist Information Office.

Victor Harbor (population 10,000), 84km south of Adelaide, is the centre of the Encounter Coast, South Australia's premier holiday location. It was established as a whaling station in 1837 and, during the era of clipper ships, it became an important port for the Murray River trade. They berthed in the lee of Granite Island, connected to the mainland from 1875 by a timber trestle causeway

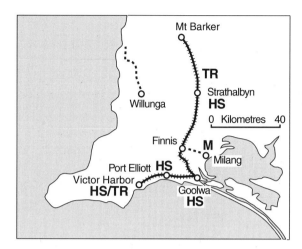

with a single 1600mm gauge railway. The line was horse-worked because of the weight-restricted causeway. The National Trust museum in the old station master's house contains memorabilia of railways in the district.

Goolwa (population 4000), 85km south of Adelaide, is the first port on the River Murray and Australia's only remaining inland port. The town is rich in river history, with many buildings dating from the 1850s.

Goolwa - Port Elliot Tramway

Heritage Site

Australia's first public railway, the horse-operated line from Goolwa to Port Elliot, opened in May 1854. It conveyed goods and passengers from the river port of Goolwa overland to the coast at Port Elliot, thereby avoiding the treacherous Murray River mouth.

The line was extended to Victor Harbor in 1864 with a branch from Middleton to Strathalbyn in 1869. Horse traffic was replaced by steam operations in 1885 when the Strathalbyn-Middleton line was routed to join the Goolwa-Middleton line.

Display: A replica of a passenger carriage from the horse tramway is preserved in a show case in Cadell Street, Goolwa. The old railway cutting to the wharf is the oldest example of railway construction in Australia, having been excavated in 1852.

Other relics of the original line, including the original Railway Superintendent's house (1852) and horse stables (1863), remain in situ as important heritage items buildings.

⛩ **RNE**

Victor Harbor Horse Tramway
District Council of Victor Harbor

Tourist Tramway (Horse)
1600mm gauge

The tramway connecting Granite Island with Victor Harbor over a causeway opened on 27 December 1894 and a horse-tram service operated until 1954. A 1.6km section of tramway was relaid and opened in June 1986 as a South Australian Jubilee Year project. It is the only seven-day a week horse-drawn public tramway in the world.

Trams: Four double-deck tramcars have been built for the tramway in the heritage style of the late 1800's.

Operations: Trams operate from 1000 to 1600 in winter months and for extended hours in the summer for seven days/week year round. Departures at 20 minute intervals during peak periods.
Fares (1995) Adults return $4, children $2.

Contact: Peter Bond, Technical Director
District Council of Victor Harbor
PO Box 11, Victor Harbor SA 5211
Phone: (08) 8552 1777/Fax (08) 8552 4360

⮢ ⛩ **RNE**

Victor Harbor Tourist Railway
SteamRanger

Tourist Railway (Steam/Diesel)
1600mm gauge

MARK CARTER

Steamranger's 4-8-4 locomotive No 520 Sir Malcolm Barclay-Harvey *makes a steamy departure from Goolwa with a Cockle Train working bound for Victor Harbor. 520 is presently undergoing repairs.*

The Victor Harbor Tourist Railway operates between Mount Barker and Victor Harbor, a distance of 80km. The line is the mos scenic in South Australia, skirting the Southern Ocean between Port Elliot and Victor Harbor. The main depot is now located a Mount Barker with a sub-depot at Goolwa.

Features: the choice of three journeys of steam nostalgia, the day-long *Southern Encounter* from Mount Barker to Victor Harbor or shorter *Cockle Train* trips between Goolwa and Victor Harbor and *Highlander* services between Mt Barker and Strathalbyn. Mainline 4-8-4 locomotive 520 hauls *Southern Encounter* trains, while 4-6-2T F 251 operates the *Cockle Train*, during holiday periods, with diesel locomotives or railcars at other times. This follows the route of the original horse tram most of the way.

Locomotives: 5 steam locomotives: 4-8-4 No 520 (Islington, 1943), 4-6-0 Rx 207 (NBL 20516/1913) and 4-6-2T F 251 (Perry 236/1922) are operational, with 4-6-2 No 621 (Islington, 1936) and 4-6-0 Rx 224 under restoration. 3 operational diesel locomotives - Bo-Bo shunters 350 (built Islington 1949), 507 (built Islington 1952), and mainline Alco Co-Co No 958. Two of the pioneer 900-class mainline diesel-electric locomotives of 1951 are retained on static display.

Rolling Stock: Ex-Adelaide *Redhen* suburban railcars 412 and 428, and trailer 824; Brill Railcar No 60; 27 operational passenger carriages and a number of freight vehicles. *Southern Encounter* trains use steel carriages built at Islington in the 1940s. Vintage *Centenary* carriages, originally built between 1908 and 1923 for suburban working and upgraded from 1936 for country use, are used on the *Cockle Train*.

Operations: *Southern Encounter* tours operate on selected Sundays from 1030 from June to the end of November. Return trains depart Victor Harbor at 1600, arriving Mount Barker at 1800. On alternate Sundays July-August the steam-hauled Mt Barker-Strathalbyn *Highlander* service operates. *Cockle Trains* operate on every Sunday of the year and more frequently in school holiday

periods. Trains do not operate on days of total fire ban or when the forecast temperature fort Victor Harbor is 35 degrees or more *Twilighter* railcar trips from Mt Barker to Strathalbyn, with coun try-style dinner at a local pub, operate on selected autumn and sprin Saturday evenings.

Fares: *Southern Encounter* Adults $35, children $18, family $8 return. Mt Barket-Strathalbyn return $18 adults. *Cockle Train* re turn fares $15 adults, $13 seniors and $8 children. Singles and sec tional fares available (correct to October 1996).

Bookings: Phone (08) 8391 1223 or Fax (08) 8391 1933. Posta bookings to SteamRanger. Bookings are essential for *Souther Encounter* trains. *Cockle Train* booking on the day from Victo Harbor, Port Elliot and Goolwa stations.

Location: Mount Barker 45 km south-east of Adelaide off South Eastern Freeway; Goolwa and Victor Harbor 80 km south of Ad elaide via South Road.

Public Transport: regular Hills Transit commuter bus services to Mount Barker; Premier Road Lines to Goolwa and Victor Harbor

Contact: SteamRanger
PO Box 960, Mount Barker SA 5251
Phone: (08) 8231 1223 or on running days
(08) 8552 2782/8555 2691
Victor Harbor station (08) 8552 2782 and
Goolwa station (08) 8555 2691 (*Cockle Train* details
Internet: www.steamranger.org.au

RNE

Port Milang Historic Railway Museum

Railway Museum
1600mm gauge

Port Milang, located on Lake Alexandrina, was established in 1854 to service paddle-wheel steamers on the Murray-Darling river system. A 14km broad gauge railway linked it to the SAR system in 1884 and the port developed into one of South Australia's busiest. A horse-drawn 1067mm gauge line connected the railway yard with the jetty. The railway closed in 1970. The museum has been established by volunteers to commemorate the contribution of the railway to the town. Railway track has been rebuilt in Milang yard and the long term aim is a link to the Victor Harbor line.

Exhibits: The 1884 station building has been returned to the site and fully restored with a 40 metre platform. Redhen railcar 406, two 1920s SAR Centenary carriages, explosives van (ABXY 3-D), SAR guard's van, flat wagon and 4-wheel grain wagon are on display. Exhibits portray the produce and goods carried by rail to Milang. Other features include a railway crane and water column. **Facilities:** a light refreshment outlet has been established in a carriage. Souvenirs, crafts and early photographs of historical Milang are displayed in the station.

Opening Times: 1000-1700 every Sunday and public holidays; 1400-1600 school holidays. Group tours at other times welcome. Entry is free.

Contact: G Chaplin, Secretary
                   Milang Historic Railway Museum
                   PO Box 6, Strathalbyn SA 5255

Phone: (08) 8536 2938

HERITAGE ITEMS

Encounter Coast Discovery Centre, Victor Harbor. Located adjacent to the railway station, this centre provides an insight into the history of the Encounter Coast. It tells the history of the first railway to Victor Harbor and explains the role of the railway in changing the trading port into a holiday centre.
Location: 2 Flinders Parade; Phone (08) 8552 5388

Port Elliot Railway Station: The station represents the final chapter in the area's rail development, when the priority of freight haulage to Victor Harbor had been supplanted by the movement of holiday makers. Architecturally, the building is a better-than-usual timber framed railway station, with interest being added by the use of wrought iron brackets and 'arches'.

Strathalbyn Railway Station: The station complex, constructed in 1883, is of a format typical of the late 19th century age of railways. The station is an elongated U- shaped building, while the goods shed is constructed of sandstone with brick quoins and has a magnificent curved roof design. The Strathalbyn complex is of great importance as a key part of the heritage of transport evolution in South Australia.

Victor Harbor Railway Station/Goods Shed: The opening of the railway in 1864 as an extension of Australia's first public railway elevated Victor Harbor to a sea port, tapping trade transported down the River Murray to Goolwa. Physically, the railway site is a key element in the Overall design of early Victor Harbor, its importance reflected by its juxtaposition between the commercial sector, the foreshore boarding houses and the causeway leading out to Granite Island, it both defines and divides the foreshore recreation area from the town.

FLINDERS RANGES AND OUTBACK SOUTH AUSTRALIA

Situated at the crossroads of Australia's transcontinental land routes, the northern region of South Australia owes its economic base to railways. Construction of a narrow-gauge (1067mm) northern trans-continental line commenced from Port Augusta in 1879, while the railway from Broken Hill to Port Pirie opened in 1887 to enable the development of rich mineral resources. The standard gauge Transcontinental Railway, which opened in 1917, provided an additional boost to the region. With lines from Peterborough to Quorn (1882), Terowie (1881) and Gladstone to Wilmington (1915), these lines constituted SAR's narrow-gauge Northern System. The standard gauge line from Stirling North to Leigh Creek is a heavy-haul coal line operated by *FreightCorp*.

To complete the link from Broken Hill to Port Pirie, the 56km gap from Broken Hill to the South Australian border was bridged by the **Silverton Tramway Company** (STC). The STC 1067mm gauge line opened in January 1888. The line continued until 1970, when the new standard gauge line made the STC main-line operation redundant. The STC is an active short line and shunting operator in today's railway scene. It shunts mineral sidings in the Broken Hill area and its brightly painted locomotives can be seen in the city.

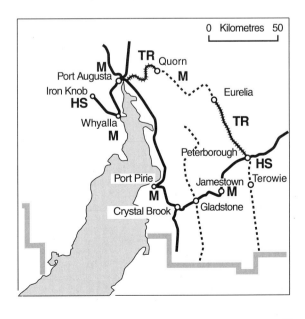

Port Augusta (population 15,000) at the head of Spencer Gulf (310km north of Adelaide), has been an important railway town since 1878 and became the operating headquarters of the Commonwealth Railways in 1917. There are extensive railway workshops in the town. Pioneer diesel-electric locomotive GM1, which established a new era for the Transcontinental Railway in 1951, is preserved at the railway station.
Tourist information: (08) 8641 0793

Quorn, 334km north of Adelaide, is a historic town which developed as the railway crossroads of Australia. Bypassed by the standard gauge Maree line in 1956, Quorn retains many heritage buildings which serve as reminders of the town's important role in the history of South Australia.

Terowie (221km north of Adelaide) was a major break-of-gauge railway centre. It has been declared a historical township with attractive main street of shop frontages which reflect the charac of life in a country town of 100 years ago.
Tourist information: (08) 8659 1092/1105

Peterborough: An important railway town situated astride t narrow gauge line from Port Pirie to Broken Hill, with lines nor to Quorn and south to Terowie. Peterborough was a divisional hea quarters of the SAR with a major locomotive depot and worksho In January 1970, the new standard gauge line to Broken Hill w brought into operation, while the line to Terowie was converted broad gauge, making Peterborough a three gauge railway junctic

National Trust Museum, Jamestown

Local History Museu

Jamestown is located 208km north of Adelaide on the Crystal Brook-Peterborough railway line which opened to Jamestow in 1878. With the advent of the standard gauge in 1968, the railway station, built in 1885, was closed and a new stati building erected to the north-east of the town. The former narrow gauge station became a museum featuring railway and loc history in 1971.

Exhibits: broad-gauge 1st class carriage No105, built in 1882, which was converted to hospital car No 229 in 1913 and to an employees sleeping car in 1951. Plans of these conversions are on display along with photographic displays, time-tables, posters, uniforms, railway publications and artefacts.
Opening Times: Monday-Saturday, 1000-1600
Sundays 1400-1600.

Contact: Jamestown National Trust Museum
PO Box 223, Jamestown SA 5491
Phone: (08) 8664 0092 (caretaker) or
8665 2036 (Branch Chairman).

♿ RNE

Homestead Park Pioneer Museum, Port Augusta
Corporation of Port Augusta

Local History Museu

This museum, based on the old *Yudnappina* homestead, a National Trust classified log-house (c 1868), features Port Augus local history including its railway heritage.

Exhibits: Ex-Port Pirie Smelters 0-6-0T *Passchendale* (AB 1546/1919), ex-CR 6wDH shunting locomotive MDH.1 (Clyde 58-192/1958), a railcar, 2 passenger carriages, steam railway crane and section cars, together with an extensive photographic collection. A miniature railway operates most weekends.
Open: 0900-1700 daily (except Good Friday and Christmas Day).

Admission: Adults $2.50; children 80c.
Location: Elsie Street, Port Augusta SA 5700
Turn off Highway to Adelaide at Ampol service station.
Contact:. Phone (08) 8642 2035

HERITAGE ITEMS

Bruce Railway Station: This 1881 station and station master's residence on the original Ghan railway has been faithfully restored as B&B accommodation. Donated railway memorabilia, including the original "Bruce" station sign adorns the walls.
Location: PO Box 173, Quorn SA 5433
Phone: (08) 8648 6344

Old Railway Station, Port Augusta: The heritage-classified railway station opened in 1878 with the opening of the first line to the Government jetty. Located on Commercial Road, it now houses Curdnatta Art and Pottery.

Oodnadatta Railway Station: This substantial building is sig nificant for its association with the historic *Ghan* Railway, a lin which played a major role in transport to and communication wit Central Australia for many decades until its closure in 1980.

A major station on the line between Marree and Alice Spring the Oodnadatta building was the line's terminal for forty year Oodnadatta Station is of further significance because of its bein the last known survivor of its particular design in South Australi The building was renovated in the 1970s and in 1983 was sold t the Aboriginal Development Commission.

Port Lincoln Railway Museum
Eyre Peninsula Railway Preservation Society

Local History Museu

The heritage-listed railway station at Port Lincoln is home to a museum of historical artefacts and memorabilia of the Eyr Peninsula railway system.

Exhibits: Telegraphic equipment, staff uniforms, office equipment and track maintenance tools including Fairmont quad fettlers' trolleys, that tell the story of the men and women who made the Eyre Peninsula through the railways.
Open: 1400-1600 Wednesday, Saturday and Sunday.
Admission by donation. Other times by appointment.

Location: Port Lincoln railway station, Liverpool Street, Port Lin coln; 42km south-west of Port Augusta by Lincoln Highway.
Contact: Mrs Alice Domagalski, Secretary
Eyre Peninsula Railway Preservation Society
Edillilie SA 5630
Phone: (08) 8676 4255 or
Robert Prout, President (08) 8682 4550

ichi Richi Railway, Quorn
ichi Richi Railway Preservation Society

Heritage Railway (Steam)
1067 mm gauge

DEREK ROGERS

One of the two railcars in use on the Pichi Richi Railway.

he Society aims to preserve the narrow gauge railway through Quorn and the Pichi Richi Pass as an operating museum. The ailway opened in 1879 as the first section of the Great Northern Railway planned to connect Port Augusta with Darwin. For many years the Great Northern Express ran to Oodnadatta and it was at Quorn in 1923 that it was dubbed The *Afghan Express* which was in time abbreviated to *The Ghan*. Following a period of hectic activity during the 1939-45 war, the Pichi Richi line was closed in 1957. A workshop and museum has been established on the original site of the former Commonwealth Railways Quorn workshops. A extension of the line to Saltia opened in 1999, with a further extension to Stirling North, near Port Augusta, scheduled to open in 2000.

Heritage significance: The whole railway is on the Register of the National Estate for its historic and scenic railway track and structures including bridges, cuttings embankments some with pitched masonry, historic rolling stock and equipment and historic buildings.
Features: A functional railway transverses rugged scenery and century old bridges and stone embankments built by early British stonemasons and Chinese workers. The workshop and museum offers a classic collection of South Australian and Commonwealth railway narrow-gauge rolling stock ranging from an 1879 steam locomotive to the first diesel locomotive to haul *The Ghan*.
Locomotives: 9 steam, 4 diesel locomotives, including ex-WAGR W-class 4-8-2s 931, 933 and 934, together with W 22 from STC built 1951), ex-SAR T-class 4-8-0 No 186 (Martin 198/1909), ex-SAR Wx-class 2-6-0 No 18 (BP 1820/1879), ex-SAR 2-6-0 Yx 141 Martin 43/1892) and ex-CR 4-8-0 NM 25 (Thompson 51/1925) which formerly operated on the Pichi Richi Pass railway. Ex-CR A1A-A1A de NSU 52 and Co-Co NT locomotives provide diesel back-up.
Rolling Stock: 2 railcars, 30 passenger carriages, more than 50 freight wagons and service rolling stock. A steam motor coach, The *Coffee Pot* (built by Kitson in 1905) has been restored to operating condition.
Operations: Steam trains or railcars from Quorn to Woolshed Flat 16.5km) on the second and fourth Sunday of the month, March to November, plus many other days (please refer to time table). Ex-

SAR Railway Commissioner's carriage, *Flinders* (16 passengers), steam motor coach *Coffee Pot* (22 passengers) and 1928 railcar (34 passengers) are available for private hire. Contact the Society for special train and group bookings. Conducted tours of the workshop and museum are available on all running days.
Fares (1999) Woolshed Flat return: adult, $20, concession $24, children $12 and family $60 (except *Coffee Pot);* Saltia return adult $30, concession, $15 child $25. Workshop-museum conducted tours: adult $5, family $12.
Bookings: All BASS SA agencies, *Dial-n-Charge* through Adelaide 131 246 or National 008 888 327; Quorn station (08) 8648 6598 (operating days only); or mail bookings to PRRPS. Group bookings phone/fax (08) 8658 1109; charter 08 8264 7439.
Location: At Quorn, 325km north of Adelaide. Australian National trains, the *Indian Pacific* and *Ghan,* allow a break of journey by prior arrangement: stop off at Port Augusta and use hire-car, taxi or bus service to Quorn (43km). Stateline buses operate from Adelaide.
Contact: Railway Station
        Railway Terrace, Quorn SA 5433
Phone: (08) 8648 6598 (operating days only)
For information on the PRRPS, phone (08) 8276 6232
recorded information 08 8395 5266
Web Page: www.prrps.com.au

   RNE

Steamtown Peterborough
Steamtown Peterborough Railway Preservation Society

Tourist Railway (Steam/Diese.
1067mm gauge

Formed in 1977, Steamtown is an operating steam railway museum which maintains a working link with Peterborough narrow gauge railway heritage. Operations commenced in 1981 and today the Society maintains some 57 route kilometres narrow gauge track over the remaining southern portion of the line, once known as the Quorn line, to Eurelia.

Heritage Significance: Peterborough roundhouse (built 1927) is the most substantial remaining structure of the former narrow gauge division of the SAR and has great technological significance and rarity value. It occupies a half circle, with 22 stalls originally and an 87ft turntable. The size and relative intactness of Peterborough make it the most significant surviving example of a South Australian roundhouse. It is Australia's only tripple-gauge round-house The roundhouse remains as an important symbol of the steam era and is National Trust classified.

Locomotives: 4 steam and 4 diesels. Steam locomotives are ex-WAGR Pmr 4-6-2 No 720 (NBL 26564/1950) W-class 4-8-2s Nos 901 (operational) and 907 (BP 737884 1951) and ex-SAR T-class 4-8-0 No 199 (Martin 201/1912). Ex-Commonwealth Railways Sulzer diesel NSU55 has been restored to operating condition, while ex-WAGR 0-6-0DM Z1151 is also operational.

Rolling Stock: 17 passenger coaches and freight rolling stock. Steam-hauled trains comprise former Commonwealth Railways wooden carriages built between 1917 and 1928 for the standard gauge Trans-Australia Railway. Some coaches were transferred to narrow-gauge bogies for use on the Alice Springs *Ghan* trains. Ex-SAR narrow gauge carriages include AV16,AV5, *Long Tom* 186 and three brake vans.

Operations: Excursions operate from Easter through to the October long week-end on most public holiday week-ends. Trains operate from Peterborough to either Orroroo (5.5 hours, 71km return) or Eurelia (7.5 hours, 115km return). All trains feature a photograph stop on the famous Black Rock Bridge, the longest on the former SAR narrow-gauge railway system. Mixed goods trains provide the opportunity to witness first-hand traditional narrow gauge o erations in the spirit of the *Quorn Mixed*. Trains are well stock with souvenirs and refreshments. Available at other times are se tion car excursions (second Sunday of the month, Septemb through March) and a 1927 Morris motor inspection car, which available for hire at most times.

Fares & Bookings: Peterborough-Orroru return, adults $25, chi $15, family $50; to Eurelia return adult $35, child $20, family $8 Peterborough Corporation, Phone (08) 8651 3566; or Tourism S. 1 King William Street, Adelaide, Phone (08) 8212 1505. Group Bookings and Carriage Hire, phone/fax (085) 22 1394

Location: At Peterborough, 243km north of Adelaide, on the ma Australian National railway line between Port Augusta and Br ken Hill. By road, travel via the historic towns of Burra and Terowi

Public Transport: Adelaide- Peterborough bus service operates days per week. Bute Buses operate from Adelaide to Peterborou and Orroroo, Mon, Wed, Thus and Fridays; Phone (08) 8826 211 The twice weekly *Indian Pacific* train stops at Peterborough b request.

Contact: Secretary
Steamtown Peterborough Railway Preservation Soc
PO Box 133, Peterborough SA 5422
After hours bookings (08) 8522 1394

RNE

MURRAY REGION
Big River Country

Australia's largest river system, the Murray-Darling, has a rich history as a transport artery to the inland pastoral areas of New South Wales and Victoria. From 1853, steam paddle-wheelers commenced operations from Goolwa, near the Murray mouth, to service centres along the rivers. Eventually 300 paddle-wheelers competed for cargoes and rival colonial governments built railways to tap the trade for their ports. Today the Murray meanders through South Australia's heartland to the sea giving its modern day explorers unforgettable encounters with abundant wildlife, historic towns, rich vineyards and orchards.

Light agricultural branch lines were built from Tailem Bend to open up the Murraylands for agricultural development between 1906 and 1928. The region is an important agricultural area producing wheat, wool, meat and dairy produce. The remaining branch lines from Montaro South to Apamurra, Tailem Bend to Loxton and Pinnaroo have been converted to standard gauge for grain traffic.

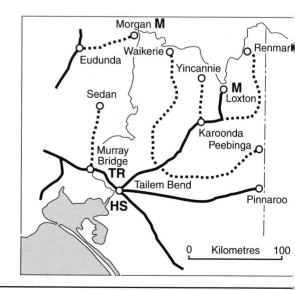

urray Bridge (population 17,000) is the main commercial and rism centre of the region. The main Adelaide-Melbourne rail-y line opened in 1886 using the first bridge over the Murray. A w railway bridge over the Murray River was built in 1925. The lway station is of heritage significance.

ailem Bend (population 1600) developed as a classic railway vn with a locomotive depot to service the Murray Lands branch es. The roundhouse has been recommended for listing by the tional Trust. Restoration of the railway station as a council tourist information centre, coffee shop and interpretative centre is planned.

Karoonda (Population 250) 146km East of Adelaide, is a peaceful farming centre and former railway junction in the heart of the mallee country and an example of how local enthusiasm can create visitor appeal.

Loxton (population 3500) was settled as a farming area in the 1890s and a village was proclaimed in 1907. The district prospered with the opening of the railway in 1914. A large irrigation scheme was established in 1948.

obdogla Irrigation Museum
obdolga Steam Friends Society Inc

Industry Museum (Steam)
610mm gauge

COBDOGLA IRRIGATION AND STEAM MUSEUM

Bagnall 610mm gauge locomotive No 1801 built in 1906 and restored in 1988 was used on the Walhalla Long Tunnel Goldmine timber tramway, on the Geelong sewerage outfall construction line, on the Glenelg Breakwater project and on the Cobdogla to Loveday railway for transporting materials at Humes Pipeworks.

he museum, at Cobdogla in an irrigation settlement in the heart of South Australia's Riverland, aims to give visitors a ealistic view of the history of irrigation and demonstrate the size of the machinery involved.

rain: Bagnall 1906 0-4-0ST locomotive originally used on the ght railway from Cobdogla wharf to the Loveday pipe factory in e 1920s, has been restored to operating condition for use at the useum. The train operates over 830 metres of track around the useum and to the north, with a new extension along 600m of rmer channel reserves to Loveday and Marmera. Trains are nor-ally operated by the Bagnall steam locomotive, with a Simplex wDM loco as back-up.

isplays: The National Trust have fitted out the former steam plant uilding as an Interpretative Centre for the Irrigation Areas. The useum's other famous Humphrey Pump (c 1925) which is the nly working example in the world (State Heritage Item). Other ems include a John Fowler steam B6 crane traction engine, pumps, actors and horticultural implements used in the development of e district.

Operation: operating days are held on Australia Day and the Sundays of the following long weekends: Easter, May, June and October, and the middle Sunday of the July school holidays. Steam Train Twilight Runs are held on the Sundays in January and during school holidays. Program details can be obtained from the Barmera Travel Centre. Tour groups and special events by arrangement.
Location: at Cobdogla, 215km east of Adelaide. It is accessible by road via the Sturt Highway or from the River Murray via the channel inlet to the pumping station.
Contact: Barmera Travel Centre
            Phone (08) 8588 2289; fax (08) 8588 3330
General inquiries: Denis Wasley
            Cobdogla Steam Friends Society Inc
            PO Box 208, Berri SA 5343
Phone: (08) 8582 2603

♿ 🚻 ☕ 📖 ⛩ **RNE**

Murray Bridge Wharf Railway
Murray Bridge River Boat, Rail & Steam Group Inc

Heritage Railway
1600mm gauge

This group is reconstructing the short branch line from the station to the historic wharf precinct as a key attraction of t▐
Murray Bridge river front development strategy. The historic railway station is also being restored as a railway history cent▐

Features: The 1.5km line connects the town railway precinct and the heritage-listed wharf freight yard where goods were transhipped to and from river boats. Displays will be established at the wharf goods shed and crane depicting the interface between the transport modes.

The heritage-listed railway station has been leased to private operators and is being restored within heritage guidelines. It will serve as a coffee shop, photograph gallery and local railway history centre. The wharf area has picnic areas and the riverfront is being landscaped with a walking trail.

Locomotives & rolling stock: 4wDM shunting tractor (ex-Yarrawonga Munitions Factory) and ex-SAR 4-6-0 locomotive Rx160 (SAR 29/1913), currently on static display; 2 Centenary passenger cars and brake van; 5 powered section cars; 9 4-wheel and bogie freight wagons.

Operations: Trains and section cars will operate over the line fr▐ the former wharf railway freight yard to the town railway precin▐ An annual *Murraylands Steam & River Boat Rally* is held m▐ November.

Location: at Murray Bridge, 78km east of Adelaide by South-E▐ Freeway.

Contact: Andrew Hill, Secretary
Murray Bridge Wharf Railway
PO Box 984, Murray Bridge SA 5253
Phone: (08) 8531 1552; fax (08) 8531 141▐

 ♿   ⚲   ☕   ⛩   **RNE**

Loxton Village Museum
District Council of Loxton Waikerie

Themepark

The historical Village Museum recreates an early 1900s farming town with 30 re-created buildings, each packed with mem▐ rabilia of a bygone era.

Displays: ex-SAR 4-6-0 locomotive Rx 55 (SAR 55/1905) is on static display. Other items of railway interest include Yinkannie railway station (reerected on site), semaphore and train order signals, and water crane. There is also a monorail truck, parts of which were used on the Loxton Farming Company monorail, constructed to the Caillet system, which operated in the district between 1911 and 1915.

Opening Times: Daily except Christmas Day
1000-1600 Monday to Friday, 1000-1700 Saturday and Sunday.

Admission: Adults $5, concession $4, children $2.50, family $▐
Location: on banks of Murray River, adjacent to Loxton shoppi▐ centre, 256km north-east of Adelaide.

Contact: Loxton Tourism & Arts Centre
Bookpurnong Terrace, Loxton SA 5333
Phone: (08) 8584 7194

 ♿   ☕   📖   ⛩

Port of Morgan Historic Museum
Port of Morgan Historic Museum & Heritage Society

Local History Museum
1600mm gauge

Morgan was once the State's largest freshwater port served by six trains daily from Adelaide. The railway closed in 196▐ This museum, housed in the old Morgan railway station, provides an excellent display of the district's rail and riverbo▐ history.

Exhibits: interpretative display of the district's rail and river boat history accredited by the SA History Trust. 3 ex-SAR freight wagons provide a background to the exchange of goods between river and rail. Section car rides are available over a section of track in the former station yard. Rides are available on the *PW MAYFLOWER*, one of the state's oldest paddle wheelers.
Opening Times: 1400-1600, Tuesday, Saturday and Sunday, or by appointment.

Admission: $2 per person or $1 per person groups (more than 10▐

Location: in the old railway station on the banks of the Murra▐ River at Morgan, 163km north-east of Adelaide.

Contact: Mary Holt
PO Box 98, Morgan SA 5320
Phone: (08) 8540 2136 or 8540 2085; Fax (08) 8535 6199.▐

OUTH-EAST REGION

uth Australia's South-East Region is home to two of Aus-
lia's most famous wine districts - Coonawarra and
dthaway - extensive pine plantations and rich grazing
untry.

Railways have played a significant role in developing
e region. The SAR south-eastern railway system from
olseley to Mount Gambier and Millicent was originally
ilt as a narrow (1067mm) gauge lines between 1876 and
87. During the 1950s, some 314km of track was converted
broad gauge (1600mm) on the understanding that it would
entually be converted to standard gauge. Conversion of
e Melbourne-Adelaide line to standard gauge in 1994-95
lated the south-eastern railway and the corresponding line
m Maroona to Portland (171km) in Victoria. The Victo-
an line, together with several western grain lines, was con-
rted to standard gauge, giving Portland a new importance
a grain shipment port. The isolated South Australian lines
re closed and their future remains in doubt.

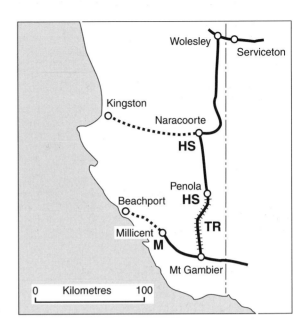

ount Gambier (population 22,500), known as *Blue Lake City,*
m the adjacent crater lake. Orderly development from it found-
g in 1854, use of local white stone for many historic buildings
d fine parks and gardens make Mount Gambier a natural tour-
 destination.

illicent: (population 8200) A town which began in 1870 as a
ntre for the pastoral industry. Rapidly expanding pine forests
d processing plants and lush grazing land now surround the town.

Naracoorte: The town, which developed from various settlements
in the 1840s, is the major service centre for the north of the region.
The World Heritage listed Naracoorte Caves Conservation park
and Bool Lagoon, a wetland of international importance, are the
main attractions.

Millicent Museum
ational Trust of SA

Local History Museum

he museum is located in a former school building and covers local history, including the role of railways. The museum
atures an outstanding display of horse-drawn vehicles.

ocomotive: Ex-SAR narrow gauge 4-8-0 locomotive T 224
Walkers 224/1914) is on static display at the museum as link to
e former narrow gauge era of the South-East Division.
ocation: 1 Mount Gambier Road (Highway One), Millicent, 50km
est of Mt Gambier.

Opening Times: 0930-1630 daily (except Christmas Day).
Admission: Adults $4, concession $3, school children 50c.
Contact: John Northwood, Curator, Phone (08) 8733 3205

HERITAGE SITES

ld Penola Railway Station: Built in 1908, the station reflects
he development of Penola as a notable town in the region.
rchitecturally, the railway station is an interesting application of
he Queen Anne style to a 'utilitarian' structure. Situated 1km south
f the present railway station, it is now a private residence.

Pioneer Park Station, Naracoorte: Former narrow gauge
0-4-4T V 9 (Beyer Peacock 1597 of 1876), the oldest and smallest
SAR locomotive, is on static display in Lions Pioneer Park. The
locomotive was presented to the Corporation of Naracoorte in 1955
as a historical relic. The protective "station" was constructed as a
1988 Bicentennial project.

Limestone Coast Railway
Mount Gambier & District Railway Society

Tourist Railway/Museum
1600mm gauge

GREG ROBINSON

Limestone Coast Railway railcars at Penola station in the Coonawarra district.

The Society seeks to maintain the rail infrastructure of the former SAR South-Eastern Division. The Society operates regular tourist trains between Mount Gambier and the popular Penola/Coonawarra Wine District. Services also operate to Millicent and Naracoorte (from late 2000)

Features: A relaxing journey through pine forests and prime farming country to Penola, in the region's premium wine growing district. 3-hour Coonawarra stopover to enjoy local heritage walks, restaurants, antiques and gift shops, galleries and heritage-listed buildings.

Rolling Stock: Ex-TransAdelaide Red Hen railcars 405, 424 and 334 restored in LCR livery.

Operations: Regular Sunday trip from Mt Gambier to Penola/ Coonawarra with special trips to Millicent and Naracoorte (from late 2000). Coonawarra trips depart Mt Gambier at 1000 Sunday and returns at 1600.

Fares: Mt Gambier-Penola return
Adult$15, concession $12, child $8.

Bookings: Through The Lady Nelson Visitor & Discovery Centre
Jubilee Highway East, Mount Gambier SA 5290
Phone: (08) 8724 9750; fax (08) 8723 2833
toll free 1800 087 187

Charter details and bookings:
Contact LCR Phone/fax (08) 8724 7589
Location: Mt Gambier railway station, Helen Street.

Contact: Mandy Suckling, Secretary
Limestone Coast Railway
PO Box 2442, Mount Gambier SA 5290
Phone: (08) 8723 9900; Fax (08) 8725 0516

WESTERN AUSTRALIA

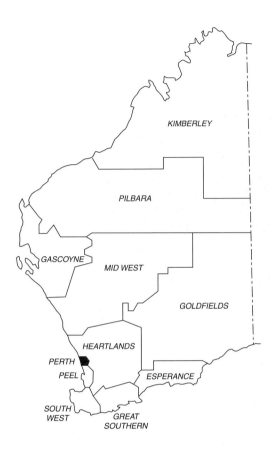

WESTERN AUSTRALIA'S sparse population and vast distances were the dominant factors shaping railway development in that State. The pioneer railways were private lines serving the timber industry and the heritage of these "bush lines" remains a dominant theme in railway preservation.

The first Government line, between the northern port of Geraldton and Northampton, did not open until 1879. The Government went on to construct an extensive network of narrow gauge (1067mm) lines to open up the State's agricultural areas and mineral fields. By the 1950s, a fleet of modern steam locomotives operated over the 6330km WAGR network. This fleet provided a number of locomotives for railway preservation groups.

The huge distances of the West need to be taken into account in planning a railway heritage itinerary. Because of the low population and resource base, there are few sites open during the week. In the Perth area, Rottnest Island, with its Oliver Hill Railway offers an interesting experience that operates on a daily basis. The **Bennett Brook Railway** at Whiteman Park operates Wednesday to Sunday (daily in school holidays) with steam in the cooler months and the **Whiteman Park Tramway** add variety on weekends and public holidays. The main railway museum at **Bassendean** is open for restricted hours on Sundays.

For those wanting to see more of the State, check with the **Hotham Valley Tourist Railway** for scheduled tours. The **Etmilyn Forest Railway** operates from Dwellingup Tuesday, Thursday, Saturday and Sunday, while the **Pemberton Tramway** offers daily scenic tram trips through spectacular forests, with steam train trips on Saturday and Sunday between May and November. There are a number of timber industry and local railway museums in the South-West and Wheatbelt that open on a daily basis. At Kalgoorlie, the **Loop Line Railway** provides daily operations. Visitors to the Gascoyne Region in the north can travel behind steam on the **Carnarvon Light Railway** between April and November.

MAINLINE OPERATORS

Hotham Valley Tourist Railway

Mainline Tours (Steam/Diesel)
1067mm gauge

DAVID WHITEFORD

Hotham Valley Tourist Railway locomotive PM 706 on a tourist journey at Walkaway.

The Hotham Valley Tourist Railway (HVTR) is Western Australia's principal rail tour operator, using both steam and diesel hauled trains. HVTR, now in its 23rd year of operation, offers steam and/or diesel-hauled tours over the State Government ra system in conjunction with *Westrail* and independently, over the restored Dwellingup-Etmilyn line.

Operations: Hotham Valley operates a comprehensive program of steam and diesel-hauled tour trains over the *Westrail* network to some 27 destinations for major destinations and events, including fully packaged three-day Safari tours. Many are steam-hauled. Diesel and steam-hauled day/evening tours, weekender and three-day tours are also operated. *Etmilyn Forest Diner* tours from East Perth operate most Saturdays and selected Fridays. (See under Peel Region).

Information, Fares and Bookings:
Phone (08) 9221 4444; fax (08) 9221 3065
Charter and group travel available to a wide range of destinations with special catering and entertainment.

Locomotives and Rolling Stock: See under Peel Region.

Location: Tours operate from Perth City Station and/or Fremant Midland and Armadale.

Contact: Hotham Valley Tourist Railway
2nd Floor, Travel Centre, Commonwealth Bank
86 Barrack Street, Perth 6000 WA
(GPO Box B73, Perth WA 6001)

ARHS (WA Division) Heritage Train Tours

Mainline Tours
1067mm gauge

The Australian Railway Historical Society (ARHS) is Western Australia's premier railway enthusiast organisation. The Wes ern Australian Division was founded in 1959 and it is the only railway Society in the State which caters for the needs of a railway enthusiasts, covering all aspects of railways from today's high-tech industry to yesterday's historical scene.

Operations: A limited tour program to a range of metropolitan and country destinations. They may use restored WAGR S-class 4-8-2 steam locomotive No 549 (Midland, 1947).

Phone: (08) 9377 1588 for details.
For recorded information, phone (08) 9279 7189.

Location: Tours operate from Perth City Station and/or Fremantle, Midland and Armadale.

Other: The ARHS meets on the second Friday of every month the Exhibition Hall of the Bassendean Railway Museum. Meeting commence at 2000 hours, with guest speakers on various aspects o railway history and operations.

Contact: Secretary, ARHS (WA Division)
Box 363, Bassendean WA 6054
Phone: (08) 9342 9751

PERTH REGION

Founded by Captain James Stirling in 1829, Perth owes its growth to the discovery of gold in the 1890s. The City became a thriving commercial and political capital, fed by a vast new railway network to the outback.

Today, Perth (population 1.3 million) is renowned as Australia's sunniest capital and the warm hospitality extended to visitors. It is a city of parks and gardens, galleries and museums, superb beaches and unpolluted skies. Electric street tramways operated in Perth from 1899 to 1958, while a second system operated in Fremantle between 1905 and 1952. Perth's electric suburban railway, opened in 1991, is Australia's newest and most modern.

Tourist Information: Western Australian Tourist Centre
Albert Facey House, Forrest Place
Perth WA 6000
Phone: 1300 361 351; facsimile (08) 9481 0190

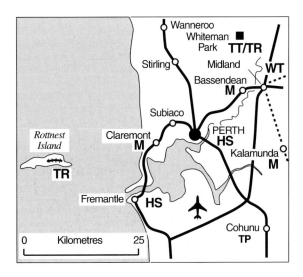

Public Transport: Public transport in Perth - comprising rail, bus and ferry services - is operated by *Westrail* and the private sector, and is managed by *Transperth*. Perth's electric railway system is the most modern in Australia. Air-conditioned electric trains operate over the Fremantle, Midland, Armadale and Northern Suburbs lines, ticketing is by computer-linked machines and there is an advanced train information system. The rail network now covers 92 route km with 55 stations and carries some 30 million passengers annually.

Feeder bus services operate to five stations on the Northern Suburbs line, while there are bus interchanges at Armadale, Kelmscott, Cannington and Midland. The City Busport, catering for 2700 bus movements daily, is one of Australia's most modern. There is a common fare system for all bus, train and ferry services, based on concentric zones, which gives a two-hour validity and enables changes between any vehicle/mode without further charge. A Free Transit Zone for bus and train travel operates within the Perth CBD.

Oliver Hill Railway, Rottnest Island
Rottnest Island Railway Trust

Tourist Railway (Diesel)
1067mm gauge

Historic Rottnest Island off Fremantle was originally used as a penal colony, then as an internment camp and military base during World War II. Two 9.2-inch coastal defence guns were established at Oliver Hill and a 1067mm gauge railway was built from Kingstown to Oliver Hill in the mid-1930s to transport military supplies from the coast. The prison buildings have been adapted to holiday uses and the island has now become an important resort for the nature-lover, historian and holiday-maker.

Description: The military railway was rebuilt in 1993 as a 8.5km 1067 mm gauge tourist railway from the old jetty and Kingstown barracks to the Oliver Hill gun batteries and a line was built into the main settlement. The line has been constructed in an "environmentally friendly" manner and provides an exciting focus on the island's natural vegetation and wildlife attractions.

Train: Bogie tourist carriages and two ex-WAGR 4wDH shunting tractors.

Access: Daily ferry services to Rottnest Island from Perth, Hillarys and Fremantle. Daily flights (*Rottnest Airbus*) from Perth Airport.

Operations: Four trains per day from Settlement Station, via Kingstown to Oliver Hill station and gun emplacements at 1030, 1130, 1245 and 1400. Round trip with gun inspection takes two hours.
Fares: Oliver Hill and return, $9 adults, $4.50 concession, including a tour through the Oliver Hill gun emplacement.

Contact: Rottnest Island Railway Trust
PO Box 418, West Perth WA 6872
Phone: (08) 9222 5600

Bassendean Rail Transport Museum
Aust. Railway Historical Society (WA Division)

Railway Museum
1067mm gauge

The Bassendean Railway Museum, operated by the ARHS WA Division, was established to display preserved locomotiʻ and rolling stock which operated in Western Australia. The museum houses the State's most comprehensive collectionʻ steam, diesel and electric locomotives, rolling stock, photographs and railway memorabilia.

Locomotives: 22 steam, 8 diesel and 1 electric locomotive (dating from 1880) from the Western Australian Railways (1067mm gauge) and industrial lines, including 0-6-0ST C 1 of 1881 (the oldest surviving WAGR loco), 2-6-0 A 11 of 1885, 2-6-0 Y 71 an ex-sawmill loco of 1886, 4-6-2 P 508 of 1925, 4-8-2 S 549 of 1947 and 2-8-2 V 1220 of 1956.

Rolling Stock: Collection of WAGR passengers cars and other items of rolling stock. Locomotive name and number plates, photographs and other artefacts are displayed in the exhibition building. The Sales Kiosk has a wide selection of railway books, videos, magazines, souvenirs and postcards.

Operations: Open Sundays and public holidays (except Christmas and New Year) between 1300 and 1700. Wednesday during school holidays, 1300-1600. Special mid-week visits can be arranged groups by phoning (08) 9279 7189.

Admission: Adults $4, children $1.

Location: 136 Railway Parade, Bassendean; a Perth suburb. car, note Perth Metropolitan Street Directory map 62.

Public Transport: Take Midland train to Ashfield (half-hourly se ice on Sundays) - the museum is 400 metres north-east of Ashfiʻ railway station.

Contact: Secretary, ARHS (WA Division)
Box 363, Bassendean WA 6054

Phone: (08) 9279 7189

♿ 📖 ⛱

Whiteman Park Heritage Tramway
Perth Electric Tramway Society (PETS)

Tourist Tramway (Electric)
1435mm gauge

This group was formed in 1981 to restore and operate vintage Western Australian and other electric tramcars. The group moved its tram collection in 1983 to Whiteman Park, a recreational, heritage, arts and crafts, conservation, education and sporting park for the people of Perth. A 4km electric tramway has been established as part of the park's public transport system.

Tramcars: Operational trams originate from the Fremantle, Melbourne and Ballarat systems. Restored Fremantle Municipal Tramways bogie car No 29 (built 1921), five ex-Melbourne W2, SW2 and W4-class trams and Ballarat tram No 31 are available to operate public transport services during periods of peak demand, such as the Classic Car Show in March. The restoration of Perth E-class tram No 66 (built 1917) is scheduled for completion in 2000. The bodies of eight Perth, three Fremantle and two Kalgoorlie trams have been acquired for future restoration.

MICHAEL STUKE

Ready for service outside the tramshed at Whiteman Park: ex-Me bourne W2 tram No 329, restored Fremantle car No 29 and e Melbourne W4 tram No 674.

Operations: Saturday, Sunday and public holidays, 1100-1630; Wednesday to Friday 1100-1500. Trams operate on 30 minute schedules. Trams are available for special hire (Phone: 08 9249 2466).

Fares: Return; Adult $2.50, child $1
Single; Adult $1.50, child 50c

Entry Fees to Whiteman Park:
Adults $2, child $1 or $5 per car (family) from Wednesday to Sunday.

Location: 8km north of Guildford, 30 minutes drive from Perth. Motorists approach by Beechboro Road (from the west) and West Swan Road (from the east) to the Lord Street entrance off Marshall Road.

Public Transport: *TransPerth* train to Guildford station, then taxi. *TransPerth* bus 336 (Mon-Sat only), Morley Bus Station to Ellensbrook, passes the Whiteman Park entrance, although this some distance from transport and other facilities.

Address Perth Electric Tramway Society
PO Box 257, Mt Lawley WA 6929

Phone: Museum (08) 9249 2777, or
Michael Stukely (08) 943 1945

♿ ☕ 🍴 🚻 ⛱

ennett Brook Railway
A Light Railway Preservation Association

Tourist Park Railway (Steam/Diesel)
610mm gauge

e WA Light Railway Preservation Association was formed in 1976 with the aim of preserving and/or operating light lway rolling stock and equipment. The Swan Valley's Bennett Brook Railway provides transport between various facilities Whiteman Park and has a total length of 5.7km.

critage Features: The main structural features of the e are the beautifully restored and re-sited East Perth laisebrook) WAGR suburban station building (dating m 1898), the replica East Perth locomotive shed, the dland workshops turntable and the Fremantle Box A gnal cabin, which are located at Whiteman Village Junc-n. The 45-lever Subiaco signal box (erected in 1901) d station canopy (1925) are outstanding items of rail-y heritage that have recently been relocated to the 3R. The railway terminus at Mussel Pool features the mer WAGR Nungarin station, Cottesloe signal cabin, llie yard cabin and the railway's workshop and stor-e area. A comprehensive collection of former WAGR erlocking and lower quadrant semaphore signalling is cluded as part of the operation.

comotives: Two 67-tonne NG[15]-class 2-8-2 steam comotives ex-South African Railways (NG 118 and 3) are operational, together with privately-owned Perry 4-2T, *Betty Thompson* (ex-Inkerman sugar mill, eensland). Australia's only surviving Mallett locomo-e is under restoration. WALRPA has an extensive llection of industrial diesel and petrol locomotives. incipal operational units are Planet 4wDH (FC Hibberd 50/1938) ex-Lake View & Star mine, Gemco 4wDM 1964 (PW27 ex-Wyndham) and Fowler 0-6-0DH of 50 ex-Isis Sugar Mill No 2.

olling Stock: Historical regauged ex-WAGR bogie agons and wagons rebuilt as carriages are used for pas-nger services. A collection of regauged freight wagons also featured.

perations: 1100-1700 hours Sundays and public holi-ys and 1100-1600 Wednesdays to Saturdays (also onday-Tuesday during school holidays). Trains oper-e from Mussel Pool to Whiteman Village Junction, then ound the loop line and return to Mussel Pool. Travel ne is approximately 45 minutes. Steam operations in ason (mid-autumn to late-spring), with diesel-hauled ins at other times. During summer months, evening in services operate in conjunction with bush dances.

ares: $4 all lines; reduced section and single fares are available. roup bookings and train hire are available. There is a $3 entry fee Whiteman Park for cars (may vary for special event days).

ocation: 8km north of Guildford, 30 minutes drive from Perth. lotorists approach by Beechboro Road (from the west) and West wan Road (from the east) to the Lord Street entrance off Marshall oad or Reid Highway.

ublic Transport: *TransPerth* train to Guildford station, then taxi. *ransPerth* bus 336 (Mon-Sat only), Morley Bus Station to llensbrook, passes the Whiteman Park entrance, although this is me distance from transprot and other facilities.

DAVID WHITEFORD

Ex-South African Railway's NG[15]-class locomotive No 123 hauling a tourist passenger from Kangaroo Flats station at Bennett Brook light railway. The shelter is ex-Pingelly WAGR bus stop shelter.

Contact: The Secretary
WA Light Railway Preservation Association
PO Box 386, Midland Junction WA 6936
Phone: (08) 9249 3861 (workshop)

Kalamunda History Village
Kalamunda and Districts Historical Society

Local History/Folk Museum
1067mm gauge

History Village is the largest folk museum in Western Australia. It is located in the former WAGR Kalamunda railway yar part of the Zig Zag Railway line from Midland to Karragullen. This was under timber company ownership from 1891 to 19 when it was taken over by the WAGR. The line closed in 1949.

Display: The museum utilises the original station buildings of 1903 and 1927. Early buildings of the district have been relocated to the museum. 2-6-0 steam locomotive G 118 (Dubs 3502/1897) is preserved at the station platform. WAGR and timber railway memorabilia is on display at the museum, including photographs of the history of the railway, particularly the zig zag by which the line climbed the Darling Escarpment.

Opening Times: 1000-1500 Monday-Thursday;
0930-1500 Saturday; 1330-1630 Sunday.

Admission: Adults $3, children $2, seniors $1.

Location: Williams Street and Railway Road, Kalamunda; 25 east of Perth.

Contact: Dianne Harrison, Secretary
PO Box 121, Kalamunda WA 6076
Phone: (08) 9293 1371

HERITAGE SITES (Register of the National Estate)

Claremont Railway Station: The group of buildings (c1881) constitutes a rare, surviving example of 19th century and early 20th century steam-train railway establishment. Designed by George Temple Poole, the architectural form and layout of the place is important for association with the Government Railways Department in the steam-train era. The 1906 45-lever high-level signal box has been restored, including levers and associated lights, track diagram panel and operating semaphore signal. The cabin is open to the public on first Saturday each month, 0930-1130.
Contact: Claremont Museum
66 Victoria Avenue, Claremont WA 6010
Phone: (08) 9386 3352

Fremantle Railway Station: The station was built to the design of WAGR engineer Mr Darvill and opened in 1907. The station is a fine example of the Federation Free Classical style in a lively design. The building is an imposing element on the streetscape of Phillimore Street with its classical and massive appearance, and is an important townscape element closing the vista from Market Street.

East Perth Terminal: Standard gauge passenger services to Northam, Kalgoorlie and eastern States (*Indian Pacific*) operate from the East Perth railway terminal, 2km east of Perth. One of the four-wheel composite carriages built for the first WAGR railway in 1876, No AI258, has been fully restored by Westrail and is on display in the foyer, while ex-WAGR 4-8-2 locomotive S 542 is on static display.

Midland Railway Workshops: The workshops, located on a 68ha site adjacent to the Midland town centre, were the largest industrial complex in Western Australia in the early part of the century. Construction commenced in 1901 and the workshops were operational by 1904. It operated as a self-contained manufacturing unit to repair and construct locomotives, rolling stock, railway fittings. More than 70 buildings are on the site. First built were the Powerhouse and three main workshop blocks, followed by followed by the Administrative Building and the Railway Institute. The three workshops buildings consist of massive brick masonry sawtooth roof structures designed to be twice the length to which they were first constructed.

Midland Railway 4-4-0 Locomotive B6: The 4-4-0 locom tive B6 (Hawthorn Leslie 2217/1891), one of the MRWA's f mainline locomotives, has been moved to Midland Workshops storage on behalf of Swan Shire Council. It is the last locomotive its type in the world and the only Midland Railway steam locom tive to survive.

Perth Railway Station: The Station, built to the design of Geor Temple Poole, opened in 1894. The brick and corrugated ir building in late Victorian Free Classical style has important asso iations with the development of the State's railway system. The s tion is an imposing element with its classical and massive appearar on the streetscape of Wellington Street, and is an import townscape element closing the vista from Forrest Place. In additi to suburban electric trains, the station serves as the terminal Bunbury and special tour trains.

WALKING TRAILS

John Forrest Heritage Trail: The Mahogany Creek line fr Midland to Northam, which included the 340 metre Swan Vie Tunnel, served as the main line from Perth to the east from 18 until the opening of the Avon Valley dual gauge line in 1966. T formation has been restored as a heritage trail. The tunnel, the on one in Western Australia, and four of the bridges on the line within the John Forrest National Park and are heritage protecte The railway formation can be walked from Swan View to Chidl (22km). Swan View railway station, with its restored platform a new shelter, can be accessed from Morrison Road, Swan View (20k from Perth) or via Great Eastern Freeway to John Forest Nation park (25km from Perth). Entry fees apply for vehicles to drive the park.

EEL REGION

is rapidly growing region to the south of Perth has a strong
onomy based on mining, agriculture and tourism. There
several outstanding natural features, including 75km of
ractive and accessible coastline, the Peel Inlet, Harvey
tuary and extensive forestry areas. The region covers nearly
700 square kilometers and is home to a rapidly expanding
pulation of approximately 75,000 people. Mining and ag-
culture are the major industries.

Railway development in the region originally focused
the needs of the timber industry. Several tourist railways
d museums have preserved features of this heritage.

andurah (population 47,000) 75km south of Fremantle, is a
rant and versatile city famed for its picturesque waterways and
ests. A new 82km electric suburban railway is under construc-
n from near Cannington in Perth to Mandurah, via Rockingham.

njarra (population 2000) 89km south of Perth, is one of the
lest settlements in the State and developed as a service centre for
timber industry. It is now known for its tourist railway operations.

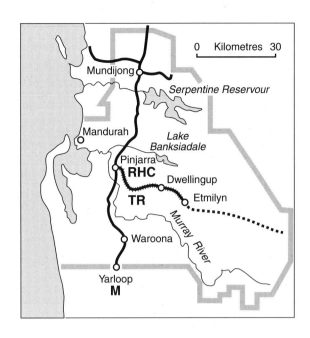

istoric Mill Workshops, Yarloop
rloop Workshops Inc

Industry/Steam Museum
1067mm gauge

e first timber mill at Yarloop was established in 1895 and the settlement became the centre of the extensive timber milling
erations of Millars' Timber and Trading Company throughout the State. A 1067mm gauge railway was constructed from
e WAGR siding at Yarloop east for 93km into the Darling Ranges to transport timber from the mills. The Yarloop work-
ops, constructed in 1896, were at the centre of the Millar's operations, with over 100 men employed maintaining locomo-
es and mill machinery. They remained in use until 1978. The Yarloop timber mill, now operated by Bunnings, is still in use.
mber from the mill was consigned by rail until 1992.

isplays: The former locomotive workshops are being restored to
erating condition in association with the Australian Heritage Com-
ission. The development includes a steam room where various
am engines are operated from a central boiler. Crafts are on sale.

ocomotives: 0-6-0DH industrial locomotive (Clyde 61-241) which
erated at Yarloop Mill (operational) and Yx 2-6-0 steam locomo-
e No 176 ex-Donnelly River saw mill (static exhibit).

pening Times: Daily 1000-1600, except Tuesday. Train rides on
ecial days.

Location: Yarloop is situated 130km south of Perth on the main
line to Bunbury.

Public Transport: Daily Westrail *Australind* passenger trains.

Contact: Colin Pusey, Yarloop Workshops Inc
              PO Box 77, Yarloop WA 6218
Phone: (08) 9733 5214

RNE

Hotham Valley Tourist Railway
Hotham Valley Tourist Railway Inc

Tourist Railway (Steam/Diese
1067mm gauge

D BRENNAN / HOTHAM VALLEY TOURIST RAILWAY

Hotham Valley Tourist Railway G-class locomotive No 123 passing over Davis Brook with a tourist train in the forest on the scenic Etilmyn Tramway.

The **Hotham Valley Tourist Railway** was formed in 1974 to preserve the scenic branch line between Pinjarra and Dwellingu 24km away, which was opened in 1910 to carry timber traffic. Dwellingup became the centre of an extensive timber milli industry, with 75km of "bush lines" hauling logs to the large mill at Banksiadale and other lines centred on Marrinup. The la timber mill at Dwellingup used the line to dispatch timber until 1984. The branch has been retained exclusively for HVT operations. The railway yard and facilities at Pinjarra is classified as a historic precinct by the National Trust. The precin serves as the base for the HVTR, where it has established its main steam locomotive depot. A light railway from Dwelling to Etmilyn, the *Etmilyn Forest Tramway*, was opened in 1986 utilising a portion of the former WAGR railway to Narrogin

Heritage Significance: The engine, carriage and goods sheds at Pinjarra are the only buildings left on the East Perth to Picton railway which date back to the construction of the line in 1893. The carriage and goods sheds contain rare cast-iron window frames.

Features: The *Etmilyn Forest Tramway* takes passengers into the heart of the Jarrah country, with a forest walk at Etmilyn, while the *Etmilyn Forest Diner* service offers a five-course dinner in a 1919 vintage dining car, 1884 lounge/buffet can and saloon carriage with a floodlit forest as a stunning backdrop. A steam locomotive depot is located at Pinjarra, with a sub-depot at Dwellingup.

Locomotives: 6 ex-WAGR steam, 6 diesel. Operational steam locomotives include W-class 4-8-2 903, 920 and 945 (BP built 1951) and Pm-class 4-6-2 706. The HVTR also operates a large fleet of heritage diesels, including ex-WAGR Co-Co DE C1701-3; 2-do-2 DE Xa1401; Bo-Bo DE Y1116 (BTH 1956, and 0-6-0DM Z1152; ex-Midland Railway Bo-Bo DE F40 and G50 (EE Aus) and ex-TGR 0-6-0DM V4/5 (DC/VF 1948, 1951).

Rolling Stock: 46 passenger carriages from the Western Australian, South African and Tasmanian systems.

Operations: Darling Range Tours depart Pinjarra station at 1100 Wednesdays from April to November, connecting with the 0930 *Australind* service from Perth. *Dwellingup Forest Ranger* trains run on selected Saturdays or Sundays between May and October, using diesel-hauled trains from Perth City station and double-headed

steam services between Pinjarra and Dwellingup. The round t takes 8 hours. The *Etmilyn Forest Railway* operates Tuesday, Thu day, Saturday and Sunday (and Monday public holidays) at 14 from Dwellingup railway station. Reservations are not necessary

Fares: Adult $8 and child $3.50 (add $1 for steam service betwe May and October). Journey time is 90 minutes and there are excelle picnic ground facilities at the station. First and tourist class far are available. *Etmilyn Forest Diner* departs Perth most Saturda and selected Fridays at 1800 and returns mid-night. All-inclusi cost for coach transfers, rail travel, 5-course dinner and fine servi is $60. The tour is limited to 40 passengers.

Location: Pinjarra is situated 80km south of Perth.

Public Transport: Daily Westrail *Australind* passenger trains. D coach tours operate from Perth in conjunction with the Etmil Forest Tramway.

Contact: GPO Box B73, Perth WA 6001
Travel Centre
2nd Floor, Commonwealth Bank
86 Barrack Street, Perth WA 6000

Bookings: Phone (08) 9221 4444; (08) 9421 1908; or
(08) 9531 1133; fax (08) 9221 3065

E-mail: hvtr@easymail.com.au

Home Page: www.iinet.com.au/~drsmith/hvrail.html

 RNE

OUTH - WEST

e southern corner of Western Australia was developed on
   wealth of its magnificent karri and jarrah forests, rich
ricultural lands and the coal deposits of Collie. Extensive
works of private timber railways, built to the *Government*
-6in (1067mm) gauge were constructed to haul logs to the
wmills and sawn timber to ports or interchange points with
WAGR system.

Today, the south-west has the largest and most diverse
tional economy in Western Australia based on timber,
riculture, mining and tourism. The timber industry and its
ociated railways offer many attractions for the tourist and
itor interested in the state's economic history.

nbury (population 28,500) is Western Australia's second city
owes its prosperity to its fine natural harbour. It is located 180km
th of Perth on Leschenault Estuary formed by the Collie and
ston Rivers. Established in 1836, the city is the economic and
ninistrative centre of the south, with surfing beaches, Land Back
rbour with its historic timber jetty, churches and museums.
urist Information: Bunbury Travel Centre (08) 9721 7922
                (at former railway station in Carmody Place).
avel: Westrail's *Australind* train services depart twice daily from
th, taking two hours for the 180km journey. By road, take South-
stern Highway and Route 1. *Westrail* coach services link other
th-west centres with the *Australind* at Bunbury.

llie (population 9,800) is Western Australia's main coal mining
a. It is an attractive town set in forest and agricultural country
h many fine public and commercial buildings. In the 1960s the
omotive depot here was one of the last strongholds of steam power.
ocomotive museum preserves this steam heritage.

sselton (population 12,650) 229km south of Perth, was the
ation for Western Australia's first locomotive-operated railway,
8km timber line, which opened in 1871. In 1895, Busselton was
nected to the WAGR rail network, via Boyanup. Passenger
vices ceased in 1957 and freight operations were closed in 1985.
blic transport is provided by *Westrail* and South West road
vices.
sselton Tourist Bureau: 22 Causeway Road
       Busselton WA 6280
       Phone: (08) 9752 1350

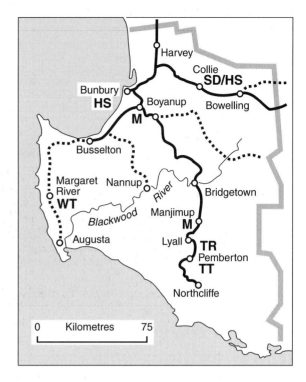

Margaret River (population 8000) 50km south of Busselton, is
an important wine growing area and popular tourist destination. A
section of the former Busselton-Augusta railway between Margaret
River and Cowaramup (12km) has been developed as a walking
and cycling trail.

Manjimup (population 4,000) 304km south of Perth, was the headquarters and workshops for the various timber railways operated by
the large sawmilling company of Bunning Brothers. It remains a
major woodchip traffic source for *Westrail*.

Pemberton (population 960) 40km south of Manjimup, is a timber town which has become a tourist base for some of the world's
finest timber stands conserved in National Parks. Local forests,
wineries, tourist railways and tramways are major features.
Karri Visitors Centre: Brockman Street.
          Phone: (08) 9776 1133 or 008 671 133

usselton Jetty Railway
usselton Jetty Management Committee

Tourist Railway (Diesel)
1067mm gauge

sselton became a major timber shipping port from 1909 based on its 2km long jetty. Closed as a port since 1973, Busselton
rives as an agricultural and tourism centre. Local enthusiasts have restored the jetty and a 1.5km tourist railway has been
mpleted along its length.

urist Train: A road-rail "locomotive" hauls four tourist carriages
the line. Passengers have spectacular views over Geographe Bay
Cape Naturaliste.

erations: Daily with hourly services between 1000 and 1700.
 Interpretative/Arts Centre will be constructed in 1999/2000.

Location: Queen Street, Busselton; 55km south west of Bunbury
(230km south of Perth).
Address: Hon Secretary
            Busselton Jetty Management Committee
            PO Box 851, Busselton WA 6280
Phone: (08) 9754 3689

Boyanup Museum of Transport and Rural Industries

Transport Museum

This widely acclaimed regional transport museum is located at Boyanup, the terminus of the first railway line from Bunb… in 1891. The transport museum, restoration and operating complex was opened at Boyanup, the original terminus of … isolated Government railway from Bunbury in 1985. It is home to the famous Vintage Train.

Features: The museum theme is transport and rural industry. It features a collection of vintage carriages (dating from 1897) which are housed in the former Bunbury goods shed and portion of the rebuilt Bunbury steam locomotive roundhouse. The museum also features rural wagons, trucks and a steam crane.

Locomotives: Operating diesel locomotives include ex-Midland Railway F40 (EE Aust, 1958) and JFK Engineering 4wDH (built 1972), which has been restored to operating condition as BM002 *Jardee*.

Rolling Stock: Historical passenger carriages built in the 1897-1912 period.

Opening Times: The museum is open daily from 1000 to 1600 year round. Tour trains operate over the Boyanup-Capel branch … on the first Sunday of the month. Bookings through museum.

Location: Adjacent to the South West Highway from Perth and Boyanup railway station, 18km south-east of Bunbury and 191… from Perth. Take Donnybrook Road from Bunbury.

Contact: Peter Goss, Boyanup Museum
PO Box 71, Boyanup WA 6237

Phone/fax: (08) 3731 5250

Collie Steam Locomotive Museum

Static Display

The Collie Tourist and Travel Bureau maintain a display of steam locomotives that once operated in the Collie district. … underground battery-electric mine locomotive is preserved at the Collie Rural Life Museum opposite the Tourist Informati… Office.

Locomotives: Ex-WAGR locomotives 4-8-0 Fs 452 (North British 1913), 4-8-2 W 943 (Beyer Peacock, 1952) and 2-8-2 V 1215 (Robt. Stephenson Hawthorne, 1956) and *Polly*, a former Aveling & Porter traction engine converted to a locomotive for use on Buckingham Bros. timber railways, are on display.

Opening Times: Monday to Friday, 0900-1700;
Saturday, Sunday and Public Holidays, 1000-1600.

Admission is free; please contact the Tourist Bureau.

Location: At the western entrance to Collie and junction of Coalfields Highway and Atkinson Street. Collie is 47km east… Bunbury.

Contact: Collie Tourist and Travel Bureau
Throssell Street, Collie WA 6225

Phone: (08) 9734 2051

Manjimup State Timber Museum

Industry Museum

Manjimup Shire Council / Bunnings Age of Steam Museum

The two museums and tourist bureau are located in Manjimup Timber Park. The Timber Museum tells the history of … timber industry and its steam-operated railways in Western Australia from inception to today. The theme follows pioneer… methods of felling and hauling logs, milling timber, home markets and export. This is achieved through displays of machine… tools, historic photographs and accompanying text.

Display: The Timber Park contains a hamlet of old buildings of the timber era. The Timber Museum features a 10m high Willamette steam log-hauler, while other notable items include two Robey horizontal 2-cylinder steam engines of 1896 and 1908 from saw mills, Bellis & Morcombe steam engine, Marshall stationary steam engine and blacksmith shop.

Railway Items: *Snorting Liz*, a unique locomotive converted from a Ransomes Sims & Jefferies steam traction engine for use on the Adelaide Timber Company line at Wilga, former State Saw Mills 2-6-0 steam locomotive (J Martin 127/1895, ex-SAR Y-class) and log bogies There is a collection of historical photographs, including prints from the John Steward collection.

Opening Times: 0900-1630 daily.

Admission: Adult $3, child/pensioner $1, family $7
- covers both museums.

Location: Rose Street in the central town area, Manjimup; 320… south of Perth.

Public Transport: Daily *Westrail* road coach services from P… Perth Terminal or Bunbury (connecting with *Australind* train).

Address: c/- Shire of Manjimup
PO Box 1, Manjimup WA 6258

Phone: (08) 9771 2111

HERITAGE ITEMS

Bunbury Railway Station: Bunbury station is a fine Federation Free classical Style building which complements the other important buildings of the gold boom period in Bunbury. The station is important for its architectural and townscape significance.

Collie Goods Shed: The goods shed is a demonstration of an industrial function now past as a result of the predominance of road transport. The form of the building is typical of the older goods sheds statewide consisting of a steeply pitched gable roof with a prominent vent at the Ridge.

Locomotive *Ballaarat*: Western Australia's pioneer steam locomotive, *Ballaarat*, is preserved in Victoria Square, Busselton. The

locomotive, built at the Victoria Foundry at Ballarat for the W… Australian Timber Company, is the oldest surviving Australian-b… locomotive. In 1994 it became the first item of moveable herita… registered in Western Australia.

Busselton Railway Station: relocated on the opposite side … the Vane River from its original site, the station is preserved … viewing and various uses.

Locomotive *Kate*: An early timber locomotive, *Kate* of 18… which was used on the MC Davies Karriedale line, previously p… served in Rotary Park, Margaret River, is undergoing restoration… Boyanup Museum to operating condition.

...mberton Tramway / Steam Railway
...mberton Tramway Company Pty Ltd

Tourist Railway (Steam/Tram)
1067mm gauge

DAVID WHITEFORD

The Pemberton - Northcliffe tourist tram on a journey through a section of scenic forest country.

...e scenic former 36km WAGR Pemberton-Northcliffe railway line, completed in 1933, was reopened as a tourist tramway ...1987. It offers a breathtaking ride through towering forest country south from Pemberton. The 21km section north from ...mberton to Lyall was leased to the Pemberton Tramway Company in 1995 for train operations. Steam trains operate over ...e historic railway from Easter to November.

...atures: Pemberton station and railway to Northcliffe, including ...dges, are listed by the National Trust for historical significance. ...e tram journey traverses one of Australia's most scenic rail lines ...d offers a comfortable means of viewing the trees and flowers ...th photo stops at the Cascades and Warren River. Tours offer an ...ormative commentary on the early timber and railway history of ... area. At Northcliffe, visitors can walk through the *Forest Park* ...d visit the Tourist Centre museum. Steam-hauled trains operate ...rth from Pemberton to Eastbrook and Lyall. This historic section ... railway was originally a State Saw Mills line completed in early ...14. Everything imaginable was transported on this railway. There ...s even a payroll robbery in 1925 between Collins Siding and ...ronhurst. In 1926, upgrading was completed and the line was ...en over by the Government Railways. In 1995 the Tramway Com-...ny was granted leasehold of the railway. The 1¾ and 3-hour return ...ps travel through beautiful forest and pasture, and the shorter trips ...n to the Eastbrook siding.

...amcars: Four light self-propelled 40-seat trams modelled on a ...07 Fremantle tram.
...comotives: The Company operates restored 2-8-2 steam locomotive ...213 (RSH 7782/1955), four Y-class Bo-Bo DE locomotives, ...m-Eng 0-6-0DH and Plymouth 4wDH (6129 of 1958) shunting ...comotives. State Saw Mills 2-6-0 No 7 (Martin 117/1895) is on ...tic display in the Mill Park, as part of the Pemberton Pioneer ...useum.
...olling Stock: Passenger stock is ex-WAGR suburban carriages of ...45 vintage. Cowans Sheldon 60-tone breakdown crane is in op-...ating condition. Various ex-WAGR freight wagons are also in use ...uling logs.

Operation - Tramway: 7 days/week, departing at 1045 and 1400 to Warren River, taking 1¾ hours for the round trip. Trips over the whole line to Northcliffe are available on Tuesday, Thursday and Saturday, departing at 1015 and return at 1545 (5½ hour round trip with five forest stops and stopover in Northcliffe). Group bookings are available to coaches, social clubs and tram hire parties.
Operation - Railway: Steam trains from Easter to November, departing Saturdays at 1030 and 1415, and Sundays at 1030. Extra services also operate during school holidays and long weekends. Various Driver courses are offered on steam or diesel locomotives.

Fares: Adults $13 to Warren River return, ($26 to Northcliffe return) for adults; child $6.50/$13; concession $12/24; family $36/66. Train trips $19.50 return to Eastbrook Siding; to Lyall $26 return. Child, student and senior concessions. A special combined tram and train ticket is available.

Location: At Pemberton, 340km south of Perth by South-Western Highway. The tramway is easily located by road by following signposts.
Public Transport: Daily *Westrail* road coach services from East Perth Terminal or Bunbury (connecting with *Australind* train).

Contact: Ian Willis, Manager, Pemberton Tramway Company Railway Crescent, Pemberton WA 6260
Phone: (08) 9776 1322; fax (08) 9777 1634

HEARTLANDS

Following the goldrush of the 1890's, the government sought to improve the colony's agricultural output by making land and financial assistance available for farming. Agriculture boomed and towns were established to service wheat farming areas. The government built new railway lines to wheat farming areas and between 1905 and 1918, more than 3200km of light lines were laid down in the new agricultural areas and a further 1310km between 1923 and 1933.

Agricultural production remains the mainstay of the region's economy. Railway activity in the region declined during the 1980s due to through working of trains from Avon Yard and seasonal operation of local district wheat lines. Rapid urban development in the Avon Valley towns of Northam and Tooday/York resulted in the introduction of rail commuter services (*AvonLink*) in 1996.

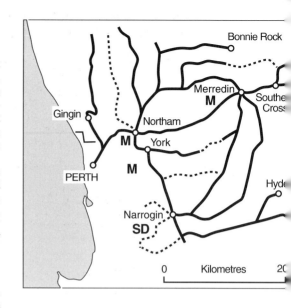

York (population 3200) is Western Australia's oldest inland town and became the first true inland rail terminus of the WAGR with the opening of the line from Guildford and Chidlow in 1885. York is classified as an historic town by the National Trust with many outstanding buildings dating from the 1840s. Although the town was overshadowed as a railway centre by nearby Northam, York remained an important depot station for the Great Southern Railway and Bruce Rock branch operations.
York Tourist Centre: 105 Avon Terrace.
Phone: (08) 9641 1301

Northam (population 10,500) in the Avon Valley, became an important railway town with the opening of the Eastern Goldfield Railway in 1886. The station in its present form was completed in 1900. The narrow gauge line and infrastructure became redundant with the construction of the standard gauge railway in 1966. The town has grown rapidly in recent years and regular *AvonLink* commuter rail services operate to Perth.
Northam Tourist Information Bureau: 138 Fitzgerald Street.
Phone: (08) 9622 2100

Narrogin (population 5600) is the commercial hub of a flourishing agricultural area 192km southeast of Perth on the Great Southern

Railway (GSR). The town became an important railway junction 1906 and expanded to one of the largest railway centres in West Australia, with six lines radiating from it to service wheat grow areas.

The town's railway heritage is remembered in a large muse collection in the Allen Street Memorial Park (off Kipling Street) pioneer XA-class 2-Do-2 diesel-electric locomotive No 1425 of 1950s and representative rolling stock are on static display.
Narrogin Information Centre: 23 Egerton Street.
Phone (08) 9881 2064

Merredin (population 3500) 265km east of Perth, is the centre a railway and wheat farming district which grew following establishment of a locomotive depot there in 1904. With the c struction of branch lines to service wheat areas, it subsequently came an important railway junction and its imposing station w built in 1923.
Merredin Tourist Centre: Barrack Street.
Phone (08) 9041 1666

York Railway Station & Railway Museum

Heritage Site/Museum

The imposing two-story stone, Victorian Gothic railway station (1885) was in WAGR use until 1987. The heritage-list building is on the Register of the National Estate.

Display: A museum of railway memorabilia with a scale model railway of the station and yard dating from the 1950s. Tea gardens operate at the complex.

Rolling Stock: Sleeping carriage AQZ 415 is the first of an intended larger display of rolling stock on the former flour mill sidings. Suburban carriage AYE 710 has been adapted as a tea room.

Opening Times: Saturday, Sunday and public holidays 1100-1600; admission free.

Location: 97km east of Perth; daily *Westrail* road services.

Contact: York Railway Station
York WA 6302
Phone: (08) 9641 1966

 RNE

Old Railway Station Museum, Northam
Northam Railway Preservation Group of WA (Inc)

Heritage Site/Museum
1067mm gauge

The heritage-listed station ex-WAGR building on the former narrow-gauge Eastern Goldfields Railway has been restored as a museum based on the railway and the history of the district.

Heritage Significance: The station building is architecturally significant, possessing Italianate decoration such as chimneys and eaves corbels and arts and crafts cum *Federation* influences such as timber worked gables. Also historically important as a reminder of effect in Northam.

Display: Railway operations form a large part of the displays, which include a HO gauge model railway.

Locomotives: Ex-WAGR Pmr-class 4-6-2 steam locomotive No 721 (NBL 26565/1950) on static display and Motor Rail Simplex 4wDM ex-Wundowie pig-iron foundry (operating condition).

Rolling Stock: A cross-section of WAGR narrow gauge rolling stock types, including 3 passenger carriages.

Opening Times: Sundays from 1000-1600;
public holidays 1300-1600 (except Christmas, New Year and Easter);
other times by appointment (08) 9622 2100.
Admission: Adults $2, children 50c, pensioners $1.
Location: 98km east of Perth.
Public Transport: daily *Avon Link* and *Prospector* rail services.

Contact: Jeffrey Pollard, Northam Railway Preservation Group
193 Wellington Street, Northam WA 6401
Phone: (08) 9622 2100

♿ RNE

Merredin Old Station Museum
Merredin Museum & Historical Society Inc

Heritage Site/Museum
1067mm gauge

Following the opening of the Perth-Kalgoorlie standard gauge railway, the narrow gauge line was closed in 1971 and the old railway station was to be demolished. The local historical society won the battle to keep four architecturally beautiful buildings intact and they were restored as a museum featuring local railway history.

Heritage Significance: The Merredin railway station represents an intact complex of railway structures, dating from 1890's to 1923, which formed the focus and catalysts for the development of the Merredin township. The buildings, with decorative elements in Federation *Queen Anne style*, have a high degree of integrity and are an uncommon example of this type. The complex includes the 1890s water tank and the prominent signal box which illustrates the period at which the Western Australian railway system reached its peak.

Features: The signal cabin, with 95 levers and steel stilts, is unique in Australia. It offers good views over Merredin township. Main collection areas are the railway history of the Merredin area, together with Merredin's social, agricultural, mining and war (1939-45) history. Charts depicting changes in the station buildings between 1906 and 1968 are on display and a signal gantry is preserved beside the signal box.
Locomotives: Ex-WAGR 4-6-0 steam locomotive G 117 (Dubs No 2501 of 1897) and diesel shunter TA 1808 (Tulloch 1970) on static display.
Rolling Stock: Various items of WAGR rolling stock from 1912 onward.

Opening Times: Open daily.
School days 0900-1200 and 1300-1430;
Weekends and public holidays 1000-1600.
Other times by appointment.

DAVID WHITEFORD

Merreden railway station museum is adjacent to operating narrow and standard gauge lines. Narrow gauge locomotive P 2001 is about to pass the museum with a grain train.

Admission: Adults $3, pensioners $2, children $1.
Phone 411 648 for appointments outside these hours.
Location: 240km east of Perth on the transcontinental railway and Great Eastern Highway.
Public Transport: Served by daily *Prospector* rail services.

Contact: Rosemary or Jim Lambert
PO Box 379, Merredin WA 6415
Phone: (08) 9041 2373; fax (08) 9041 2525

♿ RNE

GOLDFIELDS REGION

This huge region is steeped in the history of gold mining, grand Australian architecture and a rich heritage of early settlement. The discovery of gold at Coolgardie in 1892 and Kalgoorlie the following year brought prosperity and an influx of settlers to the west. To service the remote desert locations the Goldfields Railway was opened to Coolgardie in 1896, while the Goldfields Water Supply pipeline was constructed from the Darling Ranges near Perth during 1898-1902. The links bestowed permanence on Kalgoorlie and Boulder, which became recognised as the richest gold area in the world. An extensive system of private "Woodlines" brought firewood to power the mines and industries of Kalgoorlie. An isolated railway line serving the port of Esperance opened in 1910. It was extended to Norseman and Kalgoorlie in 1927, providing new prosperity for the town as a shipping outlet for the goldfields.

The region remains Australia's premier gold producer but other mining and agricultural activities are also important. Establishment of nickel mines at Kambalda in 1967 provided the rationale for conversion of the railway to standard gauge in 1974. The line now serves as an outlet for iron ore and nickel exports through the port of Esperance.

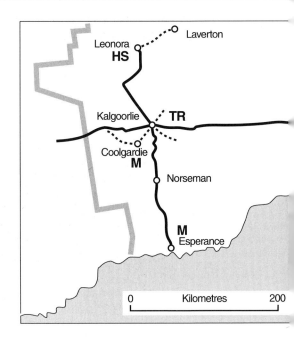

Kalgoorlie/Boulder (population 33,000) 600km east of Perth, is Australia's premier gold mining centre and a tourist base for the Goldfields Region. The city has developed into one of the State's premier regional centres with an arts centre, business park and university campus. Kalgoorlie is linked to Perth and Sydney by the standard gauge transcontinental railway and has developed as a regional transport hub for the north of the state. An electric tramway system operated until 1952. Tram No 3 is under restoration by the Kalgoorlie Museum. Local public transport services are operated by Goldlines Bus Service.
Getting There: Daily *Prospector* rail services from Perth, plus GSR's *Indian Pacific*. Westrail Goldfield Tours provide regular package holidays to Kalgoorlie and Coolgardie.

Coolgardie was once a boom gold mining town, with a populatic of 15,000 in 1898. The focus shifted to Kalgoorlie and Coolgard became a ghost-town, but is now enjoying a second gold-boom ar renaissance as a tourist destination. Some of the gold boom era ca be relived through the Goldfields Exhibition, the magnificent go ernment buildings and ghost suburbs.

Esperance (population 7500) is a flourishing commercial and tou ist centre on the southern Australian coast, 721km from Perth. It best known for its spectacular coastal scenery and national parks

HERITAGE ITEMS

Kalgoorlie Railway Station: The heritage-listed railway static of 1896 has been restored to its original style and character.

Gwalia Historical Museum Association Inc   *Museum*

The twin towns of Leonora and Gwalia were once linked by a street tramway. It was steam operated from 1903, then upgrade to electric traction in 1908. The electric tram was replaced by a petrol-powered vehicle in 1916 when fire destroyed th powerhouse. The Sons of Gwalia gold mine operated a 490mm (20inch) gauge railway to supply the mine with wood for fue The woodlines extended over an extensive area through the scrub south of the towns. Three locomotives hauled 30,000 tor of wood each year until the mine closed in 1963.

Displays: Fine examples of some 20 original miners camps, an old shop and boarding house, faithfully restored, are in the Gwalia Precinct, together with the former State Hotel, a grand two-storey building. Ex-Sons of Gwalia 0-6-2T steam locomotive *Ken* (Midland Works 1934), two woodline wagons, mining kibbles and hoppers are on static display under cover at the Museum. The body of the electric tramcar is also on display. The museum collection includes 1000 photographs and 2000 other items of days gone by.

Opening Times: Daily 1000-1600.
Admission: Adults $2. Visitors an also view the modern workings of the Sons of Gwalia Mine pit, now operating again underground since reopening in 1984.

Location: Tower Street, Gwalia; 237km north of Kalgoorlie. Leonora has two hotels, a motel and caravan park for accom modation.

Contact: Gwalia Historical Museum Association
               PO Box 111, Leonora WA 6638
Phone: (08) 9037 7210

 RNE

Golden Mile Loopline Railway, Boulder
Golden Mile Loopline Railway Society Inc

Tourist Railway (Diesel)
1067mm gauge

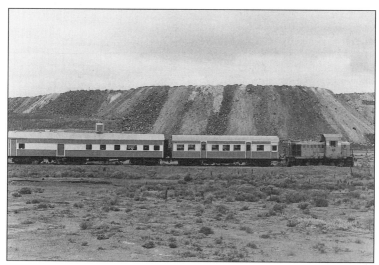

DAVID WHITEFORD

A Golden Mile Loopline Railway tourist train passing by the mullock heaps from the opencut mine workings near Kamballie.

This Society operates tourist trains over the 7km long Kalgoorlie-Boulder loop which served the rich gold mines. In the 1890's the loop line was Western Australia's busiest suburban line with over 60 steam-hauled mixed passenger and goods trains through Boulder station on weekdays. Action by a group of local rail enthusiasts in 1978 resulted in the line being retained as a tourist railway.

Operations: Trains operate along a horseshoe section of the original loop line from Boulder station out to the former township of Trafalgar before returning to Boulder, stopping at the Super Pit Lookout on the return trip. The trip takes about an hour. Passengers are provided with a full commentary of historical sites, rail and mining history along the route. The nearby Boulder station houses the Eastern Goldfields Historical Society museum, which has a large collection of rail and tram photos listed on computer and available for purchase. Steam trains are scheduled to operate on selected services from late 1999. A new line is planned from Golden Gate to the Hannans North Tourist Mine.

Locomotives: Ex-WAGR 0-6-0DH diesel locomotive B 1610 (Coming 1965), 0-6-0DM Z 1153. There are also Wickham trolleys. Ex-WAGR 4-6-0 G 233 (Martin 174/1898) is on lease from ARHS WA from late 1999.

Schedules: Trains depart at 1000 Monday-Saturday, 1000 and 1145 on Sundays, public holidays and school holidays. Functions for 20-

25 people may be booked for special Night Trains which offer a 3-course meal and hire of train for up to 5 hours ($32 per head), with fully licensed bar, dance floor and DJ music on board. Minimum booking period, 7 days in advance.

Fares: Adults $9, concession $7, children $5, family$25.

Location: Boulder City railway station, corner of Burt and Hamilton Streets; 5km from Kalgoorlie.

Public Transport: Goldlines Bus Services operate to Boulder half-hourly weekdays, every 40 mins Saturdays.

Contact:	Golden Mile Loopline Railway Society Inc
	PO Box 2024, Boulder WA 6432
Phone:	0407 387 883 for ticket office information
	Fax (08) 9093 3556

 RNE

Coolgardie Railway Station Museum

Local History Museum

Following the opening of the standard gauge railway from Perth to Kalgoorlie in 1968, the narrow gauge Eastern Goldfields Railway through Coolgardie was closed in 1971. The Railway Station, built 1896, was restored as a museum in 1990.

Heritage significance: This substantial building is historically significant in the way in which it reflects Coolgardie's development during the gold-mining era of the late nineteenth century. Architecturally, the station reflects well the characteristics of Western Australian railway buildings of the period.

Locomotive: Ex-WAGR 4-6-2 PMR 729 (NBL 26924/1950) is preserved at the station with a period train.

Display: The museum features local railway and mining history. There is a good collection of railway photographs

Opening Times: Daily except Friday from 0800-1630.

Location: Woodward Street, Coolgardie; 40km south-west of Kalgoorlie on the Great Eastern Highway.

Public Transport: *Westrail* operates daily *Prospector* rail services from Perth, connections via Bonnie Vale siding, 14km north of Coolgardie. Goldrush tours operate twice a week.

Contact:	Railway Station Museum
	Woodward Street, Coolgardie WA 6429
Phone:	(08) 9026 6388

  RNE

MID WEST REGION

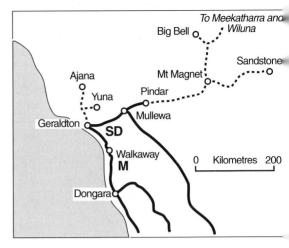

The vast region centred on Geraldton covers important agricultural and gold producing districts. Known to many as the 'wildflower region', this area is home to one of the world's finest collections of flowering plants.

Western Australia's first government railway opened from Geraldton to Northampton in July 1879 with a branch from Geraldton to Walkaway in 1887. To connect this isolated line with the Eastern Railway, a 446km private railway from Midland Junction to Walkaway was commenced in 1887 which opened as the **Midland Railway of Western Australia** in June 1895. The MRWA was the longest privately-owned common carrier railway in Australia and operated a fleet of fine American-pattern but British-built 4-6-2 and 2-8-2 steam locomotives. The line was dieselised in 1958.

The MRWA sold its assets to the WAGR in August 1964. New railways are under construction to service a steel-making complex at Geraldton.

Geraldton (population 35,000) 424km north of Perth, was established in 1849 and became the port for mining and agricultural industries. In the 1890s, Geraldton boomed through gold discoveries

in the Murchison Region and became increasingly important as supply and shipping centre for the pastoral and agricultural industries. Geraldton is the port and administration centre of the gold production, mining, fishing and agricultural industries of the Mid West Region and its renowned as a world leader in rock lobster fishing.

Walkaway Station Museum
Walkaway-Geraldton Historical Society

Local History Museum

The substantial WAGR railway station at Walkaway opened in 1887and is one of the oldest railway buildings in Western Australia. The station was closed in 1966. It has been preserved as a folk museum.

Displays: The museum contains a number of railway items, including Midland Railway Company records, photographs, railway lamps and literature on railways. There are goods sheds, cranes and a weighbridge.

Opening Times: 1000-1600 Tuesday to Friday;
1300-1600 Saturday and Sunday.

Admission: Adults $2, children 50c.

Location: 32km south-east of Geraldton.
Contact: Mrs K Criddle, Secretary
Walkaway-Geraldton Historical Society
Walkaway WA 6528
Phone: (08) 9926 1036

 RNE

HERITAGE ITEMS

Geraldton Railway Station: The original station building in Marine Terrace is of heritage significance as the first railway station in the State.

Geraldton Regional Museum: The Museum complex occupies two buildings on a waterfront site in Marine Terrace: the Old Railway Building and the Maritme Museum. The Regional Museum will be relocated to a purpose-built museum building at the marina by June 2000.

Gin Gin Railway Station: Opened in May 1891, this was one of the first railway stations built by the Midland Railway Company for its new line from Midland Junction to Walkaway.

The refreshment rooms, goods shed, crane and portion of the platform have been demolished, but the main station building still intact and marks one of the most significant events in the district.

Yalgoo Railway Station: For over 80 years (1896-1978) the stone railway station was of great importance to the town of Yalgoo and the surrounding district; first for transport linked with the mining industry and later for wool, being one of the main centres on the line between Geraldton and Meekatharra.

With the closure of the line the station buildings are disappearing and Yalgoo will probably be the only remaining example from this line.

GASCOYNE REGION

The Gascoyne region of is commonly referred to as the 'outback coast' – where the deep red soil meets the brilliant blue waters of the Indian Ocean. The region's economy is based on fishing, tourism and irrigated horticulture.

Tourism is the Region's fastest growing industry. The region has a number of unique tourist attractions including the Ningaloo Marine Park, a world heritage area at Shark

Bay and the world's largest monocline (single rock), Mount Augustus.

Carnarvon (population 7000), the service centre for the region, is isolated from the WAGR rail system. A 6km 1067mm gauge tramway which linked the township of Carnarvon with its jetty on Babbage Island was opened in 1909. The 1.6km jetty is claimed to be the longest in Australia.

Carnarvon Light Railway & Jetty Tramway
Carnarvon Light Railway Association Inc
Carnarvon Jetty Restoration Committee

Tourist Train (Steam/IC)
1067mm gauge

The original Public Works tramway, which linked the town of Carnarvon to the jetty, closed in 1965. The Carnarvon Light Railway Association has restored 5km of line between the Carnarvon Visitor's Centre and the jetty on Babbage Island to operating condition. The Jetty Restoration Committee has restored and maintains Carnarvon's famous jetty and associated railway, formerly operated by the Public Works Department. The jetty and tramway are listed on WA's State Register of Heritage Places.

Significance: The mile-long jetty at Carnarvon was the first major port established in the 1000km of Western Australian coastline between Cossack and Geraldton. It remains the longest timber jetty of its kind in Western Australia being a total length of 1660 metres. Construction began by the Department of Harbour and Lights in 1904 and extended in 1912. The timber structures are a unique example of engineering and workmanship at the turn of the century.

Train: A tourist train consisting of light carriages and a converted road vehicle takes passengers from the Babbage Island station to the end of the jetty. Fares: $4 for train; $2 for access to jetty. The steam train operates from the jetty back to the town.

Locomotive: Ex-Public Works 0-4-0T steam locomotive *Kimberley,* (A/Barclay 1754/1921). It worked on Carnarvon jetty until 1956 and was placed as a static exhibit until 1987 when the restoration project commenced. Two Simplex diesel locomotives are also in service.

Rolling Stock: 2 ex-WAGR AYE/AYF suburban carriages.

Operations: Thursday to Sunday, between April and October.

Display: Interpretative theme museums in the jetty precinct to tell

the history and culture of the region. The former jetty tramway operations are demonstrated through seven former wagons located on the area surrounding the old Public Works Department shed.

Facilities: A kiosk operating in an ex-WAGR carriage sells train tickets, a range of local souvenirs and refreshments. All proceeds are channeled to jetty restoration activities.

Location: Annear Place, Carnarvon. Carnarvon is 983km north of Perth on the Gascoyne River.

Public transport: Daily Greyhound and McCafferty bus services from Perth. Local Carnarvon bus service operates week-days on 'Hail and Ride' basis.

Contact:	Carnarvon Light Railway Association Inc
	PO Box 771, Carnarvon WA 6701
Phone:	(08) 9941 2173
Carnarvon District Tourist Bureau	
	Robinson Street, Carnarvon WA 6701
Phone:	(08) 9941 1146

 RNE

PILBARA / KIMBERLEY

Until the 1970s, railway operations were largely confined to jetty lines serving ports such as Onslow, Port Sampson, Broome, Derby and Wyndham. Cossack was the original port of the Pilbara Region and the centre of a pearling industry. A 2km 1067mm gauge horse-tramway opened in 1887 to connect the port with the town of Roebourne. It was converted to locomotive operation and operated for many years as an outpost of the WAGR system.

Subsequently, the development of huge mining operations in the Pilbara region brought the construction of modern, high capacity, 1435mm gauge iron ore railways.

Four lines:-

- **Hamersley Iron Ore Railways** (541km),
- **BHP Iron Ore Railroad,** (Port Hedland to Newman 426km),
- **BHP Iron Ore (Goldsworthy) Railway** (217km) lines, and
- **Robe River Railroad** (201km),

connect mines with shipping ports at Dampier, Port Hedland and Cape Lambert which operate some of the world's heaviest trains with 25,000 tonne payloads.

The Kimberley Region is becoming a popular tourist destination for its spectacular outback landscapes, particularly the Hamersley Range National Park, the Bungle Bungles, Mitchell Plateau and the gorges of the Fitzroy Crossing district.

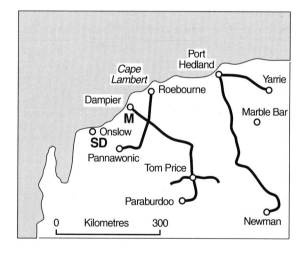

Port Hedland (population 18,000) located 1600km north of Perth, is the thriving capital of the Pilbra Region. Once a port for the fledging pearling and pastoral industries, the town is now the Pilbara's international gateway and Australia's largest iron ore port.

Broome (population 10,500) located 2436km north of Perth, originally established as a pearling port, has become an international tourist resort as the gateway to Australia's last frontier of pristine wilderness - the Kimberley.

6 Mile Railway Museum, Dampier
Pilbara Railways Historical Society

Museum/Mainline Tours
1435 mm gauge

The Museum is home to the locomotives that built the iron ore industry in the Pilbara. Its collection comprises locomotive and rolling stock of all the mining railways in the area, past and present.

Locomotives: The Society's pride is former UK Great Western Railway 4-6-0 steam locomotive *Pendennis Castle*, built at Swindon in 1924. It was imported in – to operate tour trains over Pilbara standard gauge lines. The locomotive is currently a static exhibit. The museum also features a diverse collection of diesel locomotives: pioneer NSW Railways Alco AIA-AIA DE No 4002 (built MLW 1951), subsequently No 9405 on the Robe River Railroad; ex-Hamersley Iron 007, an Alco S-2 built in 1940 for the Spokane, Portland & Seattle Railway in USA; Mount Newman 5450, an EMD F7A unit built in 1951 for the US Western Pacific Railway; BHP Iron 5502 (Alco M636 of 1976); ex-Goldsworthy Railway No H1 (English Electric B-class, 1965); and Hamersley Alco M636 3017 (rebuilt to C636R by Com-Eng 1983). Hamersley Iron 1000, an Alco C415 centre-cab (built 1966 as a demonstrator unit) is also in the Society's care.

Rolling Stock: Four ex-NSWGR FS sitting carriages, KBY luggage van and two ex-WAGR sleeping coaches. Some 1067mm gauge rolling stock from the Point Samson jetty rail system - two small

diesel locomotives, each with a "train" of rolling stock - has recently been acquired by the museum.

Operations: Museum open Sundays 0900-1200 and 1630-183 Wednesdays, or by appointment. Passenger trains are operated during the tourist season by the Society over the Hamersley Iron Railway, generally on a weekend.

Notes: The former Dampier Jail has been restored as a souvenir shop.

Location: "6-Mile", just outside the town of Dampier on the Hamersley Railway.

Contact: Wayne Carman, Pilbara Railway Historical Society
         PO Box 412, Karratha WA 6714
Phone: (08) 9143 6468
Home Page: www.holiday-wa.net/loco.htm

HERITAGE ITEMS

Broome Historical Society Museum: The former rail depot, including passenger and goods platforms, is being developed as an outdoor display area. Preserved railway items include a 4-wheel wagon of 1880 and a 4-wheel passenger carriage. The museum is located in the old Customs House adjacent to the former PWD rail depot.

Hamersley Iron 7-Mile Complex: Pioneer HI railway locomotive No 2000 is on static display at the complex.

Onslow Shire Council: The former north-west port of Onslow had a 1067mm gauge railway from the jetty to the town operated by the Public Works Department. State ships ceased calling at Onslow in 1972 and the railway was closed. The goods shed and rolling stock at the former railway depot have been preserved as a museum. A train consisting of a 0-4-0 petrol locomotive (Andrew Barclay 3202/1928), 4-wheel low-side wagon and 4-wheel passenger brake van is on static display.

Port Hedland BHP Complex: Mount Newman locomotive 549 is on static display.

Port Hedland Park: In the Rhodes open air collection are three diesel-electric locomotives from iron ore railways are on static display: ex-Goldsworthy Railway Bo-Bo H2; and ex-Mount Newman 5451 and 5497 and a few relics of the WAGR line to Marble Bar.

Port Samson: A small stub of the former Public Works jetty remains with two 4-wheel H-type wagons preserved as a monument to the jetty and depot.

Wyndham Jetty Railway: Preserved locomotives and rolling stock from the Wyndham railway maintain the heritage of the jetty railways which once operated in the North West. A Hudswell Clark 0-6-0ST steam locomotive of 1891, a small diesel locomotive built by Commonwealth Engineering, 1912 Ironside *New Century* petrol locomotive, a 4-wheel crane, a steam crane and wagons are on display.

NORTHERN TERRITORY

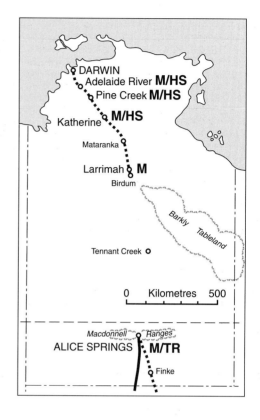

The Northern Territory occupies a vast land mass but has a population of only 170,000. It is most known for its two main geographical attractions; Kakadu National Park in the Top End and Ayers Rock (Uluru-Kata Tjuta National Park) in Central Australia.

The Great Northern Railway was proposed as a transcontinental line from Adelaide. The first section of the 1067mm gauge line opened from Port Augusta to Farina in 1882, but it did not reach Alice Springs until 1929. Construction from Darwin (then Palmerston) commenced in 1886 and opened to the mining settlement of Pine Creek (234km) in 1889. Later, under Commonwealth control, the line was extended in stages to Birdum, 504km from Darwin, where the vision of a northern transcontinental railway petered out.

The NAR saw frenzied activity as Australia's *Front Line Railway* between 1939 and 1945. The vintage steam locomotives were worn out at War's end and diesels took over in 1954. The NAR gained a new lease of life through iron ore export traffic from 1967. Following the destruction by Cyclone *Tracy* on Christmas Day 1974, the NAR was wound down and closed on 30 June 1976.

The narrow-gauge line from Marree to Alice Springs was replaced by a new standard gauge line from Tarcoola in 1980. Redevelopment of the Port of Darwin and construction of a standard gauge line to Alice Springs commenced in 1999.

The heritage of the North Australia Railway is preserved in a number of museums along its route. A section of the NAR line, including a small bridge, has been left in situ, about 5km south of Darwin, to serve "as a reminder to the Territory's engineering heritage".

Darwin (population 98,000) is the administrative centre for the Northern Territory. Since 1974 when it was levelled by Cyclone *Tracey*, Darwin has been remodelled as the ideal tropical capital, with wide tree-lined streets, inviting public buildings and hectares of landscaped parkland. Today, Darwin serves as a base for international visitors to the wetlands of the north, especially the Kakadu National Park.

Alice Springs (population 25,000), the major town of Central Australia, owes its foundation to the Overland Telegraph which arrived in 1872. Today it serves as the tourist hub of a truly magical part of Central Australia.

Tourist Information: Northern Territory Tourist Bureau
Tourism House, 43 Mitchell Street
Darwin NT 0800
Phone: (08) 8999 3900

HERITAGE ITEMS (Register of the National Estate)

Adelaide River Railway Station: This railway station, dating from 1888, was one of the earliest stations built on the North Australian Railway. It was the only one with a refreshment room and the station also played a strategic role during Second World War troop and supply movements. The station building, with its late nineteenth-century design, its scale and its form makes a notable aesthetic contribution to the Adelaide River townscape. The station has now been restored and is maintained by the National Trust of Australia (NT) and by its tenants.

Adelaide River Railway Bridge: Built in 1888, the steel lattice girder bridge, 155 metres long, is the largest on the Darwin to Pine Creek section of the former North Australia railway. The bridge is regarded as a superb example of late nineteenth century engineering in an isolated location.

Katherine Railway Bridge: The bridge, the longest on the Northern Territory Railway, was first crossed on 21 January 1926. It is a "through girder" type, patterned on a bridge at Penrith, NSW. The seven 30.5 metre length plate girder spans were manufactured at the State Dockyard, Walsh Bay, NSW. The bridge is significant for the place it has in the development of a mode of transportation in the Northern Territory; and for its role as a transport artery during the Second World War.

Pine Creek Railway Precinct
National Trust

Local History Museum

Pine Creek served as the terminus of the NAR from 1889 until 1914. The precinct contains the station (built 1888), railwa~ and associated structures.

Heritage significance: Pine Creek's railway precinct is historically important for its direct association with the construction of the North Australia Railway and the role that rail played in the Territory's development over a lengthy period. The precinct is the most complete of the surviving NAR installations and exemplifies the types of infrastructure built for the line.
Features: The historic precinct comprises the railway station, station master's residence, goods shed, crane and rail sidings. Museum displays feature the NAR, mining, World War II memorabilia, Chinese and Aboriginal culture and local history.
Locomotives and Rolling Stock: Former NAR 2-6-0 NF-5 (BP 1717/1877), which carries the plates from NF-2; CR carriage (NABP 13) and water tank wagon are displayed under cover. The diminutive NF-class locomotives handled mainline work until the

Second World War. A sister engine NF-6 was blown into Darwi~ harbour by Japanese bombing in 1942, where it still rests.
Location: Main Terrace, Pine Creek, 220km south of Darwin o~ Stuart Highway. McCafferty's and Greyhound/Pioneer provid~ regular bus services. Phone: (08) 8976 1254
Opening Times: Daily, April-October 0800-1500
                                              October-April 0800-1200
Admission: Adults $2, children/National Trust members free.
Contact: National Trust
                      GPO Box 3520, Darwin NT 801
Phone: (08) 8981 2848

 RNE

Katherine Railway Station Museum
National Trust

Local History Museum

The station was constructed in 1926 with the extension of the railway from Pine Creek. It was one of the first, if not the firs~ building to be constructed in Katherine. The building is unique in that its prefabricated construction in reinforced concret~ using traditional forms was the only use made on the North Australian Railway of this medium and to this design. A sectio~ of the North Australian RailTrail opreates from the museum to the high-level bridge.

Exhibits: Displays depict the railway history and the effect the military build-up had on Katherine. 2-6-0 locomotive Nfb-88 (Martin 37/1892), with rolling stock and a locomotive water tank, is on display at the Museum.
Opening Times: 1000-1400 Monday to Friday
                                      (closed Saturday and Sunday).
Admission: Adults $2, children/National Trust members free.
Location: Railway Terrace, Katherine.
                      310km south of Darwin on Stuart Highway.

Phone: (08) 8972 1833
Public Transport: McCafferty's and Greyhound/Pioneer provid~ regular bus services.
Contact: National Trust
                      GPO Box 3520, Darwin NT 0801
Phone: (08) 8981 2848, or
Katherine Regional Tourism: Phone (08) 8972 2650

RNE

The Old Ghan
Ghan Preservation Society

Tourist Railway (Steam/Diesel)
1067mm gauge

With the opening of the standard gauge railway to Alice Springs, the Ghan Preservation Society was formed to acquire 30km o~ the former 1067mm gauge Central Australia Railway for a tourist train. The $7 million project was opened in December 1988

Features: A 1920s style railway station - named Stuart - has been constructed at Macdonnell with museum, tea rooms and ticket office. There are also locomotive sheds, barbecue and picnic areas. The old telegraph line between Macdonnell and Ewaninga (opened 1872) has also been restored to operating condition.
   The museum features a collection of locomotives, carriages and rolling stock, plus a variety of railway paraphernalia and historic photographs which tell the story of the line from the start of construction in 1877 to closure in 1980.
Locomotives: Operational are ex-WAGR 4-8-2, W 924 (BP 7401/ 1951), ex-QR B-B DH DH.14 (Walkers 596/1969) and ex-NAR NSU 58 A1A-A1A DE locomotive of 1954. Ex-QGR C17-class 4-8-0 No 967 (Walkers 504/1950) and NSU 53 are on static display (latter on Stuart Highway opposite Norris Bell intersection).
Rolling Stock: Eight items of passenger rolling stock formerly used on the Commonwealth Railways, including two dining cars.
Operations: Trains operate between April and end of October. Departs Macdonnell at 1000 on Wednesday-Friday and Sunday with additional services June-September. Steam trains on first weekend of June, July, August and September. Refreshments are served on trains, while the Ewaninga tour includes a barbecue lunch.
   An evening dining service also operates Friday nights all year

round (check with the Society for departure times). Bookings ar~ essential and charters welcome.
Contact: The Society or Tourist Centre, Alice Springs
                      Phone (08) 8952 5199
Fares: $15 adult, $8 child. Group discounts available.
Museum Open: 0900-1700 daily. Closed Christmas holidays.
Admission: Adults $4, children $2.
Old Ghan bookings through NT Government Tourist Bureau.
Phone (08) 8952 1299; Fax (08) 8952 7404
Location: At Macdonnell Siding, Norris Bell Avenue, off Stua~ Highway, 10km south of Alice Springs.
Public Transport: The *Alice Wanderer* bus service calls a~ MacDonnell Siding regularly throughout the day.
Phone (08) 8953 0310.
ASR operates one of Australia's top luxury trains, *The Ghan*, t~ Alice Springs.
Contact: Ghan Preservation Society
                      Norris Bell Avenue, Alice Springs NT 0871
Phone: (08) 8955 5047; Facsimile (08) 8955 5220

QUEENSLAND

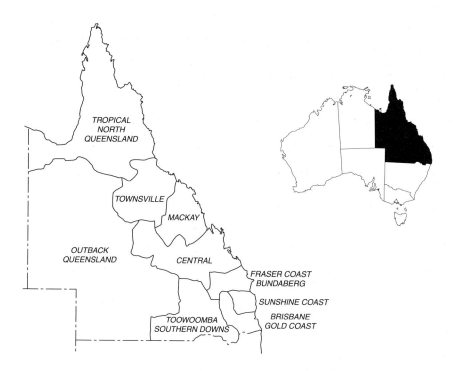

QUEENSLAND is the most decentralised of the Australian States and its railway system developed as separate regional systems connecting the vast interland with coastal ports. The vast distances demanded low-cost railways and the system was built to narrow (1067mm) gauge with light engineering works and small locomotives.

In addition the government railway system, sugar millers in coastal regions established an extensive system of 610mm gauge railways to haul cane to the mills. These cane railways added further character to the Queensland railway scene, particularly in the steam era when small tank locomotives hauled hand-harvested cane during the crushing season, between June and December.

Since the 1960s, the railways have been upgraded for heavy coal and mineral haulage, with extensive electrification, track realignment, new bridges and modern signalling and communications systems. Queensland Rail (QR) now operates Australia's largest rail network (over 10,000km) and hauls the largest volume of freight.

Preserved railways and tramways in Queensland reflects the regional structure of the State, with heritage operations in most of the major coastal cities. However, most operations are restricted to week-end running, in many cases only one Sunday a month.

The best-known tourist trains operate over the spectacular Cairns-Kuranda line in the Far North, while this region also boasts the steam-operated Atherton-Herberton Railway over the scenic Herberton Range. This operates Wednesday to Sundays. There are several other interesting heritage railway operations in the Far North, including the famous *Gulflander* train between Normanton and Croydon.

Central Queensland offers the newly-opened **Archer Park Railway Station Museum** with its unique Purrey steam tram and the **Dee River Railway** at Mount Morgan, which takes visitors on a tour over a section of the former QR line to this remarkable gold-mining town. In the Wide Bay/Burnett Region, the **Mary Valley Heritage Railway** at Gympie operates over a scenic 41km line through the Mary Valley, while cane railway enthusiasts can experience narrow gauge steam every Sunday on the **Bundaberg Botanic Gardens Railway**. Closer to Brisbane, on the Sunshine Coast, the Durundur Railway at Woodford also offers narrow gauge steam trains on Sundays.

Ipswich offers a remarkable range of railway heritage, and steam enthusiasts can experience the flavour of QR branch line operations of the 1920s on the **Swanbank Railway** (first Sunday of the month) or the **Rosewood Railway Museum** (last Sunday). The former Ipswich Railway Workshops are being developed into a world-class railway heritage centre. Finally, the **Brisbane Tramway Museum** at Ferny Grove operates well-presented vintage trams each Sunday.

MAINLINE TOURS

QR Heritage Trains
QR TravelTrain/Heritage Branch

Heritage Tours (Steam)
1067mm gauge

SHANE O'NEIL

Restored QGR Garratt steam locomotive No 1009 departing Stanthorpe with an Up tourist passenger on 27 August 1998.

Queensland Rail maintains and restores steam locomotives and wooden carriages for special operations.

Rolling Stock: A significant fleet of wooden carriages is preserved for mainline operations. Most of the carriages are based in Brisbane, with others relocated at Rockhampton.

Steam Locomotives: An ongoing program of restoration of steam locomotives commenced with the restoration of DD17 locomotive No 1051. At present, the operating fleet comprises:
- A10-class 0-4-2 No 6, (Neilson 1170/1865), the oldest working locomotive in Australia and one of the oldest in the world;
- C17-class 4-8-0 No 974 (Walkers 511/1951);
- DD17-class 4-6-4T No 1051 (Ipswich 210/1952);
- Beyer Garratt 4-8-2+2-8-4 No 1009 (BP 7349/1950); and
- BB18¼ class 4-6-2 No 1079 (Walkers 547/1956).

Undergoing restoration in Ipswich Workshops are:
- A10-class 0-4-2 No 3 (Neilson 1214/1866);
- AC16 2-8-2 No 222A (Baldwin);

- BB18$^1/_4$ No 1089 (Walkers 557/1958), the last mainlir locomotive built in Australia;

Locomotives scheduled for restoration are:
- PB15 4-6-0 No 732 (Walkers 378/1926);
- C17 4-8-0 No 1000 (Walkers 537/1953).

Operations: Regular steam-hauled charter trains are operated from Brisbane's Roma Street station by Sunshine Rail Express Tour Trainaway Tours and Suntours (see below). Diesel-hauled train with heritage rolling stock also operate in Central Queensland from Rockhampton and Gladstone.

QR Heritage Activities: QR has established a Heritage Unit, so up a Historical Centre at Ipswich and is providing training an support to its own QR Heritage Volunteers, who are active acros the State. QR has a full-time Heritage Volunteers Coordinator, wh may be contacted on (07) 3235 1140.

SunSteam Inc

SunSteam is a non-profit volunteer association with an interest in Queensland railway heritage. Its main activity is the opera tion of tours throughout the Queensland rail network. It was formed in 1992 and since 1993, it has operated an average of eight tours a year to various locations in south-east Queensland. *SunSteam* is a corporate member of the QR volunteer grou assisting with minor maintenance of rolling stock, tours, etc.

Tours: *SunSteam* operates competitively priced tours to suit the family. Tours utilise the QR heritage fleet and operate to Toowoomba, Laidley and Yandina as part of the regular itinerary. The group maintains a free mailing list to give regular supporters advanced notice of tours. *SunSteam* also runs special charter trips for companies and individuals including wedding parties.

Location: Most trains depart from Brisbane's Roma Street static and most tours have suburban pick up points.

Bookings and Inquiries: The Secretary, SunSteam Inc
GPO Box 3155, Brisbane QLD 4001
Home Page: http://www.sunsteam.org.au/

Sunshine Express Rail Tours
Australian Railway Historical Society (Qld Division)

Mainline Steam/Diesel Tours
1067mm gauge

The Queensland Division of the ARHS operates steam-hauled heritage train tours to various destinations in the state.

Trains: Regular tours using steam and diesel locomotives and heritage carriages chartered from the QR (see above).

Operations: Steam-hauled tours operate over the QR network usually on a monthly basis with additional excursions for special events. Destinations vary but are mainly contained in the area bounded by Gympie in the north and Toowoomba in the west as well as the suburban system. Special half-day tours with family fares are run several times a year. Charters for groups, societies or corporations are also arranged at reasonable rates.

Iron Road Restaurant: The ARHS (Qld Division) also operates evening dinner tours around the Brisbane suburban network. The tours, which operate under the trading name of *Iron Road Restaurant,* normally run on a Friday or Saturday evening and patrons are served a four-course meal in a wooden dining car in the style of the 1930s while viewing the *City Lights.*

Location: Trains depart from Brisbane's Roma Street station and most tours have suburban pick up points.

Bookings and Inquiries: (07) 3371 4231 1000-1500 Tuesday to Friday or fax (07) 3217 7321. A recorded information service operates outside these times.

By mail, PO Box 1119, Toowong QLD 4066

Office: The Society office at 39 Bayliss Street, Auchenflower (Auchenflower Bowls Club) is open 1000-1500 Tuesday to Friday.

Other: The *Ken Rogers Memorial Library* (same address) is open on the first and third Sundays of the month from 1000-1530.

Trainaway Tours

Trainaway Tours was formed in 1983 to organise tours for people who enjoy train travel. Rail excursions mainly use railcars hired from QR, while coach tours to closed railways and other points of railway interest are also provided. Group members have helped restore QR railcar 901. From time to time, interstate and overseas tours using scheduled railways and visiting preserved railways.

Operations: About six tours are run each year.

Location: Most trains depart from Brisbane's Roma Street station.

Bookings and Inquiries: Trainaway Tours
PO Box 1346
Toowong QLD 4066
Phone: (07) 3390 4209
Fax: (07) 3899 2784

BRISBANE / GOLD COAST REGION

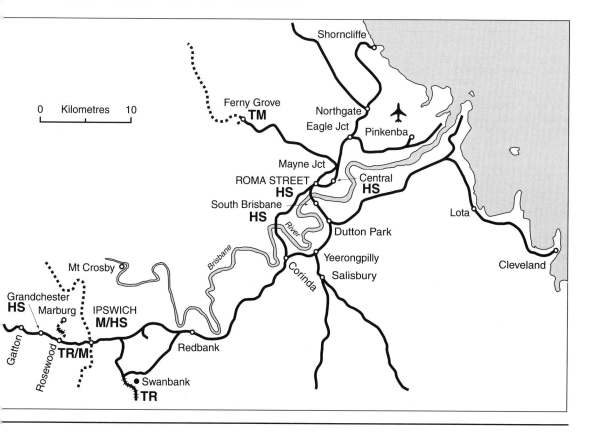

Brisbane and the Gold Coast are Australia's fastest growing urban regions. Ipswich was the birthplace of the Queensland Railways with the first line from Ipswich to Grandchester in 1865 and extended to Toowoomba on 1 May 1867. The main Western Line from Brisbane to Toowoomba (162km) involves heavy grades and curves to climb the Little Liverpool and Main Ranges which have been a significant constraint to railway operations, particularly during the steam era.

Brisbane (population 1.4 million) is the centre of one of Australia's fastest growing urban regions. The South Bank Parklands complex has become a focus for visitors and residents with its riverbank promenade, cafes, restaurants and events. It adjoins the Queensland Cultural Centre, which includes one of Australia's finest art galleries, the Performing Arts Complex, the Queensland Museum and State Library.

Gold Coast City (population 500,000) is part of Australia's fastest growing area. It is a major tourist destination with fine surfing beaches and resorts.

Ipswich (population 130,000) 43km west of Brisbane, was founded in 1827 as a convict out-station. Coal mining provided the impetus for its early development and Queensland's main railway workshops have been located here. Ipswich is the *Heritage City* of South-East Queensland and railways are a major feature of the city's ric heritage.

Tourist Information: Regional Tourist Information Centre
Cnr Brisbane Street and d'Arcy Doyle Place
Ipswich QLD 4305
Phone: (07) 3281 0555; Facsimile (07) 3281 0555

CityTrain: Modern electric suburban trains operate over a 220kr network, comprising 6 lines and 136 stations. Services are oper ated by modern air-conditioned electric trains and a range of ticke are available, including *Day Rover* and Multi-trip tickets. Fas interurban electric trains operate to Nambour, 105km north of Bris bane Central and south to Robinvale on the Gold Coast.

Steam locomotives operate special excursion trains over th sections of the suburban network during selected periods (e.g., pric to Christmas).
Train Information: Suburban 13 1230

Brisbane Buses: Brisbane City Council operates an extensiv system of suburban bus services. *CityXpress* services operate fron the City underground bus station. Normal stage services radia from the city, with many routes (eg, 170-178) following forme tram lines.

A combined QR/BCC day rover ticket, *ROVERLINK*, is avai able from railway stations and BCC ticket agencies for $7 adul and $3.50 concession.

North Ipswich Railway Technology Centre
Queensland Railways

Railway Museum/Steam Centre
1067mm Gauge

Part of the North Ipswich Railway Workshop site is being developed as a railway museum and steam locomotive depot. I will include a depot for the restoration and maintenance of steam locomotives, a station for steam train excursions an displays of rail equipment and technology.

Heritage Significance: A railway workshop facility has existed at North Ipswich on railway reserve land since the inception of Queensland Railways in 1864. The heritage-listed buildings in North Street were constructed from 1900 and offer an outstanding example of industrial architecture. The workshops are important as an example of an early 20th Century railway workshop which was regarded in its time as a model for the smaller decentralised workshops throughout Queensland. The place is important for its strong association with the industrial economy of Ipswich and Queensland, and for supplying rolling stock and locomotives used throughout Queensland. The workshops built 210 steam locomotives and numerous carriages for the QR. It also possesses what is believed to be the last operating carriage/locomotive traverser in eastern Australia.
Australian Railway Technology Centre: The Queensland Government has committed $20 million to preserve the cultural significance of the North Ipswich complex. A contract has been let for the commercial development of the site, including a museum and operating depot for QR steam locomotives.

(See QR Heritage Trains).
Railway Historical Centre, The Terrace, North Ipswich, is locate in the sole remaining building of the original railway workshop The fine Victorian era brick and stone warehouse style buildin was built in 1878 as a store which is now being developed as a integrated facility incorporating the QR Archives and a Museum The Centre houses the QR Archives containing railway document drawings and the historical photographic collection.

The Archives are open to the public by appointment betwee 1000-1600, Mondays to Fridays.
Phone: (07) 3280 5440
E-mail: historical.centre@qr.com.au
Location: The Terrace, North Ipswich, approx 1km north (10 minute walk) of Ipswich Railway station across the Brisbane River. A loc bus service is available from the Transit Centre. Parking is avai able adjacent to the premises.
Contact: Graham Wilson, Heritage Coordinator, Traveltrain.
Phone: (07) 3235 3212

St Helena Island Tourist Tramway
Rotary Club of Wynnum-Manly/National Parks & Wildlife

Tourist Railway (Diesel
610mm gauge

St Helena island in Moreton Bay operated as a penal colony from 1867 to 1933. A horse-powered tramway operated on th island during this era. The island is now a national park with day tours available to explore the history of the heritage-liste penal complex. A 1km tourist railway operates from the causeway to take visitors to the heritage area.

Locomotives: Baguley 0-6-0DM (3377 of 1953), formerly No 1 at Mulgrave Sugar Mill in North Queensland. 12 passenger cars equipped with public address system.
Display: Models of the penal complex featuring the tramway, as well as a preserved convict-powered rail car are displayed at the heritage area.

Operations: Guided tours with ferry to island, train trip and vis to ruins operate daily from for 5 hours duration. Day trip ticke $30 adult, including contribution to National Park developmen Discounts for group booking.
Bookings: For sailing times and reservations, contact St Heler Island Conducted Tours & Ferries; Phone (07) 3396 3994

 RNE

Brisbane Tramway Museum, Ferny Grove
Brisbane Tramway Museum Society

Tram Museum (Electric)
1435mm gauge

R F McKILLOP

Drop-centre Brisbane City Council tram 341 approaches the bottom terminus while four-motor tram 429 awaits its turn of duty.

Brisbane's first horse-drawn trams commenced in 1885 and electric trams were introduced in 1897. The tramways were taken over by the Brisbane City Council in 1925 and new routes were constructed. By 1940, the system had over 100km of lines and modern tramcars were being introduced. A major fire in the Paddington Tram Depot in 1962 destroyed 65 trams, and the BCC began to close tram lines. The last trams ran on 13 April 1969. The Brisbane Tramway Museum has established an operating electric tramway to preserve items from the Brisbane tramway fleet.

Trams: The museum holds 24 trams and 2 trolley buses which formerly operated on the Brisbane City Council network. Among the different types of trams preserved by the Society are a horse tram, Californian combination of 1901, ten-bench toastrack, *Dreadnought*, drop-centre and modern four-motor trams, including one of the eight *Phoenix* trams built in 1964. There are five trams in regular operation.

Operations: Open Sundays from 1230-1600, except in wet weather. Four trams are regularly operated and entry covers up to five rides on different trams with commentary on the history of each vehicle. Regular tours of the museum are also conducted. Trackwork at the museum is located in mass concrete, a form of construction pioneered by the Brisbane Tramways.

Entry: Adults $5; concession $4; children$2.50.
Facilities: Souvenir shop and display, light refreshments, toilets and picnic facilities.
Location: at Ferny Grove, a northern Brisbane suburb (terminus of a suburban electric railway line).
Public Transport: *CityTrain* services to Ferny Grove: the museum is a 10 minute walk along Arbor Street, then to Tramway Street (500 metres).
Address: Brisbane Tramway Museum Society
20 Tramway Street (PO Box 94)
Ferny Grove Qld 4055
Phone: (07) 3351 1776 for information

Dreamworld Gold Coast Railway, Coomera
Dreamworld Pty Limited

Tourist Park Railway (Steam)
610mm gauge

Dreamworld is an Australian family entertainment park set in bushland with ten distinctively themed areas. The Park features a variety of rides, shows and attractions, including the steam- operated 3km narrow gauge Dreamworld Gold Coast Railway.

Locomotives: Two restored ex-canefield steam locomotives: Perry Engineering 0-6-2T of 1951, ex-Bingera sugar mill and Baldwin 4-6-0 (45215/1917), ex- Racecourse sugar mill. A small 0-4-OT locomotive (John Fowler 16249/1923) which once operated at the nearby Rocky Point sugar mill is on static display.

Operation: Dreamworld operates seven days a week 1000-1700 (closed Christmas Day and half-Anzac Day). Steam trains operate each day with regular services to the four stations in the park.

Admission: Adults $44 and children $26 which includes all rides, shows and attractions; check on phone 1800 073 300 for details.

Location: Situated at Coomera on the Pacific Highway, 17km north of the Gold Coast and 48 km south of Brisbane.
Public Transport: Coomera is serviced by regular electric train services from Brisbane with courtesy buses to Dreamwodd.
Contact: Len Shaw, Dreamworld Parkway
Coomera OLD 4209
Phone: (07) 5588 1111; fax: (07) 5588 1110
Website: www.dreamworld.com.au

Swanbank Railway, Ipswich
Queensland Pioneer Steam Railway Co-operative

Tourist Railway (Steam)
1067mm gauge

BILL BLANNIN

Ex-QGR PB15-class locomotive No 448 with a tour train at the Swanbank Railway, Ipswich.

The Society operates steam trains with vintage rolling stock over 7km of the Swanbank branch line, near Ipswich. The line was built in 1897 to serve coal mines. It was reconditioned and extended to serve the Swanbank power station in 1975. The QPSR established a depot at Box Flat and commenced regular operations over the line by 1982. Heritage operations share the line with QR trains bringing Darling Downs coal to the power station.

Features: Typical Queensland branch line working in the first half of the century together with a collection of rolling stock provides an experience of QR operations in this era. A program of restoration of the Society's rolling stock together with the enlargement of and improvements to the depot at Box Flat is also continuing.

Locomotives: Ex-QGR PB15 4-6-0 No 448 (Walkers 93 of 1908, and *Kilrie* an 0-4-2T built by Perry Engineering in 1925 for industrial service; with ex-QR 1600-class branch line diesel-electric locomotive 1616 as back-up. There is also a 600v DC electric locomotive that formerly hauled coal trains from Murrarie to Gibson Island power station in Brisbane.

Rolling Stock: End-platform and side-loading ("slam-door") carriages date from 1883 to 1926, and some have been fully restored in an on-going program. Carriage 199, *City of Ipswich*, (built 1883) is the pride and joy of the restoration team.

Operations: Steam trains operate on first Sunday of each month, from April to December, from 1000 and 1600. Trains operate on both Sunday and Monday of public holiday weekends, such as May Day and Queen's Birthday holiday. Trains depart from Swanbank every 45-50 minutes. Charter trips are also available.

Fares: Adults $5 and children $2 (1999).

Location: Trains operate from the picnic area beside the lake o Swanbank Power Station. By road, take the Brisbane-Ipswich High way to Dinmore, then Warwick Highway (Route 15) to the Swanbank exit. Follow Swanbank Road to the Power Station. The road follows the edge of the lake to the society's station.

Contact: Kel Ayling, Secretary, QPSRC
               PO Box 5099, Brassall Qld 4305
Phone: (07) 3267 5986 or
               Mary Platt (Publicity) (07) 2381 8837; also
               (07) 3812 2394 or (07) 3265 7138

Rosewood Railway Museum
Australian Railway Historical Society (Qld Division)

Tourist Railway (Steam)
1067mm gauge

BRIAN WEBBER

Passsengers arrive at Kunkala station in RM55 and PL72 on 18 January 1999 at the Rosewood Railway Museum.

The *Rosewood Railway Museum* has been established as a tourist railway between Cabanda and Kunkala on the former Rosewood to Marburg line. The railway recreates the atmosphere of a 1940s branch line and offers spectacular scenery over the Upper Bremer Valley.

Locomotives: Restored PB15-class 4-6-0 No 738 built by Walkers in 1926. Diesel-electric locomotives 1604 and 1179, together with 4-6-0DM DL3 and B-B DH DH38 are in service. C17 4-8-0 No 720 is currently under restoration, while D17-class 4-6-4T No 855 and C17-class No 763 await restoration.

Rolling Stock: Six vintage carriages and three unique vintage railmotors – RMs 55, 64 and 1815 - in service. A variety of restored goods wagons and other vehicles are on display.

Operations: Trains operate on the last Sunday of each month, between 1000-1630. Special weekend or mid-week charters available. Souvenirs, books and refreshments are available on running days. The museum is open for static display on other Sundays.

Fares: Adults $6 return, children $3. Admission to the Museum on non-running days; adults $2, children$1.

Location: At Cabanda, on the Rosewood to Marburg Road, 4km from Rosewood (access from Cunningham Highway) or 7km from Marburg (access from Warrego Highway). Kunkala station (site of the Museum display) is reached by turning off the Marburg Road 3km north of Rosewood into Ury Road and following the signs.

Public Transport: *Traveltrain* electric services operate to Rosewood, 18km west of Ipswich on the QR mainline to Toowoomba, thence taxi to Cabanda - there is no connecting public transport.

Contact:	ARHS Queensland Division
	GPO Box 682, Brisbane Qld 4001
Phone:	(07) 3371 4231 (between 1000-1530 Tue-Fri) or
	3349 4517 (after hours) or 3376 6735
Fax:	(07) 3217 7321

HERITAGE SITES (Register of the National Estate)

Brisbane Central Station: The facade of the station building in Ann Street is heritage-listed (RNE), particularly in terms of its relationship with Anzac Square and the Post Office precinct. When opened in 1901, the station was one of the grandest buildings in the city. It is a fine example of a Victorian railway station complex with rich architectural detail typical of the era. The station was redeveloped in 1982, with restoration of the station facade to its original condition. The station clock in the tower was fully restored along with its time mechanism.

Grandchester Railway Station: 34km west of Ipswich, was the 1865 terminus of the first railway in Queensland. The attractive timber station building is of great historical importance and significance in the "townscape" of Grandchester and is listed on the Register of the National Estate. A restored steam sawmill using a C17 locomotive boiler is operational. Visitors welcome (closed Friday).

QR Monument: A monument at the corner of Downs and Lowry Streets (outside the RSL Club) marks the site where railway construction commenced on 25 February 1864. Part of the original line of 1865 serves the North Ipswich locomotive and carriage sheds and workshops.

Roma Street Station: Built in 1874 as the Brisbane terminus for passengers and freight carried on the first services through Ipswich and Toowoomba. Roma Street station is the main terminus for Queensland passenger trains. The station has been upgraded to meet the needs of modern-day travellers while preserving its heritage value. The original 1874 building remains relatively intact.

The Roma Street Travel Centre provides an interchange between train and coach services.

South Brisbane Station: is one of the few surviving remnants from the Victorian period in the region's history. The building is architecturally significant as one of the major masonry railway stations built in the Brisbane region during the Victorian era. By comparison with other surviving examples from this period it has retained much of its original character and visual integrity. The station has been upgraded and restored to serve the Southbank development. An annex at the southern end of the station houses **The Railway Shop,** a QR-operated one-stop shop for all kinds of railway related material, old and new.
Phone (07) 3235 2218.

Southport: C17-class 4-8-0 locomotive No 996 (Walkers 533 1953) is on static display in Tuesley's Park off The Esplanade, Southport as a reminder of the former QR line to that centre.

WALKING TRAILS

North Ipswich Heritage Trail: This trail - *Heritage Trail No 11* - commences at Brown's Park in Downs Street and covers the historical railway precinct of North Ipswich. It follows the original 1865 railway route from Ipswich across the Bremer River to the Railway Historical Centre, site of the original railway workshops and monument to the first railway. The present railway workshops, old Tivoli line and the former wharf line are traced. A booklet describing the walk is available from the Ipswich Regional Tourist Information Centre.

DARLING DOWNS and GOLDEN WEST

The rich agricultural lands of the Darling Downs support Queensland's most important grain producing area. The railway from Ipswich to Toowoomba opened in 1867 and onto Dalby the following year. By 1871, a branch extended south to Warwick and, with the discovery of tin at Stanthorpe, the line was extended there in 1878 and on to the New South Wales border at Wallangarra in 1887. Railway development led to grain growing and small-scale farming and numerous branch lines were constructed to serve farming settlements on the Downs.

Toowoomba: (population 90,000) Queensland's *Garden City*, is the gateway to the Darling Downs and was a significant railway

centre. There is a wide range of galleries and museums, including the Cobb & Co Museum which features Australia's finest collection of horse-drawn vehicles.

Dalby: (population 10,000) lies at the hub of the Darling Downs and is the focal point of rail and road networks.

Warwick: (population 11,300) is the main commercial centre of the Southern Downs. Established in 1847, the city features wide streets and is noted for its period sandstone and timber buildings. The railway from Ipswich opened in 1871. Warwick became an important junction for the main lines to the border at Wallangarra and west to Dirranbandi, as well as branch lines to Maryvale and Killarney.

Acland Coal Mine Museum

Industry Museum

This museum is based on the original mine of the Acland Coal Company, which operated between 1913 and 1984. When closed, the colliery was the smallest, oldest continually-worked coal mine in Queensland. It was the last mine in Australia using Samson coal cutters and small railway skips.

Exhibits: Two Bundaberg Jenbach underground locomotives and skips are on display. Surface rail lines remain on the site.
Opening Times: 0900-1600 daily (except February). Guided tours include an underground simulation, an informative talk on the life and hardships at the mine and a guided walk through the preserved buildings and works.

Admission: Adults $5, student/senior $4, child $3.
Location: Francis Street, Acland, 18km north-east of Oakey. Take Warrego Highway west from Toowoomba to Oakey and then the Cooyar road north until the sign to Acland 5km is seen on the left.
Contact: Phone (07) 4691-5703

Warwick Railway Precinct
Southern Downs Steam Railway Association

Heritage Site/Tourist Train

This community group will operate a tourist train between Warwick and Wallangarra from 2001, providing a link to the 1930s era when Warwick was on the main-line connecting the Queensland and New South Wales railways at Wallangarra.

Features: The QR railway goods shed is listed on the Register of the National estate as an example of the sandstone building technology of Warwick applied to even the railway goods shed.

Exhibits: A small museum is being established in the former Cottonvale station, located in the locomotive depot area with displays of trikes and other fettler equipment, station artefacts, locomotive repair tools and signals and communications.

Rolling Stock: An industrial 0-6-0DH locomotive (Comeng) 1029/1958) formerly worked at the Mackay sugar terminal. Four vans carriages and track maintenance wagons. A replica of a 1914 Lanhard railmotor and trailer is under construction.

Location: Cnr. Hamilton & Fitzroy Streets, Warwick.
Operations: The depot and museum are open on the second Sunday of the month from 1300 to 1600. Diesel cab rides are provided within the yard. Entry by donation. Tourist train operations to Wallangarra are scheduled to commence in 2001.
Address: Les Mullins, Southern Downs Railway Assoc
                  PO Box 978, Warwick QLD 4370
Phone: (07) 4661 9788

    ♿ **RNE**

HERITAGE SITES (Register of the National Estate)

Murphy's Creek to Toowoomba Railway: The railway, including the civil and engineering works, the station buildings and the campsites, is significant as the first range crossing in Queensland. It demonstrates a high quality of engineering for the time and earliest use of the narrow gauge for a mainline. The high number of tunnels, cuttings, embankments and curves are notable on the line and relate to the difficult terrain. The line has exceptional aesthetic qualities including distant views from the line across the coastal plain, views of forest across gullies, views of the winding track from the track and from viewpoints from roads. The visually attractive Spring Bluff Station with its hillside setting and gardens is a feature. The line is associated with the important Queensland engineer Robert Ballard, who was selected especially for the job, oversaw the works in person and lived at Ballard's Camp, the remains of which are an archaeological site.

Toowoomba Railway Station: The heritage-listed railway station (1874) features fine refreshment rooms which once served passengers on the Sydney Express via Wallangarra. They have been restored as a silver service restaurant.

Wallangarra Railway Station: The station, built in 1890, is significant for being the Queensland/New South Wales interchange station, demonstrating in its structure and layout the problem caused by the difference in rail gauges between the States and the solutions used to overcome them. It provides evidence of the pre-Federation period when the State borders were of great importance and is a good and intact example of railway architecture of the period.

SUNSHINE COAST

The *Sunshine Coast* stretches over 100km from the Glass House mountains to Noosa and Fraser Island. The region was originally opened up for sugar cane and horticulture and later flourishing pineapple and ginger industries developed. The railway line from Brisbane to Gympie opened in 1877. Two shire-owned narrow-gauge tramways from Palmwoods to Buderim Mountain and Nambour to Mapleton helped to open the districts for agriculture. The region (population 150,000) is now a rapidly growing tourist destination due to its fine beaches and scenic hinterland. Caloundra, Maroochydore, Nambour and Noosa Heads are the main centres.

Getting There: The Sunshine Coast is served by regular electric train services from Brisbane to Caboolture, Landsborough and Nambour with connecting bus services to Caloundra and Maroochydore. A new transport corridor, initially services with light rail, is being developed from Beewah to Caloundra and Maroochydore.

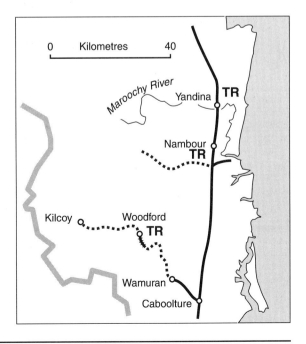

Maroochydore: (population 20,000) The geographic centre of the Sunshine Coast offers a blend of surf beach and the calm waters of the Maroochy River whose southern bank forms a virtually unbroken stretch of parkland and picnic spots.

Nambour: (Population 24,000) Maroochy Shire's administrative centre and principal hinterland town of the Sunshine Coast. Former Moreton Mill 0-4-0T locomotive *Valdora* (Dick Kerr, built 1891) is on display in Petrie Park.

Moreton Central Sugar Mill at Nambour (102km north Brisbane) is the most accessible sugarcane railway system fro Brisbane. The 120km 610mm (2 feet) cane railway system is ope ated by 8 diesel locomotives. Cane railway operations along Howa Street in the town and across the old Bruce Highway to the m offer tourists an interesting insight into Queensland's modern ra based sugar transport systems. Three locomotives are on display the mill: a Shay geared locomotive (built 1908) which former operated on the Mapleton tramway, *Eudlo,* a 0-6-0T John Fowl of 1925, and *Sandy,* a Malcolm Moore petrol locomotive built f the Army in 1943.

Durundur Railway, Woodford
Australian Narrow Gauge Railway Museum Society (ANGRMS)

Tourist Railway (Steam
610mm gauge

BRIAN WEBBER

Hudswell Clarke 0-6-0 steam locomotive Melbourne *on its return to service on 27 June1999.*

ANGRMS was formed in 1971 to establish a collection of 610mm (2ft) gauge locomotives and rolling stock from the suga and construction industries. The Society operates the Durundur tourist railway at Woodford.

Locomotives: 13 steam 5 petrol and 3 diesel locomotives most of which have been acquired from Queensland sugar mills. Historic locomotives in the collection include an 1897 Decauville from the Invicta Mill and the last locomotive built by John Fowler, a 1935 standard 0-6-2T. A locomotive rebuilding program is progressing at a steady pace. Operating locomotives include 0-6-2T No 5 from Pleystowe Mill (Bundaberg Foundry 5/1952) and Hudswell Clarke (1701/1938) 0-6-0 *Melbourne* from Victoria Sugar Mill.
Rolling Stock: Tourist carriages rebuilt from QR rail motor trailers. Numerous items of rolling stock from sugar mill operations.

Features: An operating railway has been constructed through attractive pine forest over 1.2km on the trackbed of the former QR Wamuran-Kilcoy branch line. This presents an experience of sugar industry railway operations during the steam era adapted to passenger train operations. A herb & cottage garden display and tea rooms are located at the terminus. Further extensions are planned. The d'Aguilar railway station building has been relocated to the museum site.

Operations: Every Sunday, (except where certain public holiday fall on that day) between 1100 and 1600. Steam trains operate ap proximately every 20 minutes. Group bookings for opening at othe times can be arranged.
Fares: Train rides: adults $3.00, children $1.50. Entry to the mu seum is free.

Location: Margaret Street, Woodford, about 25km west o Caboolture station (50km north of Brisbane on Main Northern line - turn into Margaret Street at the Water Tower in the main street.
Public Transport: Sunday public transport is limited to an 090: bus service from Caboolture, returning at 1630.

Contact: ANGRMS, PO Box 270
        Brisbane Albert Street QLD 4002
Phone: (07) 3202 6582 (Laurie) between 1700 and 2030, or
        (07) 3265 6834 (George).

he Ginger Factory, Yandina
uderim Ginger Limited

Tourist Park Railway (Diesel)
610mm gauge

1km tourist railway operates to transport visitors around the world's largest ginger factory.

comotive: Former Moreton Sugar mill 0-6-0T steam locomo-
e built by Krauss (4687 of 1900). The locomotive has been con-
ted to diesel operation.

erations: Open every day, 0900 to 1630 (except Christmas Day).
e Ginger Train takes visitors on a leisurely tour through the land-
ped gardens offering an informative commentary.

cation: 50 Pioneer Road, 2km east of Yandina railway station,

8km north of Nambour. Access by regular *CityTrain* services to
Nambour, with limited trains to Yandina.

Contact: Manager, Buderim Ginger
50 Pioneer Road, Yandina, QLD 4561
Phone: (07) 5446 1700

unshine Plantation, Nambour

Tourist Park Railway (Diesel)
610mm gauge

is tourist complex, located, is based on tropical fruits and features *The Big Pineapple*. A tourist train transports visitors
ound the complex.

comotives: Two small 4wDH industrial locomotives Birrima
lliery (NSW), rebuilt as steam outline units.

pening Times: Daily 0900-1700. Admission free.

cation: Forest Glen, 6km south of Nambour.

Public Transport: *CityTrain* to Nambour railway station, then regular
bus services.

Contact: Phone (07) 5442 1333

RASER COAST / BUNDABERG

nis agricultural and mining region has become a popular
urist destination based on Fraser Island, Hervey Bay and
e heritage towns of Gympie and Maryborough. Settlement
ates from 1842 when an expedition explored the Mary River
d led to the first pastrol runs. The first sugar mill com-
enced production in 1867, the same year as the discovery
the Gympie gold field brought an influx of immigrants
rough the port of Maryborough. A pioneer logging rail-
ay was constructed by William Pettigrew and William Sim
om Tin Can Bay into the Cooloola Forest in 1873. To serve
e goldfield, the Maryborough-Gympie railway opened in
881. A branch line was built north to the Burrum coalfield
1883 and another to Pialba and Urangan in 1896 to trans-
ort cane to Maryborough.

Sugar was grown on the Burnett from 1872 and discov-
ry of the Peak Downs copper field resulted in approval for
onstruction of the Bundaberg Railway in 1877. The fist sec-
on opened in 1881. The copper field was short lived, but
ugar traffic developed with the opening of Bingera sugar
ill in 1885. The sugar mills at Fairymead, Millaquin,
ingera and Isis operate some 640km of 610mm gauge cane
ilways, which offer interesting operations for the railway
thusiast during the crushing season (June-December).
undaberg Foundry built steam locomotives for sugarcane
ilways to John Fowler design in the 1950's and has re-
ently entered the locomotive-building market again.
undaberg Foundry locomotive No 1, an 0-6-2T of 1952, is
n display at Millaquin Sugar Mill.

ympie (population 16,000) is known as "Queensland's Golden
ity" following Queensland's first gold rush in 1867. Deep mining
as introduced in 1880 and continued until 1927 by which time,
me four million ounces of gold had been found. The field has
njoyed a new lease of life in the 1980s with the reopening of the
onkland Mine for commercial operations. Gympie is located on
e Mary River, 160km north of Brisbane via the Bruce Highway.

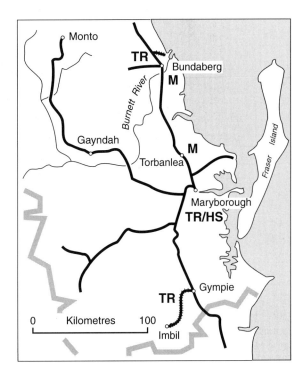

Maryborough (population 27,000) 265km north of Brisbane, is
Queensland's *Heritage City*, offering many classic examples of
colonial architecture, historic precincts, walks and drives,
Queenslander style homes, parks and gardens. First settled in 1847,
the district was one of the first to be opened for sugar growing and
a sugar mill still operates. The Wharf Street precinct retains many
of the city's early buildings and an atmosphere of old world charm.
The **Bond Store Museum** in Wharf Street has displays on early
exploration and settlement, the Port of Maryborough, immigration,
kanaks and the Maryborough Sugar Factory.

The famous engineering and locomotive building firm of **Walkers Limited** commenced operation in Maryborough in 1867. Three pioneer locomotives were built from 1873 and the firm became a major locomotive builder from 1896, building 553 steam, 161 diesel and 69 electric locomotives, together with some 200 electric mu trains, for Australian railways systems. It remains the major industrial enterprise in the city and continues to build locomotives and rolling stock for Australia's railways.

Olds Engine House and Works produces commercial internal combustion engines, steam engines and Stirling cycle hot air engines. Overhaul and maintenance of steam equipment for industry is one of the specialties of the company. Every Thursday the vertical test boiler provides steam to a restored steam engine to operate some of the plant.

Tourist Information: Maryborough & District Information Cen
     30 Ferry Street, Maryborough QLD 4650
Phone: (07) 4121 4111

Bundaberg (population 45,000) located 378km north of Br bane, is the commercial centre for the Burnett district. The city w established in 1867 and it grew rapidly with the sugar industry the 1880s. Bundaberg is a city of parks and botanical gardens w fine displays of poincianas in spring.

Getting There: The region is served by daily QR electric *T Trains* from Brisbane, as well as the *Queenslander* and *Sunlanc* services.

Mary Valley Heritage Railway, Gympie
The Valley Rattler

Tourist Railway (Steam/Diese
1067mm gauge

BRIAN WEBBER

A small crowd watch C17-class locomotive No 45 arriving with the Mary Valley Rattler at Imbil station on the inauguration day of 23 May 1998.

Steam/diesel tourist train operate through the scenic (and historic) Mary Valley on the old Gympie to Imbil line (41km). Th former QR Gympie Railway Workshops serve as a base for the railway.

Features: After passing through the City of Gympie, the line climbs the scenic Mary Valley, through forests and pineapple plantations with an abundance of curves, gradients and bridges. Passengers can stop over at Kandanga to explore the museum in the station with its pictoral record of the Mary Valley line and enjoy the town, or continue onto Imbil. After Kandanga, the line traverses an interesting gorge, timbered country and a short tunnel before descending to Imbil. Lunch can be taken in the town before rejoining the train for the return journey.

Locomotives: Restored 4-8-0 C17 No 45 (built 1923); C17 No 819 (AW 867/1927); three 1620-class diesel-electric locomotives. 4-8-0 C17 No 819 (AW 867/1927) is awaiting restoration to working order.

Rolling Stock: Two ex-QR 2000-class rail motors and restored heritage carriages dating from the 1920s.

Operations: Steam-hauled trains operate every Sunday departir Gympie at 1000. Regular rail motor tours operate on Tuesdays ar Sunday, enabling travel one way by railmotor and the other b steam on Sunday. The Society's workshop operates six days a weel Group bookings and charters available.
Fares: Gympie-Imbil $17 single, $25 return; family return $67.
Location: At Gympie railway station, 168km north of Brisbane c Bruce Highway. QR courtesy coaches connect with trains at Nor Gympie station.
Address: Mary Valley Heritage Railway
          PO Box 385, Gympie Qld 4570
Phone: (07) 5482 2750; Fax (07) 5482 7622
Internet: http://www.cooloola.org.au/mvhr/

Maryborough Heritage Railway
Maryborough City Council

Tourist Railway (Steam)
1067mm gauge

Maryborough's association with Queensland locomotive building is being brought to life through this City Council heritage railway project.

Locomotives: A replica of the first locomotive built in Queensland, *Mary Ann*, a unique 0-4-0 vertical-boilered locomotive built by John Walker's Union Foundry in 1873 for William Pettigrew's timber line, is under construction by Olds Engineering. The first locomotive built by Walker's of Maryborough for the Queensland Railways, 4-6-0 B15 (con) No 299 of 1897, has been restored to operating condition and is on display at the railway station.

Operations: B15. 299 is steamed for special charter trips. A small museum featuring railway bric-a-brac and memorabilia is located on the main platform. From 2000, *Mary Ann* will take passengers from Maryborough's historic railway station through Queens Park along the Mary River bank to terminate at the Wharf Street station. Here the locomotive will demonstrate her timber-cutting ability (as of old). The return trip will take passengers from the Wharf Street precinct to the Maryborough railway station. An extensive live steam miniature railway operates in Queens Park on the last Sunday of the month.

Location: Transit Centre, Old Railway Station, Lennox Street, Maryborough. Courtesy buses operate from the QR Maryborough West station to the old station.

Contact: Maryborough City Council
PO Box 110, Maryborough QLD 4650

Phone: (07) 4123 8888

Model Engineers and Live Steamers Association
PO Box 355, Maryborough QLD 4650

RNE

Bundaberg Botanic Gardens Railway
Bundaberg Steam Tramway Preservation Society

Tourist Park Railway (Steam)
610mm gauge

MARK PLUMMER

The Bundaberg Foundry locomotive No 3 arriving at the station in the Bundaberg Botanic Gardens.

The Preservation Society operates a tourist railway in the Bundaberg Botanical Gardens using restored sugar industry locomotives over some 1km of track.

Locomotives: Operating locomotives are Bundaberg Foundry 0-4-2T (3/1952), John Fowler 0-6-2T (11277/1907) both ex-Qunaba Mill; and Orenstein & Koppel 0-4-0WT (6805/1914) ex-Millaquin mill. Ex-World War I Baldwin 2-6-2T *FELIN HEN* (46828/1915) is stored partially restored.

Rolling Stock: Tourist carriages built on ex-sugar cane trucks.

Operations: Every Sunday and public holiday (and Wednesdays during school holidays) between 1000 and 1600.

Fares: Adults $2, children $1.

Location: Botanical Gardens, corner Gin Gin Road and Young Street, North Bundaberg. Follow main road via Tallon Bridge across Burnett River and continue Gin Gin for about 1.5km. The gardens also contain Hinkler House, Fairymead House, a district museum and garden cafe.

Contact: Paul Roberts, Secretary, BSTPS
PO Box 1569, Bundaberg Qld 4670

Phone: (07) 4159 3341; Facsimile (07) 4153 4884

Burrum Mining Museum, Torbanlea

Mining Museum

This museum features exhibits relating to the history of the Burrum Coalfields, including the role of railways in developi
the field from 1883.

Features: The museum has been built on the site of a railway siding which served the original township and the original Burrum railway station building of 1883 is located in the grounds.
Exhibits: Bundaberg Jenbach 4wDM locomotive, mine skips and ex-QR passenger carriage No 498 of 1908 (converted to brakevan).
Opening Times: 1300-1600 Wednesday
1000-1600 Friday and Saturday and
1100-1400 Sunday.
Guided tours operate on the hour.

Admission: Adults $3, pensioners $2, children 50c.
Location: Union Street, Torbanlea, 20km north of Maryborou
on the North Coast railway and Bruce Highway.

Contact: Jack Vali, 110 Thomas Street
            Howard Qld 4659
Phone: (07) 4129 4122

Bundaberg Railway Museum
Bundaberg Railway Historical Society Inc

Railway Museum
1067mm gauge

Displays: The museum is housed in the old QR North Bundaberg railway buildings. Historical railway artifacts, buildings, rolling stock, plans and photographs are on display.
Opening Times: 0800-1600 Saturday or by appointment. Guided tour provided.
Admission: Adult $2.50, children/seniors $1.

Location: 1 Wilmot Street, North Bundaberg.
Contact: John Lebsant
            13 Tarakan Street, Bundaberg Qld 4670
Phone: (07) 4152 1267

HERITAGE SITES

Gympie Gold Mining Museum was opened in 1970 to display and preserve all facets of Gympie's colourful mining and historical past. Displays include working, steam-driven mining machinery,

the railway museum and historical Monkland railway station.
Phone: (07) 5482 3995

CENTRAL QUEENSLAND

The region was founded on wool and gold, but these commodities were replaced by beef and coal as the major source of wealth. The first European settlement was at Port Curtis (now Gladstone) in 1847. Gold was discovered in 1858, followed by rich copper deposits at Peak Downs, which generated demands for a railway. Construction of the **Central Railway** began in 1865 and the first section from Rockhampton to Westwood opened in 1867. An extension to the Peak Downs copper field commenced in 1873. The Central Railway reached Emerald in 1879 and Longreach in 1892.

Local branch lines were opened from Rockhampton to the seaside resort of Emu Park in 1888 (isolated line until 1899), Mount Morgan in 1898, Yepoon in 1910, Port Alma in 1912 and Alton Downs in 1914. Local commuter passenger services ran to Emu Park, Yepoon and Mount Morgan. The Central Railway was connected with Gladstone and the southern system at Gladstone in 1903 and with the northern system at St Lawrence in 1921.

Today only the Yepoon branch remains open, but the Central Railway has been electrified to Emerald for the haulage of heavy coal traffic from the Blackwater and Moura coalfields.

Rockhampton (population 70,000) Australia's *Beef Capital,* was founded in 1855 and developed to serve primary industry and a number of goldfields in the area, including the famous Mount Morgan mine. The city was founded on railways and QR remains a major employer with its large railway workshops and depots. The

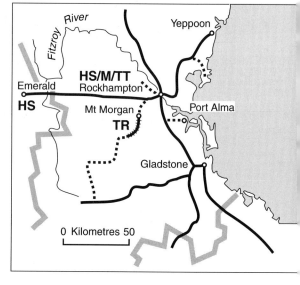

railway was constructed in the middle of Denison Street for eigh
city blocks in 1899 and forms part of the main North Coast Line
The City Council operated a steam street tramway system from
1909 until 1939 using French-designed Purrey steam tramcars and
trailers.
Tourist Information: Capricorn Information Centre,
                 Tropic of Capricorn Shire, Gladstone Road
                 (PO Box 1313), Rockhampton QLD 4700
                 Phone: (07 4927 2055; Fax (07) 4922 2605

adstone (population 27,000) is the focus for heavy rail opera-ns to the world-class coal and grain export port. Gladstone is the gest multi-cargo port in Australia. The alumina refinery is the rld's largest, there is an aluminium smelter and the State's largest wer station.

urist Information: Gladstone Area Promotion
      56 Goondoon Street.
      Phone (07) 4972 4000

ount Morgan (population 2000) 38km south-west from ckhampton, was one of the world's greatest gold mines. From discovery in 1882 until production from the huge open-cut ceased 1981, the ore body yielded 225 tonnes of gold, 360,000 tonnes copper and 50 tonnes of silver. A 21km branch railway from abra, near Rockhampton, including a 2.4km Abt-rack section, as opened in 1898. A deviation enabled closure of the rack rail-ay in 1952. With the opening of the Moura short line in 1968 and clining mine output at Mount Morgan, the Kabra-Mt Morgan

line was closed in 1987. The historic museum has a collection of memorabilia and photographs which depict the boom and bust periods of the town and mine.

Emerald 263km west of Rockhampton, is the gateway to the Central Highlands and gemfields. The pride of the town is the heritage-listed railway station built in 1900. Emerald is the termi-nus for the electrified sections of the Central Railway.

HERITAGE ITEMS

Emerald Railway Station: Listed on the Register of the National Estate as an example of the fine Victorian railway buildings erected by the central division of the Queensland railways. It is an attrac-tive structure with a timber-frame with chamber board-cladding and corrugated-iron roof, arranged symmetrically about an elabo-rate central entrance porch which consists of a louvered arched pediment with elaborate wrought iron lace and pillars for is portico.

rcher Park Station Museum, Rockhampton
ockhampton City Council/Capricorn Heritage Rail Association Inc

Museum/Steam Tram
1067mm gauge

PETER NEVE

The Archer Park Station Museum's Purrey steam tram in Denison Street,
Rockhampton on 9 August 1998.

rcher Park Railway Station was built in 1899 for local trains and Capricorn Coast services. Due to its close proximity to the ity centre, it became the main station for Rockhampton until closed in 1969. The station building has been listed on the egister of the National Estate for its excellence of architectural design. It has been fully restored as a railway museum, unction centre and sales centre for railway-related items.

eatures: The museum relates the social impact of railways, the istory of the station and the steam era generally. The elegant tim-er station building features a long frontal verandah with cast iron olumns, brackets and particularly fine central half-round-edimented entry; the latter also displaying very fine cast-iron rackets and spandrel panels of Indian-like design.

olling Stock: Pride of place is held by one of the unique ockhampton Purrey steam tramcars which was fully restored to perating condition in 1988. It is believed to be the only operating urrey steam tramcar in the world. Other items of rolling stock clude a restored French-built Billard 4wDM industrial locomo-ve and hand-pump trikes and trolleys.

Operations: The museum is open [days/times]. The Purrey steam tram operates over 1km of track between Fitzroy and Albert Streets each Sunday, with expanded services planned in future. The sta-tion has catering facilities and is available for functions.
Location: Denison Street, Rockhampton.

Contact: Denis Sheehan, President
             PO Box 573
             Rockhampton QLD 4700
Phone: (07) 4928 7780

 RNE

Roundhouse Railway Museum, Rockhampton
Queensland Rail Heritage Volunteers

Heritage Site/Depot
1067mm gauge

The 360-degree roundhouse at Rockhampton was built in 1915 as one of Australia's largest storage facilities for stea
locomotives. The Roundhouse serves as a base for the QR heritage fleet and for volunteers engaged in rolling stock restor
tion. Longer-term plans are to develop the complex as a museum.

Heritage significance: The roundhouse is classified for its industrial archaeological significance and architectural interest. The
roundhouse is probably the finest to have been built in Queensland
and is the last to remain; the central turntable serviced 52 locomotive bays.
Locomotives: AIA-AIA DE 1170 (Walkers 558/1956), the first
Queensland branch-line diesel-electric (60-ton) locomotive; 1614
and 1620 60-ton AIA-AIA DE (EE Aus A077/1963; A 138/1967)
and 90-ton Co-Co DE 1281 *CENTURY* (EE Aus A103/1965) painted
gold for the QR Centenary.
Rolling Stock: Key objects in the collection include Rail Motor
RM16, the last of the converted motor cars used by QR. There is an
important collection dating from 1896, including 3 State Cars, 453
(General Manager SE Division), 491 (Commissioner's car) and
kitchen car 991 (built 1924 as a TPO); and a variety of goods wagons.

Operations: The Group operate regular tour trains to Yepoon a
other Central Queensland locations using heritage carriages. Op
days will be held as the museum is being developed.
Contact   (07) 4932 0512
Notes: There are long-term plans to develop a museum to pres
the heritage of the Central Railway around topical themes wh
place the railway in the broader economic, political, social a
environmental context of the region.
Location: Corner of South and Bolsover Streets,
                  500m north of Rockhampton railway station.
Public Transport: Daily QR high-speed tilt trains from Brisba
Contact: Peter Draper, Queensland Rail Heritage Volunteer
                 PO Box 1566, Rockhampton QLD 4700
Phone: (07) 4932 0283 or 4928 7247 (after hours)

RNE

Dee River Railway, Mount Morgan
ARHS Qld Division (Central Qld Committee, Rockhampton)

Tourist Railway (Steam
1067mm gauge

To provide transport to the mine, the Queensland Railways constructed a steeply graded line with a 2.4km Abt rack secti
in order to avoid the high cost of tunnels. Eight Abt tank locomotives operated the rack section (Moongan to Moonmer
from November 1898 until a deviation through Bundaleer opened in 1952. This tourist railway operates over a section of t
former branch line south of the town.

Heritage Significance: The railway station is classified on the basis
of its architectural merit, an example of the excellent railway stations
built in the central railway district of Queensland. The railway water
tank is an example of a structure now mostly phased out of existence by the demise of steam. The formation of the Abt incline
remains to the east of the town. Part of the formation is now used
as the road down the Razorback Range (Razorback Road).
Features: The elegant railway station (built 1898) provides the
operating base for the railway and serves as a tourist information
centre and the site for monthly markets. The 3.5km railway line
from Mt Morgan to Kenbula traverses three bridges, passes through
a short tunnel and offers scenic views of mine workings and the
Dee River. A short section of track with rack is located in the main
street as a monument to the Abt line.
Locomotives: Former Mount Morgan Mines 0-4-0ST No 3 (Hunslet
854/1903) was restored to operating condition in 1996 and hauls
trains over the line. A sister Mount Morgan Mines 0-4-0ST locomotive (Hunslet 797/1902) is on static display in East Street near
the museum.
Rolling Stock: 2000 class rail-motor, tourist carriages, composite
carriage, brakevan and Fairmont section cars.
Operations: The complex opens daily 0800-1600 (except Christmas Day and Good Friday); Anzac Day 1300-1600); with steam
trains on Sundays and fettlers trolleys or railcar rides on other days.
A commentary of the history of Mount Morgan is provided. Train
rides, including steam-hauled trains, are available to tour groups
by special arrangement.
Fares: Adults $6, child $3, family $15 (2+2), seniors $4 (1999).
Group discounts available.
Facilities: Morning/afternoon teas and cool drinks available from
the refreshment rooms. Bookshop and souvenir shop. Mine tour
information can be obtained from the tourist information centre.
Location: Mount Morgan railway station, 38km south-west of
Rockhampton.
Public Transport: Youngs bus service from Rockhampton to
Mount Morgan operates on weekdays and Saturdays.

PETER NEVE

*The Dee River Railway's Hunslet 0-4-0ST locomotive built 1903
with a tour train on the Dee River bridge having emerged from
a tunnel on 9 August 1998.*

Contact: Dee River Railway
                 PO Box 1523, Mount Morgan Qld 4714
Phone: (07) 4938 2312; Fax: (07) 4938 2310

 RNE

MACKAY REGION

Mackay is Australia's traditional *Sugar Capital*, based on industry which dates from 1865. The first steam-powered sugar cane railway, a 1067mm gauge line on River Estate, commenced operating with a locally-built vertical-boiler locomotive in 1880. The Colonial Sugar Refining Company (CSR) opened its Homebush central mill in 1883 with a 2ft (610mm) gauge railway system which established the foundations for cane transport in Australia.

The **Mackay Railway** (1067mm gauge) serving the Pioneer Valley was opened in 1885 and enabled independent farmers to send cane to the sugar mill of their choice. It was extended in stages to Netherdale (67km from Mackay), with a branch to Eton. Cane and sugar provided the main traffic on the railway. The line has been closed beyond Marian Mill and the formation converted to a 610mm gauge cane railway. The railway from Mackay to Sarina opened in 1913.

Today, the district's sugar mills at Pleystowe, Marian, Racecourse, Farleigh and Sarina (Plabe Creek) transport million tonnes of cane over 820km of 610mm gauge cane railways for crushing. Mackay Harbour boasts the largest bulk sugar terminal in the world and the largest coal exporting facility in the Southern Hemisphere at Hay Point/ Dalrymple Bay (25km south of Mackay). QR heavy-haul coal trains up to 2km long arrive daily.

Mackay (population 70,000) located 992km north of Brisbane, is a vibrant tropical city founded on the richness of sugar and mining. It is a growing tourist destination based on its proximity to the Great Barrier Reef and tropical rainforests. Conservation of Mackay's built heritage is a priority of the City Council.
Information Centre: The Mill
    320 Nebo Road, Mackay Qld 4740
Open: 0900-1700 (0900-1600 Saturday and Sunday)
Phone: (079) 52 2677
Public Transport: QR *Spirit of the Tropics* and *Queenslander* train services, plus daily coach services.

Proserpine (130km north of Mackay) is a sugar town based on the Proserpine Cooperative Sugar Mill which opened in 1896. The mill operates 155km of 610mm gauge cane railways. A 4-6-0T steam locomotive which originally saw service in the First World War (Hunslet 1317/1916) has been preserved by the local historical museum.

Mirani Museum
Mirani Shire Council

Local History Museum

This museum documents and displays the pioneering era of the Pioneer Valley, with particular emphasis on the development of the sugar industry and the mills at Marian, North Eton and Cattle Creek.

Displays: The museum holds records of the Cattle Creek and North Eton sugar mills and there is an excellent collection of photographs, including cane railways. Two early cane railway trucks form part of the collection of pioneer transport and machinery items. The adjacent Mirani railway station has been restored as a heritage project. The former QR Mackay railway line here has been converted to the main line for Marian Mill.

Opening Times: 1000-1600 Sunday to Friday.

Admission: Adults $3. Group concessions available.

Location: 16 Victoria Street, Mirani. 32km west of Mackay.

Contact: Phone (07) 4959 1101; Fax (07) 4959 1275

Mackay Heritage Railway Inc

Mainline Tours/Railway Museum
1067mm gauge

This group is restoring a 4-6-2 express locomotive to operating condition to provide steam tours around Mackay and operates a railway museum at Paget railway station.

Heritage Significance: Paget Railway Station and associated railway equipment was a part of the complete Mackay railway complex prior to 1993 when QR removed its railway facilities from within the city boundaries. Paget station was built in 1911 and was the junction from the Mackay Railway and the Main Southern line to Rockhampton and Brisbane.

Features: Ex-QGR BB18½-class 4-6-2 express locomotive No 1037 (Vulcan Foundry 5963/1951) which worked the last QR steam-hauled revenue train at Mackay in December 1969. The Society is restoring Paget railway station to its original layout, including installation of railway lines, signals and operating equipment used in the train controls.

Operations: MHR operate diesel-hauled charter trains to locations in the Mackay region (check for details). Steam locomotive 1037 is expected to return to service in 2000.

Location: Archibald Street, Paget, Mackay.

Contact: Greg Bennett, Mackay Heritage Railway Inc
    PO Box 3536, North Mackay Qld 4740
Phone: (07) 4957 4976; Facsimile (07) 4952 4811

     RNE

TOWNSVILLE REGION

The region owes its wealth to sugar and its service role for the north-west minerals province. Construction of the **Great Northern Railway** from Townsville toward the rich gold field at Charters Towers began in 1879 and trains commenced running to Charters Towers in 1882. The line was extended to Hughenden in 1887 and eventually to Cloncurry and Mount Isa. In 1901 the Ayr Tramway Joint Board opened a 3ft 6in gauge tramway from Stewart's Creek (now Stuart) to Ayr.

Townsville (population 140,000) 1457km north of Brisbane, is Australia's largest tropical city. The City was established in 1864 as a port for the region's thriving cattle industry. Mineral finds and railway construction fuelled its growth, as did its role as Australia's garrison city during World War II. Townsville has a strong railway heritage with its locomotive depot, large workshops, the heritage listed railway station and, more recently, a locomotive building works. Townsville has a strategic location as the hub of Australia's links with South East Asia and the Pacific. The city has a diverse economic base with a busy port, an international airport, a wide range of heavy industries, the James Cook University, defence bases and tourist attractions linked to the Great Barrier Reef and World Heritage rain forests.

Information: Townsville Enterprise Tourism, Enterprise House
6 The Strand, Townsville Qld 4810
Phone: (07) 4771 3061

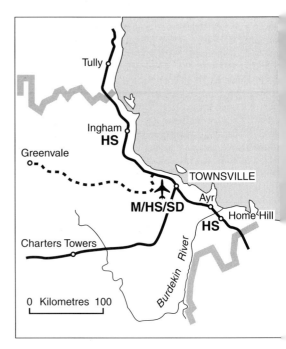

Ingham (population 5000) It is the southern gateway to the Wet Tropics World Heritage listed rainforests of Tropical North Queensland. Ingham, known for its large Italian community, celebrates in May the Australian-Italian Festival, a feast of Italian wine, cuisine, music and colour. It is the centre of one of Australia's most productive sugar producing areas. Victoria Sugar Mill, established in 1883, is the largest in Australia. The two-foot (610mm) gauge sugar railway system established here provided the model for the transport systems which today provide the base for Australia's world-class sugar industry.

The **Burdekin River** district is a major producer of irrigated sug and other agricultural produce. The four Burdekin sugar mills Pioneer, Kalamia, Inkerman and Giru operate over 520 km of ca railways and the mills are expected to crush 10 million tonnes cane by the year 2000.

Getting There: QR *Queenslander* and *Sunlander* services to Bi bane and Cairns, while the *Inlander* connects with Mount Isa. L cal *Sunbus* services operate over five routes from the Transit M in the city centre.

Great Northern Railway Museum, Townsville
Townsville Railway Workshop Historical Committee

Museum/Heritage Si.
1067mm gauge

The heritage-listed 1880 machine shop of the North Yard Railway Workshops has been retained on its original site and being developed as a railway museum depicting the history of the Great Northern Railway and the workshops. The adjace western area (designated Special Purpose) is to be transformed into a railway theme park and terminus for scenic heritage ra tours.

Exhibits: ARHS-owned heritage diesel locomotives 1150 (IGE 31090/1952), Queensland's pioneer DE locomotive, and 1263 (EE Aus A051/1961) are being restored to operating condition by the museum. Heritage workshop machinery, historic photographs and other railway items have been retained for the museum.

Location: Off Flinders Street, Townsville.

Opening Times: The museum scheduled to open in the year 2000. The North Queensland Committee of the ARHS is negotiating for a restored steam locomotive and rail motor for tourist services from Townsville over scenic lines.

The ARHS meets on the third Friday of the month at 1930 the training rooms of the Townsville Railway Station.

Contacts: Ron Aitken, TRWHC Historian
PO Box 974, Hyde Park Qld 4812
Warren Butterworth, Secretary, Townsville ARHS
PO Box GE119, Garbutt East Qld 4814
Phone: (07) 4779 4083

RNE

HERITAGE SITES

Townsville Railway Station. The Federation Romanesque style building (RNE), opened in 1914 as headquarters of the GNR, is one of the finest station buildings in Australia. Through its bold details and texture, simple massing, parapeted gable and groups of round-arched openings it displays the typical characteristics of the Federation style of architecture. The Railway Station makes a significant contribution to the streetscape of Flinders Street, the main street of Townsville, which contains many heritage buildings.

Victoria Sugar Mill. Victoria, the largest sugar mill in the southern hemisphere, was established in 1883. The mill operates over 90km of permanent 610mm gauge railway with 20 diesel locomotives. 0-6-0 Hudswell Clarke steam locomotive, *Homebush* built in 1914, has been restored to operating condition. It is on public display at the mill, together with two passenger carriages, including one built by Decauville in 1885. An original Mirrelees, Tait &

Watson 120hp steam engine which operated the No.3 mill from 1883 to 1971 is on display next to the historic train.

Burdekin Bridge. The 1097 metres bridge over the Burdekin between Ayr and Home Hill is Australia's longest railway bridge and the district's best known landmark. A diorama at the southern approach includes an early rail cane truck and bullock wagon.

Railway Park, Townsville. The Park, which provides a base for the Townsville & District Society of Model Engineers miniature railway, contains the historic Oonoomba railway station which was the disembarkation station for troop trains during the Pacific War. Ex-QR C17 4-8-0 locomotive No 251 (Walkers 327/1920) is on static display, together with several carriages and a heritage signal tower from the Townsville North Yard.

TROPICAL NORTH QUEENSLAND

Tropical North Queensland is a vast region stretching from reefs and islands, through to beach and coastal wetlands to mountains, tablelands and Gulf Savannah grassland. The region's economy has been based on minerals and agriculture, particularly sugar, but has recently become a major tourist destination.

Railway construction has followed the demands of these industries. Narrow-gauge (610mm) sugar railways date from 1882 when a steam-operated line was opened to serve Mourilyan Mill at Innisfail. Today, the six Far North sugar mills operate nearly 1000km of 610mm gauge sugar railways over which heavy cane trains operate under sophisticated control systems.

The first 1067mm gauge line was constructed from Cairns to Gordonvale by the Mulgrave Shire in 1886 to service the sugar mill there. Mineral finds inland brought pressure for improved transport, but first the obstacle of the Great Dividing Range had to be conquered. The 34km railway from Cairns to Kuranda via the Barron Gorge took 5 years to build and was completed in 1891. Once the Tablelands were reached, the line was extended to Atherton in 1903 and over the range to the tin mining town of Herberton in 1910. Isolated lines were constructed from Cooktown and Normanton.

Far North Queensland offers a range of tourist railway experiences. Both the Cairns-Kuranda and the Atherton-Herberton railway lines are listed by the National Trust as major heritage items on account of their engineering feats and scenic beauty.

Cairns (population 120,000) 1790km north of Brisbane, is the regional city and gateway to the tourist attractions of the Far North, including the Great Barrier Reef and tropical rainforests.
Getting There: Cairns is served by the QR *Sunlander* and *The Queenslander* trains. By air, international flights link Cairns with Europe, North America, Japan, South East Asia and New Zealand; domestic airlines offer regular services from southern ports. By road, the Bruce Highway links Cairns with Brisbane.
Information: Visitor Information Centre
Cnr. Sheriden and Aplin Streets, Cairns Qld 4870
Phone: (07) 4051 3588

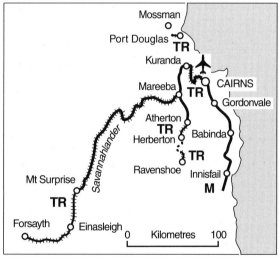

Innisfail (population 8,000) is an attractive sugar town situated 88km south of Cairns. A sugar plantation was established here in 1880 and the first mill commenced crushing the following year. A 2 ft gauge shire-owned railway, the Innisfail Tramway, provided public transport in the district prior to the opening of the North Coast Railway in 1924. Following initial development by the Shire Council and Mourilyan Mill, the 46km system was operated by the QR until taken over by the Mourilyan and South Johnstone sugar mills in 1977. These two sugar mills now operate 400km of cane railways in the district, including the lines of the former Goondi Mill which closed in 1989.

The Tropical Tablelands to the west of Cairns offers a range of tourist attractions, including World Heritage listed mountains and rainforest, waterfalls and rich agricultural areas. The two tourist steam railways at Atherton and Ravenshoe are outstanding examples of the efforts of volunteers to revitalise rural communities through the preservation of their railway heritage.

Atherton (population 5500) is the main commercial centre for the Tablelands and provides a convenient base to explore the features of the sub-region. It is the current terminus of the QR railway line which transports out bulk maize from the district.

Mareeba developed as a coaching stop for the Herberton mineral fields and became the railway junction for the Tablelands and Chillagoe lines. The **Mareeba Heritage Museum**, located in Centenary Park, is the local tourist information centre and features the Mareeba rail ambulance which served isolated communities to the west until 1972.

The Savannahland Sub-Region to the west of the Tablela⬛ features natural attractions and the poignant remains of attem⬛ by pioneers to open up the interior. The chimneys and decay⬛ remains of Chillagoe's smelters bear testimony to past efforts⬛ exploit and profit from the mineral riches of the district. T⬛ Etheridge area features fascinating, rugged country and ⬛ pioneering history of gold mining settlements.

Australian Sugar Museum, Mourilyan
Industry Museum⬛

This museum was established in 1977 to preserve the heritage of the sugar industry, through collection, preservation a⬛ display of machinery and implements used in the sugar industry since its beginnings in the 1860s. The development ⬛ Queensland's unique 2ft gauge sugar railways is given prominence.

Locomotives: The world's only remaining John Fowler jackshaft drive steam locomotive which pioneered narrow-gauge canefield railways in Australia and Hawaii, a 0-4-2T engine built in 1882, is on display, together with the 0-6-0 locomotive, *Townsville*, (Hudswell Clarke 1099/1915) used at Victoria Sugar Mill.
Exhibits: Manual and motorised pump trolleys, a rail-laying navvies trolley and tools, and an early wooden whole-stick cane truck. Professionally-equipped theatre with video presentation of the development of the Australian sugar industry. Audio-visual points throughout the Museum tell the story of the narrow-gauge canefield railways of Queensland and the development of mechanical cane harvesting. The Museum also features the largest stationary steam-engine in the Southern Hemisphere - a massive 500hp crushing engine formerly used at Goondi mill - running in slow motion as a two-story display.

Opening Times 7 days a week 0900-1700.
Admission: Adults $4, children and concession $2; family $12⬛
Location: On the Bruce Highway at Mourilyan, 7km south⬛ Innisfail in North Queensland.
Public Transport: The Information Centre is a booking agent a⬛ scheduled pick-up point for regular coach services, including Pa⬛ rama Coaches buses four times daily (Mon-Fri).

Contact: The Secretary, Australian Sugar Museum
PO Box 39, Innisfail Qld 4860
Phone: (07) 4063 2656; fax (07) 4063 204⬛
Home Page: www.sugarmuseum.org.au

Port Douglas Commuter Railway
Port Douglas & Mossman Railway Company
Tourist Railway (Diesel⬛
610mm gauge

The Mossman Sugar Mill restored the former 610mm gauge shire tramway to Port Douglas in 1986. The line was extend⬛ to the marina in 1988, some 20km from the mill. A tourist commuter train operates over the line between Marina and Crispins (6km) hauled by a former canefield diesel locomotive.

Operation: *The Ballyhooley Railway* operates six return commuter services daily between Marina and St Crispins at Port Douglas. Special three-day, weekly and family passes are available.
Location: 70km north of Cairns on the Captain Cook Highway.
Public Transport: Coral Coaches operate daily bus services from

Cairns to Port Douglas and Mossman.

Contact: Ron Smith, Mossman Central Mill
PO Box 97, Mossman Qld 4873
Phone: (07) 0498 1400

Freshwater Connection
Museum⬛

The Freshwater Complex offers passengers on the Kuranda Scenic Railway the option of *Royal Class* service on the train a⬛ a tropical breakfast at the complex which comprises a ticket office, station, gift shop, restaurant and museum. A priva⬛ steam-hauled tourist train from Redlynch to Kuranda is planned to commence in 2000.

Rolling Stock: The restaurant features 3 wooden vintage carriages formerly used on the QR *Sunshine Express*.
Display: The museum interprets the history of the Cairns-Kuranda railway with historic photographs, a relief model of the line and the original cottage of the railway's colourful construction supervisor, *Red* Lynch.

Location: At Freshwater 5km on the Kamerunga Road. Take first t⬛ left past Airport entrance heading north on Captain Cook Highway.
Contact: Ed Bone, Supervisor
Phone (07) 4055 2222

Savannahlander Tourist Train
QR TravelTrain
Tourist Railway (Railca⬛
1067mm gauge

Railways west of the Great Dividing Range were built by Chillagoe Railway and Mines Limited to serve their mine operatio⬛ A pioneer line was built to serve copper and gold fields at Etheridge in 1909. The Government took the lines over in t⬛ 1920s. The scenic line has been retained for heritage train operations. *Savannahlander* tours, operated by refurbished Q⬛ 2000-class rail motors, have become a popular adventure train experience.

Operations: Depart Cairns Wednesday at 0630 for a leisurely journey to Forsayth in the heart of the Gulf Savannah. Overnight stay at Almaden and continue to Forsayth on Thursday. Return train departs Forsayth at 0745 Friday, arriving Cairns 1840 Saturday. On board, experience first-hand a unique encounter with the region's uncanny geological formations, its history and legends. The train is available for charter groups.

Fares: Cairns to Mt Surprise:
one way - Adult $60, concession $30
To Forsayth - Adult $85, concession $43
Mt Surprise to Forsayth - Adult $35, concession $1⬛
Tour Information and Bookings: QR Reservations Centre
Phone 13-2232 or
Cairns Railway Travel Centre, Phone (07) 4052 62⬛

uranda Scenic Railway
ueensland Railways Kuranda Tourist Train

Tourist Railway (Diesel)
1067mm gauge

DAVID JOHNSON

QR locomotive 1770D with the Kuranda tourist train climbing the range on 27 September 1998.

e 34km railway from Cairns to Kuranda is Australia's most popular tourist railway. Many of the line's original features nain and the National Trust records its historical significance due to its relationship to the establishment of Cairns as a imary north Queensland settlement, its role in developing the mining, pastoral and agricultural industries of the hinterland, outstanding engineering achievement and the high degree of integrity of the engineering works and construction.

atures: The 90 minute journey offers Australia's most spectacular in ride on its way to the Barron Gorge National Park. The line mbs from sea level to 328 metres through 15 tunnels and over merous bridges, including the famous Stony Creek Falls via- ct. Trains stop at Barron Falls for passengers to alight and view 275 metre drop. Kuranda railway station is surrounded by dense nforest with an occasional palm tree, while the platforms are corated in a myriad of pot plants, ferns and hanging staghorns. **ain:** Restored vintage carriages hauled by QR diesel locomotives. **erations:** Daily return services departing Cairns at 0830 and 30 (except Christmas Day) - 20 minutes later for Freshwater -

and the journey takes about 90 minutes. Markets operate at Kuranda village on Wednesday to Friday and Sunday.
Fares: Adult $25 single and $40 return - *Royale Service* $36 adults. Included in the fare is a historical souvenir booklet on the railway.

Contact/Bookings: QR Reservations Centre
Phone 13-2232 or
QR Cairns Travel Centre, Phone (07) 4052 6249

 RNE

avenshoe-Tumoulin Tourist Train
avenshoe and Atherton Insteam Locomotion Company (RailCo)

Tourist Railway (Steam)
1067mm gauge

e *Millstream Express* steam train operates over the 7km Ravenshoe-Tumoulin section of the scenic Atherton to Ravenshoe ilway line.

ain: 1930s vintage timber carriages formerly used on the *Sun- ne Express* between Cairns and Brisbane. The 4-6-4 locomotive ilt in 1925 for Brisbane suburban services is the only operating ember of the former QR D17-class.
atures: The journey covers picturesque rural countryside, cross- g the Millstream River on the highest railway line in Queensland 30m). The locomotive *Capella* uses Tumoulin "Y" to reverse for e return journey.
erations: Ravenshoe railway station departure each Thursday 1230 (ETA 1400) Saturday Sunday and most public holidays xcept Christmas Day and Good Friday) departure 1430 (ETA

1600), EXCEPT February when the line closes for maintenance. Charters are available by arrangement.
Fares: Adult $10, children $5, family $25.
Location: Trains depart from Ravenshoe railway station, 45km south of Atherton on the Kennedy Highway.
Contact: Secretary, RAILCo
PO Box 1365, Atherton Qld 4883
Phone: (07) 4091 4871; fax (07) 4091 5871

Atherton-Herberton Steam Railway
Ravenshoe and Atherton Insteam Locomotion Company (RailCo)

Heritage Railway (Stea.
1067mm gauge

RAILCo

Ex-QGR C17-class steam locomotive No 812, Roger, with a tourist train for Herberton awaiting departure at Platypus Park, south of Atherton.

One of Australia's outstanding rail journeys is the 22km steam-hauled *Tableland Express* between Atherton and the forr tin-mining town of Herberton. Restored steam locomotives from the 1920s re-create the pioneering spirit of mining, tim and agricultural development in tropical North Queensland.

Heritage significance: The Atherton-Herberton railway, built over a ten year period from 1905-1915, is listed on the Register of the National Estate as an outstanding example of railway engineering with its substantial stone lined tunnel, massive cuts through granite, stone pitching, and its incorporation of steep gradients and sharp curves. The route contains many original railway structures that are now becoming uncommon such as the small early 20th century timber stations of Ravenshoe, Herberton and Tumoulin and a number of timber trestle bridges particularly the bridge across the Wild River. The railway line is valued by the community and visitors for providing an outstanding aesthetic experience due to the number of viewpoints which command extensive panoramas, the Carrington Waterfalls and the varied travelling through narrow rock cuts, across rivers, through forests and tunnels and steep gradients.

Features: The heritage listed railway includes the range section with a 200 metre climb up 1 in 33 grades, past the spectacular Carrington Falls, through deep rock cuttings and round double horseshoe bends to the 181 metre long tunnel at the crest of the range. Diverse and changing flora and abundant wildlife are observed during the steam train journey which takes 80 minutes in each direction. Silkwood railway station has been relocated to Atherton, fully restored by the Society as Platypus Park Station. The heritage town of Herberton retains the character of the 1920s with a large number of historical buildings.

Locomotives: Restored C17-class 4-8-0 No 812 (A/Whitworth 8 1927).

Rolling Stock: Open tourist and closed carriages.

Operations: 1030 departure Atherton, Wednesday to Saturday Sunday. 1 hour 20 minute stopover in Herberton with sched ETA Atherton at 1430. Trains also operate on most public holid (except Christmas Day and Good Friday). A range of refreshme light meals and souvenirs are available at Platypus Park Stat and Herberton Station.

Fares: Adult return $25, children (5-14yrs) $12.50, family $62. Charter trips available on request.

Location: Trains depart from Platypus Park Station, 1km south Atherton town centre on the Herberton Road, 110km from Cair

Contact: Secretary, RailCo
              PO Box 1365, Atherton Qld 4883
Phone: (07) 4091 4871; fax (07) 4091 5871

    RNE

he Gulflander
ormanton-Croydon Vintage Train

Heritage Railway (Rail Motor)
1067 mm gauge

ie 152km Normanton-Croydon Vintage line is the last isolated section of the Queensland Railways network. It was con-
ucted between 1889 and 1891 under the supervision of George Phillips who designed and patented the steel sleepers used
the line. The goldfields which the line was built to serve soon petered out, but the railway has remained in operation as it
comes the sole means of transport to isolated communities during the wet season. The line has been declared a significant
ritage item with its original infrastructure still existing relatively intact.

ritage Significance: The Normanton-Croydon Railway line is
nificant for its integrity as a late nineteenth century railway route
d complex. It is important for an array of features including; the
row gauge line which Queensland adopted to reduce the cost of
nstruction, the successful use of the *Phillips* sleepers, the his-
ic relics of the rolling stock, the many steel and timber bridges,
ter tanks and buildings which include the grand Normanton
tion Complex as well as the smaller more modest stations at
oydon and Blackbull. The railway is historically important for
role in opening the area to settlement and as being the route to
Croydon Goldfields. The line is important to local communi-
s as a communication route particularly during flood time. It is
o of national renown as one of Australia's great rail routes and is
ued by visitors for providing an appealing rail travel experi-
ce. The railway station is significant on the basis of its great
ue as a live industrial archaeological site, and the architectural
rit of the station buildings. Remnants of rolling stock
cumulated during the years of operation lie at Normanton.
atures: The railway is maintained by the Queensland Railways
a historical passenger service for the community. The vintage
l-motor service on the line is affectionately known as the

Gulflander. It offers a unique experience of Australian *Outback*
hospitality and style which has long disappeared from railways elsewhere. The entire railway is a one-man operation, covering station
master, driver, mechanic, supervisor, accountant and public relations
officer. A journey on the *Gulflander* now attracts rail enthusiasts
and adventure tourists from all over the world.

Operations: The weekly service departs Normanton 0830 on
Wednesdays; returning 0830 Thursdays. Accommodation is available at The Club Hotel, Croydon. Tour operators offer coach services
connecting with the north-bound service at Glenore, 22 km from
Normanton. From June to September there are many special trains
operating from Normanton to Glenore and the public may join these
if space is available.

Location: Normanton is 700km inland from Innisfail; 500km by
road from Mount Isa and 70km from Karumba on the Gulf of
Carpentaria. There are public transport services to Normanton from
Cairns, Mount Isa and Cloncurry.

Bookings: Queensland Rail
PO Box 270, Normanton Qld 4890

Phone: 07 4745 1391

QR Reservations Centre, Phone 13-2232

UTBACK QUEENSLAND

eensland's Outback spans just over 800,000 square kilo-
etres north from the New South Wales/Queensland border
Burke and Wills Junction and west from Mitchell,
rcaldine and Torrens Creek to the Northern Territory
order. The vast and fascinating slice of Australia supports
leveloping tourist industry based on the *Spirit of the Out-
ck* and offering a variety of unique cultural experiences.

Politicians and engineers have sought to conquer this
st slice of the continent through railway construction. Land
ant railways were promoted in the 1870s to fulfil the dream
trans-continental railways from east to west, but in the
stralian context, government loans rather than specula-
e capital drove the lines westward. The Central Line was
tended from Emerald to Longreach between 1880 and
92. The dream of a *Great Western Railway* was behind
rther extensions. An extension of the Northern Line from
ughenden, south-west to Winton opened in July 1899, while
e extension from Longreach to Winton finally opened in
26.

Copper discoveries at Cloncurry early this century
ought pressure to extend the Great Northern Railway to
rve the new field. Construction west from Hughenden to
chmond (114km) began in 1902 and the additional 275km
Cloncurry was approved in 1905 and 1906. The first train
amed into Cloncurry in December 1907. Further mineral
ds resulted in new lines to Hampden (1910), Selwyn
920), Ballara (1915), Trekelano (1917), Mount Cuthbert
916) and Mount Isa in 1929. Most of these branch lines
ve closed, but the Mount Isa mine continues as a major

source of wealth in the region. With expansion of the mine
in the 1950s, the line was upgraded for heavy mineral traffic
to the refinery at Townsville. There has been an upsurge of
mining in recent years and the region is a major producer of
copper, zinc, lead, silver and phosphate.

Today the diversity of the *Outback*, its dramatic landscapes and the warmth of its people attract visitors from
around the world. Railway travel offers a comfortable and
relaxed means of conquering the vast distances: an appreciation of railway heritage provides insight into the hopes
and heartbreak of the frontier.

Mount Isa (population 23,000) is founded on the world's largest
silver and lead mine, developed from 1924 with the opening of the
railway. It is the world's biggest single producer of silver and lead
and is amongst the world's top 10 producers of copper and zinc.
New smelters were established in 1953 and the railway was upgraded to transport greatly increased mine production to a refinery
at Townsville.

Longreach (population 4000) as a transport hub for outlying
stations and settlements following the arrival of the railway from
Rockhampton in 1892. The present station, built in 1916, reflects
the traditional rural architecture of the era. The **Stockman's Hall
of Fame**, which pays tribute to the pioneers of the inland, has
become an international drawcard for tourists. Longreach has an
important role in Australian aviation history through its association with Queensland and Northern Territory Aerial Services (now
Qantas). The Qantas Founders' Outback Museum is located opposite the Hall of Fame. Branch-line DE locomotive 1616 is on static
display at the station.

Winton is billed as the home of Australia's national song, *Waltzing Matilda* and birthplace of the international airline, Qantas. The town remains a centre for livestock shipments over the QR network.

Getting There: The QR *Spirit of the Outback* train, which departs Brisbane for Longreach (via Rockhampton) on Tuesday and Friday, provides an outback rail adventure. Features include sleeping c riages, the Stockman's Bar, Tucker Box Diner and entertainm in Captain Starlight's lounge. The *Inlander* provides a twice wee service from Townsville to Mount Isa and the *Westlander* li Brisbane twice weekly with Charleville. QR has a range of t packages with each train, including a *Westlander-Spirit of the O back* touring combination.

Aramac Tramway Museum
Aramac Tramway Museum Committee

Railway Museum
1067 mm gauge

The Aramac Shire Council constructed its own 66km line from Barcaldine on the Central Railway to Aramac which oper in 1913. The last of 10 shire-owned railways in Queensland, it operated until 1976 with four mixed trains per week conne ing with QR services at Barcaldine.

Exhibits: Classic ex-QGR railmotor RM28, *AUNT EMMA*, and its trailer which provided passenger services on the line after 1963. Other relics and rolling stock are also on display.
Opening Times: Daily.
Admission: By donation.
Location: Old goods shed, Boundary Street, Aramac, 67 km north

of Barcaldine.
Address: Aramac Tramway Museum
Lodge Street, Aramac Qld 4726
Phone: (07) 4651 3311; fax (07) 4651 3156

    RNE

Beta Railway Station Historic Museum, Alpha

An early-this-century Central Queensland railway station containing railway station working equipment relevant to the ste train era and historic photos of local railway establishment around 1890-1900 era.

Opening Times: By appointment, admission free.
Location: Dryden Street, Alpha, Qld

Contact: c/- Secretary
Prior Park, Pine Hill via Alpha Qld 4724

Mount Isa Mines Tours
Campbell's Tours

Mine Tour
912/1067 mm gauge

Mount Isa Mines (MIM) operates 130km of underground railway, together with extensive surface operations. Battery-ele tric and overhead electric locomotives operate underground and industrial diesel locomotives on the surface. There i central train control on 19 level and ore trains run continuously from the ore stopes to the undergound crushers. A 0-4-0 steam locomotive from the mines, No 3 (Hudswell Clarke 928/1910), is on static display alongside the Barclay Highway

Underground mine tours, which cover tramway operations are generally booked out three months ahead, so forwa booking is essential. Daily surface tours cover much of railway interest and include the John Middlin Mining Display Cent

Operations: Tours depart from Campbell's Travel Centre at 0900 and 1300 Monday to Friday and 0900 Saturday-Sunday, April to September and 0900 Monday to Friday only October to March. Cost $13 adult.

Bookings: Campbell's Coaches
27-29 Barkley Highway, Mt Isa.
Phone: (077) 432 006

Qantilda Pioneer Place, Winton

Local History Museun

This folk museum in Elderslie Street includes historic modes of transport and offers historical literature and photos on Winton district.

Locomotive/Rolling Stock: Ex-QR BB18½-class 4-6-2 No 1077 (Walkers 545/1956) and carriage are included in the display.
Opening Times: 0900-1600 daily. Qantilda Place is the local tourist information centre.

Admission: Adults $5, student/seniors $3.
Contact: PO Box 93, Winton Qld 4735
Phone: (07) 4657 1618